MW00605416

NAVIGATING
the
FUTURE

L. Gregory Jones
& Andrew P. Hogue

NAVIGATING
the
FUTURE

Traditioned Innovation
for Wilder Seas

Abingdon Press

Nashville

NAVIGATING THE FUTURE:
TRADITIONED INNOVATION FOR WILDER SEAS

Copyright © 2021 by Abingdon Press

All rights reserved.

No part of this work may be reproduced or transmitted in any form or by any means, electronic or mechanical, including photocopying and recording, or by any information storage or retrieval system, except as may be expressly permitted by the 1976 Copyright Act or in writing from the publisher. Requests for permission can be addressed to Permissions, The United Methodist Publishing House, 2222 Rosa L. Parks Blvd., Nashville, TN, 37228-1306 or emailed to permissions@umpublishing.org.

LCCN: 2020951061
ISBN 978-1-7910-1595-4

Scripture quotations marked (NIV) are taken from the Holy Bible, New International Versionr. NIV®. Copyright © 1973, 1978, 1984, 2011 by Biblica, Inc.™ Used by permission of Zondervan. All rights reserved worldwide. www.zondervan.com The "NIV" and "New International Version" are trademarks registered in the United States Patent and Trademark Office by Biblica, Inc.™

Scripture quotations marked NRSV are from the New Revised Standard Version Bible, copyright © 1989 National Council of the Churches of Christ in the United States of America. Used by permission. All rights reserved worldwide. http://nrsvbibles.org/.

21 22 23 24 25 26 27 28 29 30—10 9 8 7 6 5 4 3 2 1
MANUFACTURED IN THE UNITED STATES OF AMERICA

Dedication

Andy: In memory of Dr. Jeffrey L. Bain-Conkin, a dear and caring friend who had many books still to write.

Greg: In honor of grandchildren, both those already born and those who might come in the future—sources of joy as well as hope.

Contents

Acknowledgments

Our first thanks go to colleagues and friends at Lilly Endowment Inc., who have believed in this project and these ideas from the start. When we first posed to Chris Coble and Chanon Ross our hope to build a project around an idea called traditioned innovation, they were supportive, imaginative, and eager to help. Our initial proposal for the Traditioned Innovation Project was to host some convenings and conversations, then to swiftly produce a reader that articulated what we meant by the term and idea. We quickly realized there was too much to say that hadn't been said in the ways we wanted to say it, and so we proposed a pivot of sorts—one that led eventually to this book. We owe our deepest appreciation to Chris and Chanon and all our friends at Lilly for supporting that change, even though it meant a longer wait for the book. They also are responsible for commissioning the many fruitful conversations that enhanced our thinking and improved our work.

We are grateful also to the folks at Abingdon Press, especially the publisher, Brian Milford, and our editor, Michael Stephens, for their support and assistance. Brian in particular has been a longtime friend and conversation partner, and we appreciate the many discussions that have shaped our thinking about ministry, institutions, and ideas.

This work would be woefully incomplete if not for the team at Leadership Education at Duke Divinity, especially Dave Odom and Rebecca Hymes-Smith. Many of our ideas were greatly enhanced by the opportunity to gather with colleagues at the JB Duke Hotel or the downtown Durham offices of Leadership Education, and those gatherings—not to mention all the behind-the-scenes work of the Traditioned Innovation Project—would not have been possible without their leadership and support. Dave not only helped us convene these conversations, he also was the most insightful, faithful, and consistent contributor. And if that weren't enough, he read an early draft of this book, offering important enhancements and some needed early course correction.

Others joined us, sometimes repeatedly, to explore these ideas and contribute meaningfully to the final product. We would especially like to thank David King, Mark Sampson, Thad Austin, Kenda Creasy-Dean, Elizabeth Lynn, Abi Riak, Prince Rivers, Paul Heidebrecht, Edgardo Colon-Emeric, Ann Bezzerides, Danielle Gladstone, Justin Coleman, Doug Wilson, Stephanie Boddie, Curtis Chang, David Goatley, Peter Cha, Michael Lamb, Christine Pohl, Tiziana Dearing, Josh Yates, Kevin Dougherty, Heath Carter, and Jeremy Thornton.

Likewise, we gathered a group of young people to explore these themes. Their insights—and indeed, some of their pushback—were helpful and compelling. We offer our deep gratitude to Mark Richards, Sarah Dyer, Isaiah Jeong, Lauren Hovis, Billy Tabrizi, Angelica Ortiz, Calia McIntyre, Emily Wirzba, Preston Hogue, Max Ramseyer, Eunice Santana, Cameron Silvergate, and Aaron Villareal.

Throughout this book we tell stories of people who are doing faithful, even heroic, work to innovate and shift equilibriums in their communities and beyond. In many cases, we could only tell their stories because they were willing to tell them to us, and often, that meant taking time from the demands of their work and opening their doors to welcome us. We hope our telling does some justice to how important they are to the work of human flourishing. Special thanks to Mike Mather and De'Amon Harges of Broadway UMC in Indianapolis, Indiana; Susan Cowley of Talitha Koum Institute in Waco, Texas; Gregory Boyle at Homeboy Industries in Los Angeles, California; La Wonda Bornstein at The House DC in Anacostia, Virginia; Mark Elsdon at Pres House in Madison, Wisconsin; and Lynn Mann of Whittenberg Elementary and Jeremie Smith of Fisher Middle

School in Greenville, South Carolina. We also learned from visits to The Next Door in Nashville, Tennessee, and Nurya Love Parish and Plainsong Farm, Rockford, Michigan.

David Goatley and Edgardo Colon-Emeric have been wonderful conversation partners at various stages of this book's conception and writing. Kavin Rowe and Norman Wirzba were the first to read a draft of this book in its entirety and offer indispensable feedback. Dave Odom, Thad Austin, and Susan Pendleton Jones read early versions of the initial chapters and offered important perspectives shaping both the substance and tone of the book. Nathan Jones and Ben McNutt, along with Kelly Ryan, all offered insights, writing, and comments on earlier versions of ideas related to "traditioned innovation," and we are grateful for those perspectives, insights, and turns of phrase. And Laken Stewart provided valuable research assistance at various points. With so much good help, surely any remaining errors or misjudgments are ours.

Greg would like to thank people whose judgments and support have offered enriching perspectives over the years of his work on "traditioned innovation"; this includes especially invitations by John Witvliet (at Calvin University) and Carlos Colon (at Baylor University) for Greg to develop lectures with jazz combos, and invitations from pastors and churches, bishops and other judicatory leaders, and academic institutions too numerous to name. He is also grateful for his leadership team at Duke Divinity School, especially Kristi Spencer and Katherine H. Smith, for their support, encouragement, and insight along the journey. He is grateful to Andy and Sarah for making the writing process fun and a great learning experience (often enhanced by Greg's absence at key moments). Greg is grateful especially for the long-standing, and long-suffering, love and support of Susan Pendleton Jones, who surely has wondered more than once if this book would ever be finished.

Sarah would like to thank Andy and Greg (Dad) for generously sharing their wisdom, humor, and curiosity with a young cynic whose imagination became richly shaped by working together, and whose life story will undoubtedly be marked by this shared project and by the gift of their deep engagement and encouragement.

Andy would like to thank Baylor colleagues Thomas Hibbs and Elizabeth Corey for their backing of this project, especially their support of a research leave that carved space for drafting key portions of this book. Andy would also like to thank Susan Pendleton Jones, along with Greg and Sarah, for their kind and perpetual hospitality during his many visits to Durham and extended stays in the Jones home. Word to the wise: if you coauthor a book, do so with friends who will extend the kind of care and provide the kind of laughter that nourishes you, mind, body, and soul. Most of all, Andy would like to thank his family—Anna and Caroline for maintaining disbelief that a book could take this long to write, which was always a source of motivation to keep writing, and especially Tiffany, whose support has been concrete, measureless (love "that both is and isn't confounding," to borrow a phrase from C. G. Hanzlicek), and means everything.

A Poem

Disturb us, Lord, when
We are too well pleased with ourselves,
When our dreams have come true
Because we have dreamed too little,
When we arrive safely
Because we sailed too close to the shore.

Disturb us, Lord, when
With the abundance of things we possess
We have lost our thirst
For the waters of life;
Having fallen in love with life,
We have ceased to dream of eternity
And in our efforts to build a new earth,
We have allowed our vision
Of the new Heaven to dim.

Disturb us, Lord, to dare more boldly,
To venture on wilder seas
Where storms will show your mastery;
Where losing sight of land,
We shall find the stars.

We ask You to push back
The horizons of our hopes;
And to push into the future
In strength, courage, hope, and love.

—Sir Francis Drake (attributed), 1577

Traditioned Innovation: An Introduction

Human beings live and are sustained by hope. We yearn innately for life abundant. We want to trust in the future. We want to be inspired to set out for wilder seas with a boldness born of confidence and trust in God. For Christians, this hope is not a naive optimism, nor is it simply an antidote to the cynical despair often prevalent in our age. Our hope is rooted in God, far more than in any reading of the times in which we live or the complex histories of our failures and brokenness.

Focusing on the past and dwelling on present realities can lead to despair rather than hope. The COVID-19 pandemic of 2020 and the heightened awareness of centuries-long systemic racism and injustice are only the latest causes for despair as we reflect on the ways that life can be hit by what feels like a wrecking ball. We are mindful of overwhelming suffering and brokenness, both caused by humans (e.g., genocides, including the Holocaust, enslavements and persistent racism, betrayals, injustices) and those that seem random yet are destructive (e.g., natural disasters; illnesses and diseases; systemic racial, health, and economic inequities). We are discouraged if not devastated by the complicities of religious communities. Associations of religious faith and institutions with partisan political power, or with complicity in sexual abuse, have significantly undermined the credibility of Christian witness. And we often despair because of a loss of transcendence in late modernity. As the British writer Julian Barnes notes at the beginning of his memoir, *Nothing to Be Frightened Of,* "I don't believe in God, but I miss Him."[1]

Sustaining a belief in God appears to face long odds. For one, life-shaping belief in God seems to be on the decline. There is plenty of talk about God in the abstract, or in spirituality or providence, but it tends either toward Gnosticism or superficiality. That kind of talk or belief doesn't, in fact, *shape life.* Instead, life-shaping belief in God requires things like conviction, formative discipleship, and habits and practices that don't make sense apart from that belief. It also requires, as we'd like to contend here, ongoing immersion in traditions—of inquiry, of practice, indeed of living and being—that can illumine our present circumstances and draw us toward hope-filled futures.

How might we discover and navigate that kind of future? How might we do so in a world in which it feels as if things fall apart, in which, as Yeats put it a century ago, "the centre cannot hold"[2]? Is there, in fact, a center that can hold our lives together? Is there something that can point us toward a hope-filled future, that can enable us to live not only with purpose but with a sense that there is ultimate Purpose—the sort that can guide us even if our own lives, our own organizations, and our own relationships are rife with failure, brokenness, vulnerability, and sin?

We believe there is a hopeful future because of God—a God who creates the world *ex nihilo,* out of nothing, because of Love. A God who redeems the world through Christ, who sustains the world through the Spirit, and who promises to bring the creation to its fullness in God's good time. This is the same God who created humanity in God's own image and who—despite our complex human histories of sin and evil and brokenness and vulnerability to pandemics and plagues—enables us to discover a promising future, a future full of what 1 Timothy 6:19 (NIV) calls "life that is truly life."

An authentically Christian vision seems to be in relatively short supply these days, especially in popular consciousness. That's not without cause, of course: the "brand" of Christianity is too often associated with partisan politics, sexual scandal, infighting, irrelevance, or shallow promises of prosperity unable to cope with suffering and injustice. And even when Christianity is associated with radical virtues such as love and kindness, it tends to be rooted more in cultural accommodation than in Christianity's unique and compelling story about the origin and destiny of the world and of human life in all of its complexity and disorder.

At its best, and from the very beginning, Christianity has surprised the world with what our colleague Kavin Rowe calls "a story of everything."[3] It is a story that is surprising because, by pointing back to the creation of everything by God and forward to the consummation of everything in the New Creation yet to come, it leads Christians to act in the world with a vision of faith, hope, and love that has often astonished observers. This story takes human sin and evil seriously, yet it offers a robust vision of what it means to be human in the light of Christ—to be capable of sin and prone to it, and also to be part of God's redemptive work in the world. This story, in all its ability to surprise, only comes to life when it is lived in and through institutions that are willing to bear witness to it, when those institutions resist the disenchantment from which our modern world seems to suffer.

Institutions that embody "Christianity's surprise" are not only "Christian" institutions. In addition to congregations, colleges, camps, and hospitals that are explicitly Christian in their commitments and practices and ownership, also include all kinds of institutions, Christian or otherwise, that implicitly or explicitly embody faithful and effective ways for us to navigate toward a hope-filled future.

Talk of institutions is complicated, of course. One thing that seems to unite us across modernity is the belief that institutions are at best necessary evils, and at worst are things to be ignored or disrupted or torn down.[4] Institutions have often failed us, and it's not hard to recognize their shortcomings across time and space. Especially in modernity, they have too often become lifeless bureaucracies that depersonalize and dehumanize people—in common language today, to "institutionalize" something is roughly akin to sterilizing or killing it. Worse, institutional exercises of power have often manifested a complex combination of what Hannah Arendt called "the banality of evil" and a destructive witness to "principalities and powers." Christian institutions are far from immune: they have too often been complicit in (if they haven't outright perpetrated) such failures and brokenness.

These failures and brokenness, both within and beyond Christian institutions, have left people cynical about the present as well as the future. Too often, people live and act as if all we need to do is tear down institutions or pretend they aren't important, and then we can cultivate an "innovative" path forward. Yet boundless faith in innovation—or in its methods and proxies, such as "design thinking" or "hack-a-thons"—has too often become for us something that is supposed to cure our ills and help us avoid the burdensome constraints posed by institutions.

Set within a broad, well-ordered framework, rooted in mindsets such as the value of tradition (to accompany innovation) and the importance of holistic formation (to accompany methods and techniques), innovation is important. Indeed, it is vital to forming our imagination and to discovering new ways to navigate through and beyond our bewilderment about the present age and the future. This book is an attempt to cast such a framework, emphasizing the centrality of answering questions of purpose and meaning that are rooted in, though not always fully beholden to, the traditions that have borne us faithfully to the present. In other words, we don't innovate just to innovate; we're not interested in simply "keeping things fresh" or disrupting institutions so we might escape them.

Instead, we propose rooting innovation in questions of purpose, which means, as Simon Sinek suggests, we "start with why." But we don't simply start there. Instead, we hold the "why" question, the purpose question, always before us. In Christian terms, innovating means anchoring to the End of God's Reign to which we are called to bear witness. It means framing innovation within the "story of everything" that is Christianity's surprise.

To state that succinctly, innovation is necessary but not sufficient for navigating the future. Innovation can't be just about "making things up" and starting from scratch. We believe that the innovation that matters is innovation that draws on the best of the past, carrying forward its wisdom through "traditioned innovation."

If indeed Christianity is truly to surprise, if we Christians are to offer the sort of faith, hope, and love that can astonish the world and bear witness to God's reign and God's redemptive purposes, then traditioned innovation can offer a way of seeing and being that is crucial to navigating toward those purposes in what David Epstein calls "a complex, interconnected, and rapidly changing world."[5] This book focuses on traditioned innovation as an approach to articulate how and why institutions and their leaders are crucial to helping us navigate the future.

Our understanding of traditioned innovation is rooted in our belief in the triune God, and that understanding undergirds the approach in this book. Yet, even as our understanding of God animates this articulation, and even as Christianity (in more than one form) provides much of the rich tradition(s) on which we base the practice of traditioned innovation in our own lives and leadership, we think traditioned innovation can help all people—whether or not they share our particular religious convictions—navigate the wilder seas of our world and our time. We have attempted to write this book in such a way that is faithful to our own traditions and beliefs, yet adaptable, we hope, to many others.

What Is "Traditioned Innovation"?

Traditioned innovation is a way of thinking and living that holds the past and future together in creative tension. That is to say, our feet are firmly on the ground with our hands open to the future. It requires an ongoing learning in which we are encouraged to live into the future by immersing ourselves in the best of our past, formed with a practical wisdom—what Aristotle called *phronesis*—that enables us to discern what we ought to carry forward and what we ought to leave behind. Traditioned innovation is at once obvious, counterintuitive, transformational, and urgent as a mindset for leadership and institutions nurtured by a Christian imagination. Why is that the case?

Traditioned Innovation Is Obvious

It is obvious because we know that we all come from somewhere (the past/tradition) and that we are all headed somewhere new (the future/ innovation). We depend on continuities among past, present, and future. This is as true of us as persons as it is of communities, institutions, and the world. We are narrative creatures, and we make sense of our lives through narratives. Whether we are Steve Jobs or Nelson Mandela or ordinary folks navigating our local communities and institutions, we draw on the past to discover opportunities for the future.

We do so by narrating those stories in the context of overlapping traditions. The past inevitably reflects brokenness and destructiveness that we need to unlearn and discontinue; it also offers life-giving resources and understandings on which we depend. By cultivating a rich appreciation for the life-giving aspects of the traditions of our forebears, we discover meaning in the present and patterns to pass on to future generations. Yet the destructive features of the past and the violence, brokenness, and vulnerabilities in the present create discontinuities. Such discontinuities are often associated with systemic sin and injustice and radical evils such as slavery, economic inequities, and war and violence—as well as, most recently, pandemics.

And when discontinuities occur for a variety of reasons (such as our own failings, complexities that emerge in our lives and in the world, and new discoveries or inventions), we always seek ways to fit even the most radical discontinuities into something intelligible in relation to what has gone before us. We find meaning when we can locate the discontinuities in a larger narrative that connects the past to the future with a life-giving present. This seems obvious when we articulate virtues such as hope and their centrality for people, communities, and institutions. The more we narrate the twists and turns of the trajectories of people's lives, of communities, and of institutions, the more obvious it appears that traditioned innovation is integral to human flourishing and to the vitality of communities and institutions that cultivate such flourishing.

This vision has, classically, depended on a transcendent vision in which there is an author and guarantor of a story that encompasses everything—a trustworthy origin and beginning of the story, and a promised vision of the consummation of that story in a life-giving *telos* or end. Through much of history, we have situated even radical discontinuities within the larger story. This is the power of the book of Job, or even of accounts of the horrors of slavery in Toni Morrison's hauntingly beautiful *Beloved*, where in each case suffering was understood within a larger narrative.[6] This abiding sense of an overarching, transcendent purpose to the world made obvious for many of our forebears a mindset that seamlessly held past, future, and present together in a complex narrative full of unexpected twists, turns, and brokenness.

Traditioned Innovation Is Counterintuitive

Why, then, is traditioned innovation so counterintuitive? Why is it not even a well-established notion, but rather a phrase that Greg developed in part to make sense of his own leadership? It is counterintuitive because central features of modernity have undermined any real hope for the future. The burdens of the past and of the present seem overwhelming even to religious people who have typically been a source of hope-filled storytelling but whose communities have been complicit in, and even responsible for, the brokenness.

Our modern moral imagination suffers from disenchantment because of the collapse of any transcendent vision—a collapse in which we are often complicit. We live in what Charles Taylor calls an "immanent frame" in which we assume that this world is all there is, and so the future doesn't seem to offer any transcendent hope.[7] We tend to oscillate between naive optimism (see our expectations for the techniques of innovation or our faith in "disruption") and cynical pessimism (see the narratives of decline across the political spectrum or the alarming statistical trends in depression, loneliness, and suicide).

At the cosmic level, a truncated vision of an "immanent frame" has left us with minimal resources for any hope for the future; at the individual level, a hyper-individualistic culture is undermining our moral commitments and our character; and at the social level, a bureaucratic approach to organizations is stifling human productivity and creativity, leaving us hating the institutions whose creative vitality we desperately need. We currently lack the resources and vocabulary to navigate a more life-giving future. So traditioned innovation seems counterintuitive.

It is only if we can reclaim a sense of Purpose that we will be able to articulate a fully human and cosmic sense of flourishing and address our crisis. Is there such a story that can offer a compelling vision of the future? Can we overcome our disenchantment, our hyper-individualism, our bureaucracy? Can we cultivate a sense of flourishing in which people, communities, and institutions create virtuous cycles of what 1 Timothy 6:19 (NIV) calls "life that is truly life"? Can we address long-standing systemic injustice and spirals of violence, depression, destructiveness, and corruption and bear a more faithful witness to God's Reign?

Our account of traditioned innovation depends on positive answers to these questions. But we can't do so simply by invoking Christian convictions and practices, as if nothing has changed since the pre-Enlightenment world in which these convictions were taken as given. Indeed, many people find religious belief, or any sense of Purpose, to be incomprehensible, or perhaps not necessary, meaning that neither a pining for a return to lost values nor a declension narrative portending our imminent doom is likely to resonate. Our cultural naive optimism and cynical despair are mirror images that, paradoxically, contribute jointly to our contemporary anxiety, distrust, and fear.

Traditioned Innovation Is Transformational

Traditioned innovation offers a vision that transcends both the naive optimism of progressive thinkers who benefit from the current sociopolitical dynamics in the world, and the cynical despair of people who are suffering from systemic injustice or are paralyzed by either fear, hatred, or anxiety, or all of these.

People, especially cosmopolitan people in the West, are tempted by narratives of optimism. Living within the immanent frame isn't all bad. Modernity isn't yet completely in rubble. Indeed, some "stories" have emerged that, while not shaped by a vision of divine purpose or a clear *telos* in a comprehensive sense, are designed to encourage greater confidence and optimism in the present. For example, at a macro level, Stephen Pinker and Hans Rosling have documented dimensions of the material progress that people around the world have experienced over the last centuries. They are optimistic that the world is getting better and that human life is improving on a variety of metrics. Their confidence is rooted in science and technology, though without any overarching sense of Purpose or End.

On a personal and more micro level, Martin Seligman has led a movement focused on optimism. His specific research has focused on "positive psychology," and it has spawned interest in other dimensions of human life such as "positive organizational behavior," "positive health," and "positive education."

A key challenge for people like Pinker and Rosling on the one hand, and "positive psychology" proponents on the other, is the reality of human suffering and the propensity of humans to behave in ways that create, intensify, and magnify suffering. Narratives rooted in an optimistic reading of data or in an optimistic outlook on the world invite us to focus on the positive while minimizing those dimensions of life that might lead to pessimism, despair, or fear. But is it a matter of becoming Optimists with a capital *O*? Is that sufficient to live happily in the immanent frame? Can narratives of optimism help the world navigate the challenges being posed by brokenness, including externalized violence as well as internalized despair and bitterness? Can Optimism about reason and love triumph over irrationality and hatred?

Likely not. Optimism isn't resilient enough to overcome the despair that occurs when spirals of injustice, distrust, violence, corruption, and brokenness create cynicism. Optimism is woefully insufficient when events beyond our control, such as global pandemics, blindside us, weaken our perceived invincibility, and make us vulnerable. We spiral downward into fear and anxiety.

We have developed cultures that embody such destructive spirals that now seem inevitable and more "realistic" than optimism. And it is exceedingly more difficult to practice justice, restore trust, cultivate peace, heal brokenness, or foster flourishing than it is to rupture and intensify the destructive spirals.

Is there a way both to remain positively focused on the future *and* to acknowledge the difficult realities of the world and of our own lives without giving in to cynical despair? We believe a rich sense of Purpose is rooted in convictions, practices, and friendships that embody a hope that the world ultimately does make sense, that there is a God who will, in the end, redeem even the most difficult and horrifying realities of our world and of our own lives. This is the God who, in the life and death and resurrection of Jesus Christ, takes all of the world's suffering and redeems it for the sake of flourishing: yours and mine, that of communities and institutions, indeed, that of the whole cosmos. People and communities that find ways to bear witness through suffering are focused on hope—a concept far richer than optimism and pessimism alone—that embraces both the gifts of optimism and recognition of the realities that give rise to pessimism.

There is a virtuous spiral that occurs when people, communities, and institutions practice traditioned innovation by reflecting and bearing witness to the beauty of the End that they have beheld in God. Their sense of Purpose, and how that Purpose shapes diverse purposes, illumines a world that can easily get caught by darkness and despair. As that illumination offers cracks in the immanent frame, so also others can discover reasons to hope, trust, and believe that the world has meaning and life worth living, that the purpose of life is more than a contest of who can accumulate the most power, the greatest adulation, or the most resources. And the more people, communities, and institutions are inspired and informed by the beauty of the End, the more we create flourishing ecologies. A virtuous spiral cultivates life that really is life.

Traditioned innovation is transformational because it aims to cultivate this robust ecology, nurturing leaders and institutions to bear witness to the beauty of the End as well as the generativity and grace of the Beginning. We discover through traditioned innovation ways of fostering human flourishing and life that really is life. Could it help us navigate the future more faithfully and fruitfully?

We believe so.

Traditioned Innovation Is Urgent

Yet the paradox of something that should be so obvious being counterintuitive, of a mindset that is so transformational being largely ignored in late modernity (or even opposed by modernity), points to the urgency of learning to practice traditioned innovation.

Why such urgency? Is this just another occasion of hyping up the current age's challenges in a way that forgets all of the complexities of previous times, cultures, and transitions? What makes our time so different from previous times?

We are living in a time of extreme disorientation, even though there have been other times of disorientation as well. Jeremy Begbie offers a helpful framework for understanding this disorientation in his book *Resounding Truth* by attending to the "home-away-home" dynamics in both music and scripture.[8] In great music, composers will help us feel at home and then take us on journeys away before bringing us back—ultimately, to a transformed and new sense of home. In Begbie's terms, musical time is "multistoried." Some of the journeys away are very brief, while others are long, difficult, and disorienting.

For example, a composer might start a piece in a joyful home key like C major and then shift to a sad key like A minor, a key of feeling lost, forlorn. The composer might come back to C major to return to a sense of home in the short term, or she might eventually modulate to D major, a place that feels like home but is more triumphant and offers a transformed vision of that home. The composer has numerous opportunities to offer touch points of home—sometimes in just a measure or two, other times over a more sustained interval—all the while taking listeners on a much longer journey of being away before returning to a new vision of home.

Biblically, the story of the Fall is the longest span of our being away; the whole of humanity's history with God is a journey of being away, of longing to return home to the Reign of God in its fullness. On that journey, we face many disorienting times, some short and some long, such as in the story of Joseph. Some of our times away from home stretch out for generations, such as Israel's time in the wilderness and its exile. The longer we are away, the more bewildered we become and the more we worry that we won't find our way home. This leads to a loss of hope and to despair. We have some experiences of home on which we can draw, especially if we have regular practices of worship and other life-giving practices and if we cultivate institutions that are life-giving. But if we are in the wilderness or in exile, the experience of being away often feels existentially overwhelming. We fear we're destined to remain in A minor.

The urgency of practicing traditioned innovation in our time is that we are in an extended period of finding ourselves away, a time of extended bewilderment. This is caused in part by the factors described above that make traditioned innovation seem counterintuitive. But it is also because we are living in profoundly transitional times. The Czech poet, playwright, and politician Vaclav Havel notes: "I think there are good reasons for suggesting that the modern age has ended. Today, many things indicate that we are going through a transitional period, when it seems that something is on the way out and something else is painfully being born. It is as if something were crumbling, decaying, and exhausting itself, while something else, still indistinct, were rising from the rubble."[9]

In this transitional period, there is tremendous anxiety and uncertainty. Even sober-minded optimists such as Michael Ignatieff are discouraged, as evidenced by his reflection in *The Ordinary Virtues*, an account of intensive visits to seven regions around the world. He finds dark clouds on the horizon: a world in which people may find ways to live side by side, but with very little aspiration to live together. He observes that the contemporary world has competing organizing principles and narratives, while noting that the only thing we really have in common is procedural rather than substantive.

Through his encounters, Ignatieff concludes that the momentum of contemporary history creates profound ethical pressures on people around the world. He observes: "Explosive, disorienting, and destabilizing change is the defining feature of our era of postimperial globalization."[10] And what he consistently finds in contexts as diverse as the United States and Myanmar, Brazil and Bosnia, is that secular narratives such as the inevitability of technical progress, the spread of democracy, and the triumph of liberalism are all in crisis. In their place are polarized competitions to fill public space with new narratives, such as the populism of the left and of the right.[11]

Ignatieff also notes that while institutions are crucial for human flourishing, we do not have the institutions we need: "If ordinary virtue is social—that is, if it requires tolerably good institutions in order to flourish—there isn't a place on earth, not even those societies that originated liberal freedom, where these institutions are in good health."[12] This means even the ordinary virtues are consistently under threat, unless we can cultivate stronger institutions. That in itself is a daunting task, because many institutions are corrupt or weak, and because there is an overall sense that most of our institutions are inadequate for navigating the changes occurring in our world. They are too often embodiments of bureaucracy and thus tend towards corruption.

Ignatieff's analysis cries out for a rediscovery of the End. The beauty of the End is that it can help transform ordinary people, communities, and institutions into environments where extraordinary things happen and extraordinary lives are lived. Such a rediscovery depends on cultivating a mindset of traditioned innovation as we cultivate a sense of Purpose, a commitment to flourishing, and practices of leadership that nurture new and renewed institutions. Traditioned innovation is a crucial mindset for helping people, communities, and institutions discover what will rise from the rubble of modernity.

The Significance of Traditioned Innovation

Traditioned innovation is a mindset that enables us to focus on flourishing, creativity, and the life that really is life. It does so by articulating the significance of those institutions that Ignatieff longs for but can't quite find. It points to a more robust account of virtues that can lead us into the future, can enable us to cope with the horrors and embrace the triumphs of our pasts, and can foster vibrant life in the present.

In this sense, then, traditioned innovation is about much more than "innovation" as it is popularly described. It is also distinct from popular notions of "entrepreneurship" to which innovation is often closely linked. Traditioned innovation has implications for how we think about entrepreneurship and innovation more broadly. It is worth noting briefly how traditioned innovation relates to such notions as well as to some related Christian understandings.

- *Entrepreneurship* is a term typically associated with start-up
  organizations. It involves a mindset and a commitment to
  cultivating what is new. It often is associated with for-profit
  motives, which has led to a variant of social entrepreneurship.

- *Redemptive entrepreneurship* is a term used by the Praxis organization. It describes "the work of joining God in creative restoration
  through sacrifice, in venture building and innovation."[13] It has
  tended to be a term focused more on business, though recently
  it has broadened to include social ventures and cultural
  renewal.

- *Innovation* is a term typically associated with creative work to
  renew existing organizations (thus different from the "start-
  up" culture of entrepreneurs). Social innovation has often
  been used to describe new efforts to renew society at large
  or organizations focused on the social sector as distinct from
  business organizations.

- *Christian social innovation* is a term Greg uses to describe a
  Christian vision of that social innovation. In Greg's use of that
  term, it is focused on transforming the equilibrium of current
  realities, whether in for-profit, not-for-profit, or hybrid economic contexts.

- *Christian innovation* more generally describes the work of
  Christians in fostering newness. This is often focused on congregations or other institutions, and it is also used to describe
  patterns by which Christians foster hope for the future. For
  example, Scott Cormode describes his vision of Christian innovation as follows: "The goal of Christian innovation is to create
  shared stories of future hope that make spiritual sense of the
  longings and losses of the people entrusted to our care."[14]

Traditioned innovation is related to, and complementary with, each
of these descriptions. Yet it describes and encompasses a wider horizon,
focused on how to integrate the future, the past, and the present. Drawing
on the story of God's love in Christ, and the vision of the End of God's
Reign that also returns us to the beginning of God's creation, traditioned
innovation enables us to cultivate the commitments that are necessary to
navigate the future with confidence and hope and to live in Sir Francis
Drake's wilder seas.

Practicing traditioned innovation will invite us into patterns of transformational Christian social innovation and redemptive entrepreneurship,

as well as into broader hope for the future through Christian innovation. In addition, it offers opportunities to situate secular organizations, practices, and mindsets into a broader framework that helps articulate their implicit intuitions and deepen their best insights.

Traditioned innovation provides a framework to critique "Christian" institutions, patterns of leadership, and practices that fail to situate themselves fully or coherently within the broader narrative of God's creating, redeeming, sustaining, and transforming love. In our world, secular understandings, institutions, and practices often embody traditioned innovation better than do understandings, institutions, and practices that are self-proclaimed "Christian" ones.

Thus, our argument in this book draws deeply on Christian wisdom and the broader Christian narrative, while nonetheless being intended for an audience broader than those who consider themselves Christian.

We add to the original definition these implications that will shape the story we tell:

> Traditioned innovation is a habit of being and living that cultivates a certain kind of moral imagination shaped by storytelling and expressed in creative, transformational action. Moral imagination is about character, character depends on ongoing formation, and formation takes place in friendships and communities that embody traditions oriented toward the End and that are sustained by institutions.

Our Hope for You, Our Reader

There is no quick fix or set of techniques that will create a mindset of traditioned innovation. But we do believe that you can learn to cultivate it by becoming immersed in an imaginative engagement with the story of God told through scripture; by learning from exemplary institutions, communities, and people practicing traditioned innovation; and from discovering new skills for integrating character formation and dense networks of friendships, communities, and institutions into your leadership and life. Along the way, we will share stories and tips for cultivating traditioned innovation that we hope will stimulate your thinking and inspire your imagination for more faithful and fruitful living and for the cultivation of more vibrant, life-giving institutions.

We believe that the account we develop here will help us navigate the future in the wilder seas in which we find ourselves. We think it will help us cultivate thriving communities, vibrant institutions, and a sense of flourishing for you and me, for us, and for the broader world and cosmos. There is a lot at stake—and a tremendous opportunity and adventure ahead of us.

Chapter 1
Navigating

Disturb us, Lord, to dare more boldly,
To venture on wilder seas. . . .
And to push into the future

—*Sir Francis Drake*

We love to hate the institutions we need. In the midst of modernity's ruins, we are aware that we do not have the social infrastructure that we need to flourish. We look for quick fixes: we want networks instead of institutions, we want to be spiritual without being religious, we want a future that has no connection to the past, we want policies that will achieve justice and eliminate suffering.

Yet we are also at least dimly aware that the quick fixes aren't working—and likely won't work. We sense that we need a broader vision of the future and of the past that enlivens the present and points to transcendence and purpose for the future. We need an understanding of what it means to flourish that can help us overcome our despair and discover life that really is life. We need to be able to cultivate institutions that encourage networks of relationships to serve thriving communities.

In the midst of brokenness, injustice, and personal and systemic suffering, can we develop institutions that bear witness to purpose; cultivate flourishing; and offer signs of justice, reconciliation, joy, and love?

1

We yearn for stories of hope that can inspire, for exemplary people and organizations whom we can follow, and for communities and institutions in which we can invest. We long for institutions that bear life-giving traditions, are laboratories for learning, and are incubators for leadership.

These institutions may be explicitly Christian, but they need not be. They might be secular organizations that draw on Christian sensibilities and serve as secular parables of the institutions we need and for which we yearn.

We won't be able to navigate the future well if, as Drake's poem suggests, we "[dream] too little" and settle for "[sailing] too close to the shore." We need to cultivate a bold imagination, rooted in traditioned innovation, and "venture on wilder seas." There we will again "find the stars" that will enable us to navigate the future faithfully and well. We "push into the future" while staying focused on the God who enables us to hold the future and the past in creative tension in the present.

We begin with three exemplary stories that embody different organizational contexts, all of which point to the power of traditioned innovation as a pattern of thinking and living. Only two of them are explicitly Christian, yet all reflect important dimensions of an imagination that offers rich wisdom informed by faith. People who work in these organizations discover possibilities for life they wouldn't otherwise have imagined.

Meet Sergio. He was six years old when his mother told him he was too much of a burden, and he should go kill himself.

"I guess you could say my mom and me, well, we didn't get along so good," he recounts, and you're not sure how aware he is of this understatement. "Trust me," he says, "it sounds way worser in Spanish."

Terrible as this was, Sergio's life actually got even worse before it got better. He was sniffing glue by the time he was eight, a high that turned into a habit. Next came an addiction to crack, then PCP, and then heroin—all as easy to find as glue on the streets of East LA. Sergio was arrested for the first time at age nine; it was for breaking and entering. Then at twelve he found a gang, his first real sense of family, and his homies toughened him. When his mother's boyfriend tried to abuse him, that toughness paid off—sort of. Sergio stood up to the man, but then Sergio stabbed him. The result? Two and a half years locked up.

"My mom beat me every single day of my elementary school years," Sergio recalls with surprising matter-of-factness, "with things you could imagine and a lotta things you couldn't. Every day my back was bloodied and scarred. In fact, I had to wear three T-shirts to school each day. The first one cuz the blood would seep through. The second cuz you could still see it. Finally, with the third T-shirt, you couldn't see no blood."

Kids at school would make fun of him: "Hey, fool . . . it's a hundred degrees. . . . Why ya wearin' three T-shirts?" Sergio still chokes up when telling this part of the story, the wounds still surprisingly raw.

"I wore three T-shirts well into my adult years," he finally musters, swallowing back his tears, "cuz I was ashamed of my wounds. I didn't want no one to see 'em."

Out of jail, Sergio was in his mid-twenties when he met Father G, a Jesuit priest who helped him get a job at Homeboy Industries, a conglomeration of businesses—a bakery; a silkscreen and embroidery business; an online market; a line of chips, salsa, and guacamole; a clothing company; an electronics recycling business; a diner; a farmer's market; a café—that Father G founded and leads. The successful businesses are just one part of the constellation at Homeboy; the main work is providing hope, training, and support to formerly gang-involved and previously incarcerated men and women hoping to reroute their lives and contribute meaningfully to the world. Job skills, an employment record, and a reliable reference come hand in hand with opportunities for parenting classes and anger management. It was the perfect stop for Sergio: Homeboy helped him develop skills, recover from addiction, find redemption, and launch toward something altogether different from his previous life.

It wasn't a straight path, of course, but today, Sergio is flourishing, living a version of what the First Epistle to Timothy calls "the life that really is life" (1 Tim 6:19 NRSV), one in which he is off substances, out of gang life, and gainfully employed. Not only that, he helps younger men as they struggle with the scourge of substance abuse and life on the streets, and in this line of work, his scars—the ones he used to cover with three shirts—now give him all sorts of credibility. "I welcome my wounds," he says. "I run my fingers over my scars. My wounds are my friends. After all, how can I help others to heal if I don't welcome my own wounds?"[1]

Cristina, meanwhile, works as a frontline crew member at ArcLight, a movie theater across town in Southern California. The work is what you'd expect of an ordinary movie theater job—rotations of taking tickets, selling snacks, cleaning the theater at the end of a movie. But because ArcLight is not an ordinary theater, Cristina's work also entails a whole lot more.

ArcLight is a subsidiary of a company called Decurion, and if you think movie theaters are a dying industry, somebody forgot to tell Decurion, which is thriving in all sorts of innovative ways. It all starts with the fact that Decurion is on a perpetual quest to align all of its operations—including how Cristina develops, both inside and outside work—with their "fundamental beliefs about people and work." Because work gives meaning to people's lives—it's not *just* a means to make money, Decurion knows—the company has designed a variety of interesting structures and practices that empower employees to develop themselves, to create something excellent and enduring through their work, and to contribute to the good of other people. While Decurion honors the roles that everyone plays within the organization—whether popping popcorn or planning business expansion from a corner office—they also believe that reducing people to a role in a process can dehumanize them.

4

This is why they do all they can to create conditions that pull people into greater levels of complexity and wholeness, that enable them to grow and develop in their working lives. And this, they are quick to say, is not a trade-off with profitability, or even a "double bottom line." Pursuing profitability and human growth is one coherent strategy and way of life at Decurion, and they are emphatic that "nothing extra is required." Their success on both fronts speaks for itself.

So what does all of that mean for Cristina when she shows up to work at ArcLight? All sorts of fascinating things. For one, her team meeting before the shift will involve "checking in," a practice of allowing all employees to say whatever they need to say to bring themselves fully, as whole people, into the work space—whether that's a feeling or a goal or a story that overturns the rampant workplace assumption that work is public and personal is private.

It means that if Cristina's work for the day is at the popcorn machine, she won't see herself as a "popcorn maker." Instead, she is a businessperson, part of a group of businesspeople running the theater, encouraged to review cost and revenue numbers, as well as targets and actuals from shift to shift.

It means that if she's making popcorn today, she'll do something else tomorrow. She will rotate from task to task as a way to see the full operation of the theater and to grow as a person and a skilled worker.

It means that Cristina will get to think continually about how her tasks at work align with a deeper sense of purpose in her own life and in the life of the company—the same invitation afforded to everyone from the frontline employees like Cristina to the CEO at corporate headquarters.

And it means that throughout this reflective process, Cristina will get to develop a "line of sight" that will enable her supervisors to find new opportunities for her to grow. In Cristina's case, the eventual goal of leaving her theater job for a career as a film set designer means that her manager offers special opportunities to join the team creating decor for events at the theater, practice for the Hollywood set design to which she aspires, and a tangible opportunity to connect her future goals—whether or not they involve ArcLight or Decurion—to her present work.

Cristina is just one example at Decurion. Go to the C-suite or the custodians, and you'll find that they are all afforded these opportunities to develop. It's because, as Decurion executive Bryan Ungard explains it, "We see our deepest purpose—'flourishing,' as we call it—reflected in every aspect of our day-to-day operations, whether we are talking about something as simple as tearing theater tickets, or as complex as formulating a long-range business strategy."[2]

Mike and De'Amon are an unlikely leadership pair. One is an Anglo United Methodist minister, the other an African American artist. Yet they have come together in leadership at Broadway United Methodist Church, and their distinctive gifts offer a transformed vision of what it means to be and do "church."[3]

Broadway is a historic church. In its glory days in the middle decades of the twentieth century, thousands of people were members. It was a leading institution in Indianapolis and throughout the Midwest.

Over the last decades of the twentieth century, however, Broadway declined in membership and influence. It embodied a familiar narrative—changing demographics in the neighborhood, establishment mindset, and uncertainty about how to adapt to changing realities.

Mike Mather served as an associate at Broadway in the mid-1980s. He noted the well-intentioned but largely ineffective strategies the congregation was employing to meet needs in the surrounding area: food pantry, summer programs for kids, offers of tutoring.

Yet Mike also glimpsed deeper possibilities, possibilities deeply rooted in the Christian tradition: a vision for hospitality, a focus on gifts and assets rather than needs and weaknesses, and a ministry of innovation and empowerment rather than only service or advocacy.

Mike was assigned to a congregation in South Bend from 1992 to 2003. That congregation became an incubator for a developing new vision of ministry and congregational life. When Mike was asked to return to Broadway in Indianapolis in 2003, he brought his new imagination along with a deep understanding of the congregational and community context.

Mike was reintroduced to De'Amon, whom he had first met in South Bend. Mike recognized a powerful gift for relationships and community development in De'Amon, and he hired him for the church in a role they called "roving listener." De'Amon's responsibility was to get to know the community, listening to neighbors and learning more about them. He began to discern rich stories and imagination, along with distinctive gifts that the church began to find ways to cultivate.

The result has been a transformation of the congregation as well as its imagination. Through Mike and De'Amon's friendship and collaborative leadership, they have been "finding abundant communities in unexpected places" (the subtitle of Mike's book). They have incubated new businesses by uncovering assets and gifts among their neighbors; they have transformed their own imagination from a service-oriented mindset to a transformational, entrepreneurial one; and they have discovered remarkable signs of life that really is life—even amid challenging circumstances.

Broadway, as with Decurion and Homeboy, emerges as the kind of institution most of us want to be a part of. They value people, engender trust, and strive toward the well-being of individuals and communities. True, most of us don't want to be part of a "glory days" congregation that struggles to pay its bills, go into the movie theater business, or sell bread or guacamole. But those missions, frankly, are just part of why Broadway, Decurion and Homeboy exist, and they are not nearly the most important part. These organizations are doing something that is likely to strike a deeper chord in all of us, whether we lead or work in businesses, universities, churches, school systems, government agencies, or social sector institutions.

Each of them draws on deep wisdom in the past, fosters a rich vision of what it means to be human, and is focused on cultivating a broad trust in the future. Broadway is a familiar Christian institution, a congregation, yet one that practices its mission in highly distinctive and transformational ways. Decurion is a secular parable, because it trades on traditions of which it is perhaps only implicitly aware. Homeboy, led by Father Boyle, is deeply rooted in the Christian tradition and articulates ways of acknowledging the reality of suffering with a hope-filled vision of transformation.

Human beings are much more than a job title within a company, a warm body that pays tuition or occupies a hospital bed, a client who receives goods or services, a parishioner who shows up at services, or a cog in some machine that institutions otherwise maintain. If pressed, most people would agree. Yet people increasingly mistrust institutions because they have failed to live up to what we hope and expect of them. As Lex Rieffel, a senior fellow at the Brookings Institution, has put it, even our most cherished institutions "are on the defensive—they are having a hard time meeting user expectations and struggling to stay relevant." This is no small development, representing, at one extreme, the possibility of what Rieffel calls a "global dark age," or, perhaps more likely, an era in which our trust in one another and our ability to promote flourishing drastically diminish.

Flourishing people and flourishing societies rely on flourishing institutions. And flourishing institutions are in retreat. Navigating the future, then, requires us to bring fresh imagination to our leadership and participation—regardless of our positions—in institutions across sectors.[4]

Broadway, Decurion, and Homeboy are organizations that are doing something different, and they are doing it exceptionally well. In the ways they direct their attention and strategy, they help us remember that human flourishing is a more vital and transcendent purpose than any single activity or strategy or tactic. They remind us that flourishing is something we all deeply yearn for, as they provide shining examples of what is possible—for the bottom line, sure, and most important for fulfilling the human vocation and bearing witness to hope for the future. We are living things created for flourishing and for helping others to flourish.

We have mounting evidence that human flourishing does not happen inevitably or automatically in a world that is changing quickly and being environmentally degraded, where, for too many people, the ways of the past are unfit for the challenges of the future. In fact, human flourishing is a state, and never a static one, that is always under threat by deep forces in our world that bewilder us, by technological changes that are quickly altering our work and our lives, by eroding trust in society, by inequality of opportunity or injustice in its pursuit, by deep suffering around the globe and across the street, and perhaps even by the simple ways we see and treat one another in our daily interactions.

We need better imaginations as we consider how to navigate a future on these wilder seas, because what got us here won't get us there, to paraphrase Marshall Goldsmith. If institutions are vital to human flourishing, and if flourishing, trustworthy institutions are largely in decline, how might we navigate these and other threatening waters? Is a belief in innovation sufficient? Should we just learn new techniques? Or maybe we should turn the boat around and head back to shore.

The world is changing quickly, and our flourishing is doubtful. If our deep yearning to flourish is to mean anything as we navigate these wilder seas, then several fundamental questions—some old and timeless, others new and reflective of this unique era—need answers:

- What kinds of new and renewed institutions are necessary to enable flourishing? How might we nurture and advance them when institutions are globally under existential threat?

- What does it mean to be human in a milieu of artificial intelligence and machine learning? Is human flourishing possible given the changing nature of work and interaction?

- Is there purpose for my life, for the institutions in which I participate, and for the world?

- What is the future of life itself when every living thing is being commodified?

- In the face of suffering, injustice, and mistrust, how might we cultivate flourishing and create a purposeful, life-giving, hope-filled future?

In this book, we propose traditioned innovation as a way of life that is central to addressing these questions. Traditioned innovation is a way of thinking and living that holds the past and future together in a creative tension that enlivens our imagination and action in the present.

Traditioned innovation begins with the End that points back toward a generative Beginning, Flourishing, and holds the past and future together in creative tension as a way to strive toward that end—for ourselves, for our friends, families, neighbors, and coworkers, for our communities and institutions, and for our societies and the cosmos at large. Traditioned innovation is a habit of being, living, and working together that maintains both a strong fidelity to the patterns of the past that have borne us to the present and a radical openness to the changes that will carry us forward as we engage deep forces in our world—some of which foster, but many of which imperil, human flourishing.

Traditioned innovation offers a different way of seeing, and thereby a different way of thinking and acting. This book explores what is involved and what is at stake in the practice and mindsets of traditioned innovation. It encourages the cultivation of certain key dimensions of character, the development of certain mindsets and practices, and the nurturing of a Christian imagination, which together offer ways of seeing the manifold possibilities that lie before us as we navigate a future on wilder seas.

Certain virtues and character dimensions that feature prominently in this book are essential to the work of traditioned innovation: love, awe, hope, curiosity, gratitude, wisdom, discernment, humility, trust, and generativity. Following philosopher Christian B. Miller, we believe there is good reason to devote ourselves to virtue and good character, because, at the very least, virtuous lives are inspiring and infectious, good character typically makes the world a better place, the development of virtue is in keeping with divinely inspired human callings, and good character is deeply rewarding—evidence of our own flourishing. Who we are contributes in important ways to how we see, and therefore, how we navigate the future.[5]

In addition, developing a Christian imagination—by fostering unlikely friendships, cultivating vibrant institutions, and committing to entrepreneurial collaboration—can transform how we navigate complexity. Traditioned innovation emphasizes these things while also encouraging practices and mindsets, such as creative experimentation, ongoing learning, and storytelling, that spark our imaginations for the sort of innovation that promotes human flourishing.

Together, the cultivation of these perspectives, practices and mindsets, and dimensions of character are marks of the deep and ongoing formation that is required of us if we are to see the possibilities for human flourishing. But because it is an abiding challenge to see clearly amid complexity, and because we human beings are limited in our individual capacities, traditioned innovation emphasizes an expansive, and perhaps unusual, view of formation, suggesting that it must occur in multiple ways and locales:

- in people,

- in relationships,

- among teams,

- within organizations and institutions, and

- throughout communities.

This sort of deep formation, we contend, equips people and the institutions they lead and serve with a different set of navigational tools. In an era in which so much talk about innovation focuses solely on the future and suggests that techniques will save us—design thinking, hack-a-thons, or strategic plans, for example—we believe that formation is much more deep-seated, durable, and dependable. Like many of these techniques, which can be valuable in doses, traditioned innovation emphasizes the need to look forward, to embrace a nimble and adaptive stance toward a world that is always changing. But unlike the techniques of innovation and planning, which tend only to look forward, traditioned innovation encourages us to look simultaneously backward and all around—to the past, across the landscape of the present, and toward a future the particulars of which we can never predict.

Where, though, should we look? Many traditions are damaged, perhaps beyond repair. This is even the case with Christian traditions, especially as they are understood and practiced in the United States. For many, Christian traditions are associated with partisan politics, sexual abuse, infighting, and irrelevance. Christians are often clearer about what we are against than what we are for. Where might people turn to cultivate life-giving appreciation of the past, and what traditions are redeemable? Which are worth carrying forward? And how might those traditions be renewed and nurtured to help us navigate the future?

We need to be honest about the complexities and wounds of the world. Practicing traditioned innovation is neither a "fix-it" technique for institutions nor nostalgia for a past that is gone or never existed. There is nothing either intrinsically conservative or radical about traditioned innovation. Rather, it is a way of thinking and living that requires discernment of traditions that are a resource for the future, traditions that enable us to envision the future in creative tension with the past for the sake of imagination in the present.

For us, the deepest and richest imagination for navigating the future is found in the broad, ecumenical Christian tradition. That will shape and undergird our overall perspective and argument in the book. Even so, we believe that those of other faiths, and of no faith, will glean from our stories—including secular parables of people and organizations that have no explicit connection to the Christian tradition—hopeful frameworks for navigating wilder seas.

Plan of the Book

Throughout this book we emphasize important virtues, mindsets, and perspectives that help form us to see the possibilities for flourishing. While the essential virtues, mindsets, and perspectives we identify are much more interwoven than distinct, we tend to describe them distinctively throughout this book in order to unpack what is at stake. Even so, we believe these things should interact in an integrative fashion within people, teams, institutions, and communities.

The first part of this book starts—perhaps counterintuitively—with the End, focusing on what it means to commit ourselves and our institutions to flourishing. Chapter 2 is about purpose, contending that, too often, focused people and institutions dwell on mission, vision, and strategies to the exclusion of the more imperative question of purpose. Mission, vision, and strategies are all important, of course, but we suggest shifting focus first toward the broader purpose of flourishing, which helps us cultivate, perhaps paradoxically, the kinds of institutions that are poised for innovation and effectiveness in mission, vision, and strategy. To commit ourselves to a purpose of flourishing compels us to discover, hone, and deepen the virtue of love, a virtue that reorients and reorders how we navigate the future.

In chapter 3, we shift focus to the present—on diagnosing our bewilderments in the face of a world that is complex and changing quickly and unpredictably. This is a world in which flourishing is not inevitable or automatic, so we examine some of our tendencies as we react to changing complexities.

Chapter 4 looks again toward the future, contending that people, teams, institutions, and communities would do well to face the future with four key virtues: hope, curiosity, awe, and humility. With the rapid acceleration of change in our world, navigating the future requires us to hold together two seemingly contradictory ideas: that human beings are worthy of awe, and yet human beings are too limited, and the world is too complex, for us to shape the world in our own image. This should invite a sense of both curiosity and humility, even as we navigate these wilder seas with a sense of hope. Indeed, hope is central to all that we believe about traditioned innovation, because committing to flourishing in a complex world summons us toward a hope-filled assessment of what is possible.

Next, we look to the past—sort of. Chapter 5 is about traditioning, a process of transformation in which we carry forward the wisdom of the past in order to equip ourselves for the future. This means that we ought to understand our place in a broader story, and that story ought to transform us. That requires the cultivation of two key virtues—gratitude and discernment—that we develop in part through a habit of storytelling about who we are, to whom we're connected, and what we're moving toward and why.

Chapter 6 focuses on developing, in the context of relationships, teams, and organizations, the Christian imagination that equips us to see more vividly the possibilities for innovation. In this chapter we explain and advocate for what we call "unlikely friendships," "vibrant institutions," and "entrepreneurial collaboration," which together help us see the world differently, in all its many hues. Three important virtues are important for this work—trust, generativity, and wisdom—because they can draw us out of ourselves and help us understand the importance of working collaboratively in teams, networks, friendships, and institutions.

The concluding chapter points to improvisation as vital for navigating the world as it evolves. Traditioned innovation is neither fixed nor static; it requires us to adapt and improvise. It requires an awareness that we are also practicing "innovative traditioning," which is to say that our innovation is becoming tradition as we advance into the future. As Polish poet Wisława Szymborska has written, "When I pronounce the word Future / the first syllable already belongs to the past."[6]

To be fully human is to be a person who is characterized by a rich and capacious "soul." By continually orienting ourselves toward flourishing—of our own selves; of our friends, neighbors, and coworkers; of our institutions, societies, and the created world at large—we invite a new imagination for the future. Traditioned innovation focuses on forming soulful people of character, on cultivating transformational relationships and networks, on developing a pioneering spirit that pushes into the future in ways that illumine the present through the wisdom of the past, and on building communities and vibrant institutions that have the potential to shift equilibriums and promote the flourishing of all.

On the wilder seas of a complex future, we need new capabilities to see vividly the manifold character of reality and of our challenges and opportunities. How do we attain such capabilities? We believe that traditioned innovation invites a new imagination to guide us toward the flourishing for which we're all created and for which we all yearn.

Chapter 2
Purpose

Where losing sight of land,
We shall find the stars.

—*Sir Francis Drake*

Ever have a lurking sense that there is something missing in your life? That you are yearning for something deeper, hoping to discover something more in what you do, the places you spend time, the life you are living? We all long for a sense of purpose, an answer to the questions of *why*, not just what and who and where.

This is also true of our institutions, those places that shape us and form us, perhaps mis-shape and mal-form us, lowering our sights and leading us to despair. When we encounter bureaucracies that seem to exist for their own sake, discover abuses of power by leaders and organizations that are more focused on narcissistic self-preservation than a commitment to others and to a broad sense of purpose, we become cynical. And yet we continue to yearn for something more.

Purpose itself isn't quite enough. It needs to be purpose that is directed outward toward flourishing—our own, to be sure, as well as the flourishing of our friends and neighbors, our broader communities and institutions, and indeed of the whole cosmos. Cultivating a sense of purpose is natural for us as human beings, and it is natural as well for institutions. In the world in which we live, we need to renew that sense of purpose for

17

ourselves and for institutions. That might mean tapping into our own dissatisfactions and frustrations and yearnings, and being willing to venture out onto wilder seas—"to push into the future in strength, courage, hope, and love." How might we do so?

Susan Cowley recalls how she changed because of her weekly commute home from church. It was the late-1980s, and Susan, the owner of a successful marketing firm, attended a large, historic church in downtown Waco, Texas. It was, by all the standard measures, a thriving church. It was populated by families, college students, and a who's who of commuters from all around the city who kept both the pews and the offering plates full.

In those days, when Susan left church to return home each week, she did so by way of Clay Avenue, a street that changed quickly within a block or two of the church's south boundary. Stained glass windows became boarded-up windows. Men gathered on street corners; kids roamed unattended. Street signs warned passersby what the residents knew all too well: this was a "High Crime Area." Susan explained, "the very pavement seemed to ooze with sadness and despair."

The disparity didn't sit well with Susan, not when this reality seemed so at odds with what she believed to be true about humanity—that human beings are created for that "life that really is life." Then she read *The Cost of Discipleship* by Dietrich Bonhoeffer, and the die was cast. Susan and a couple of her friends in town—Sherry Castello and Marsha Martie—kept coming back to the theme of loving the poor, aware that although there were plenty of people in their city like them who did quite well, the poverty rate was high, and with that, a whole host of other complex problems persisted. It seemed as though a lot of people, including the ones Susan passed on her drive home from church, were engulfed in a "surround of force" that would not let go.

As Susan and her friends experienced that deep yearning embedded in us for purpose, expressed also in a sense of helping others discover the best they could be, they felt certain that they could offer something of themselves to help their neighbors glimpse and experience it. They were under no illusions that they could or should fix it all. In fact, they weren't sure if they could fix *anything* at all. But they knew they could do something, and they felt compelled that they *had* to do something—that intervening for good was their calling, a shared vocation. They were led by a deep love and a clear sense of purpose—that those in South Waco who struggled so mightily might be, as they called it, "loved into life."

Amid these conversations and dreams, Marsha and Sherry called Susan at work one afternoon to run an idea by her. They had discussed many times that they could only pursue this purpose in relationship, in love, and there were many structural barriers to that—racial, economic, social, and otherwise. So, with a dose of humility, they pitched the idea of buying a small home in the "High Crime Area" Susan had passed each week near her church. It was counterintuitive in so many ways—there was little or no real estate investment in the neighborhood in those days. However, once they went together to see the property, something about it felt right —right to invest in the South Waco public housing area where they envisioned learning from and loving the poor.

They bought that house, did enough renovations to make it habitable for their meetings and times of worship, and established it as a place of hospitality, open to new neighbors.

"We didn't know what we were doing," Susan recalls, "but we did know why we were there. We were there for love. There were lots of drugs; there was lots of crime, lots of poverty and despair. And we didn't look like our new neighbors. We didn't have their trust, nor should we have at that point. We didn't know exactly *what* to do. But we knew we were there to help love these neighbors into life."

In this era of declining trust, rapid technological change, nasty polarization, and suffering not unlike what Susan and her friends witnessed among

South Waco neighbors, it can be difficult to know what to do, much less why to do it. We feel disoriented. Confused. Dizzied. A little fearful. Bewildered. Why be a schoolteacher, for example, or lead a theological school or a university, if MOOCs (massive, online, open courses) and online modules are the wave of the future? Why accept leadership in an institution—be it a business, nonprofit, hospital, or public sector institution—if it seems like institutions just chew leaders up and spit them out? Why join forces with an institution at all, when institutions fail to live up to our expectations or seem only to fail us and betray our trust? Why not just find a job, earn a check, put bread on the table, and live my own life?

Why?

As the world changes, and as we find ourselves attempting to navigate the future, often uncertain about where to go and what to do and how to do it, it's safe to say that we can only begin to make sense of our malaise if we develop a clear and transcendent sense of purpose. This chapter sets out to explore that topic, acknowledging that for many of us, terms like *purpose* might have a bit of a mysterious, if not a mystical, ring. We're accustomed to talking about things like mission, vision, and strategy, perhaps—but purpose?

No matter what our particular circumstances or our position might be, our work, institutions, and lives develop meaning and effectiveness, and we begin to fulfill the human vocation, when we align what we do, how we do it, and where we're going to a transcendent sense of purpose. When, in keeping with Sir Francis, we "lose sight of land" and "find the stars," we're more likely to become those "soulful" people whose work and lives shift equilibriums and leave lasting marks. This means that:

- WHAT we do (our "mission," perhaps, in the terms usually deployed in institutional contexts) is important, even if it varies for all of us across circumstances;

- WHERE we're going (our "vision") is important, too, and surely we're not all headed to the same place; and

- HOW we set out to get there ("strategy") matters a great deal as well, and there are multiple pathways to pursue our desired end.

But to navigate our complex, bewildering present and our evolving, unpredictable future, leaders and institutions should start with, and hold to, an unwavering commitment to WHY—and to a particular kind of why: to the promotion of flourishing in our own lives, in our relationships and institutions, in our communities, and in the larger world. This is something we can commit to as individuals, and as Decurion and Homeboy and Broadway UMC demonstrated in chapter 1, it can also guide our institutions.

Pursuing purpose is no trivial matter. As psychologist William Damon has argued, purpose endows us "with joy in good times and resilience in hard times, and this holds true all throughout life . . . bringing people outside themselves and into an engrossing set of activities."

People with purpose, Damon has found, "stop thinking about themselves, becoming fascinated instead by the work or problem at hand." Not only that, "they may discover powers that they never thought they had: untried talents, new skills, reservoirs of untapped energy. They feel a surge of excitement as they move toward their objective. They lose track of everyday cares and woes, of where they happen to be, of what time it is—in short, of all the mental boundaries usually posed by our physical and material worlds."[1]

Losing sight of land, people compelled by purpose find the stars. A bit like Susan Cowley and her friends, they venture out on wilder seas not always clear about what to do or where to go or how to get there. But a devotion to transcendent purposes—to why—leads to imagination, innovation, and "powers they never thought they had" to blow past "the mental boundaries usually posed" when we focus on the land and sail too close to shore. Those transcendent purposes also lead us to cultivate the deepest sources of wisdom from traditions that precede and form us.

This kind of thinking is powerful. And it is essential, we believe, to navigation in turbulent times.

❖ ❖ ❖ ❖ ❖ ❖

If developing, articulating, and pursuing purpose sounds a bit too fuzzy, there's also a stronger case to be made. Sociologist Paul Froese has observed that people who believe their lives have a purpose are happier and more fulfilled, while people who cannot articulate a purpose tend to be, at very least, mildly pessimistic about life. The saddest people are those who are without purpose but who find themselves urgently searching.[2]

As Damon notes, this has something to do with the fact that, when we never get to the why question, we fail to satisfy one of our species' truest and deepest desires: "the universal yearning for a life with meaning." We start to exhibit tendencies toward self-absorption and self-indulgence in the absence of purpose. We end up feeling empty, resentful, and emotionally unstable.

But for those who are willing and able to articulate and pursue a *why*, the opposite is true. People with clear purpose discover "a life that combines forward movement with stability." They begin to maintain "a stable and generalized intention to accomplish something that is at the same time meaningful to the self and consequential for the world beyond the self." They encounter that sublime-sounding loss of "everyday cares and woes" and of "all the mental boundaries usually posed by our physical and material worlds."[3]

It's worth pointing out that in Froese's studies, and perhaps also in Damon's articulation, this mystical-sounding sense of purpose is heavily individualized. In other words, purpose sounds like something we mystically divine or discover—from the cosmos, perhaps, or from within, or from sources unknown—that is unique to us as individuals. That so many people think of purpose this way is not surprising, given the fact that we in Western society have subtly migrated over the last few generations from a robust sense of "we-ness" to a much more atomized "I-ness" or "you-ness." As David Brooks notes, we're told annually by commencement speakers things like: "follow your passion, march to the beat of your own drummer, listen to your own heart, you do you." Supreme Court Justice Anthony Kennedy perhaps best articulated this sentiment: "At the heart of liberty is the right to define one's own concept of existence, of meaning, of the universe, and of the mystery of human life," he wrote for the majority in *Planned Parenthood vs. Casey*, a 1992 Supreme Court opinion.

Be that as it may—and the merits of Kennedy's thinking are certainly subject to debate—the result is that we outsource thinking about purpose, if we do it at all, to the realm of the private: it becomes something we do on our own, for ourselves, and certainly not for someone else. Purpose and meaning, then, are things we neglect in the contexts of our institutions and shared spaces, and the result, as Brooks notes, is that we wind up with a society in which our schools, our public culture, our cherished institutions, and even our parents say in effect: "It's not our job to think about or impart such things. That's something you have to do on your own."

This, perhaps, is why we feel ill-equipped to think about purpose, or perhaps why it has such a mysterious ring to it. We consider it relativistic in a world in which we define our own truths—if not our own facts—and we maintain no sense that we are part of traditions that get carried forward by institutions that have the power to form us, even as we form them.[4]

Perhaps in this atomized era, when "the mystery of human life" is supposedly ours to figure out alone, it seems anathema to suppose that purpose is something we can share, that there is a "we-ness" to our why that applies across contexts. But that's precisely what we want to suggest—that a significant part of the human vocation is to fulfill the deep yearning we share for creation to flourish and for all of us, along with our institutions, to be the best we can possibly be.

You need not be Christian to share this sense of ultimate Purpose, or even a significant sense of purpose with a small *p*. There is a richness to the varied ways in which this is a shared human yearning across religious and humanistic traditions. Yet there is deep Christian wisdom to this notion that we are created for relationship with God, and that we are called to begin by focusing on the End of God's Reign—the Purpose to which we have all been called, and which signifies the overarching significance that connects the work of the Trinity: the Holy Spirit who is making all things new by conforming us to Christ, the one who has redeemed us and the Cosmos, and the One in whom Creation came to be.

So if this transcendent summons for people, institutions, communities, and the world at large to flourish is a shared one, why don't we better articulate it, anchor to it, and pursue it? To a significant degree, this has to do with where we set our gaze. In the context of our institutions, most of us focus on mission and strategy to the exclusion of purpose, and we never get to "why." This is understandable, of course, when we perceive the day-to-day first-order questions to be something like keeping the doors open and lights on, making our widgets profitably, and feeding our families. Staying focused on these kinds of concerns, we sense on most days that, even if we don't have a clear sense of what the future looks like, we know what to do right now. And that's reassuring.

But that sort of assurance is fleeting over time, especially with how quickly the world is changing and with how daunting are the challenges we need to address. The problem is that when we neglect thinking about purpose in favor of only these concerns, or when we neglect to align our mission, vision, and strategy toward a transcendent purpose, we risk all sorts of misadventures. We never "find the stars" until we lift our gaze one day to realize we're lost, in some place we shouldn't be, and scratching our heads as to why we're there or what we're doing.

Too often, our what and where and how, which seem like easier and more concrete questions, distract us from ever asking why. That's a mistake. In fact, not only should we *get to* why; we should start there.[5]

When most of us stop to ponder purpose in our institutional contexts, our instincts direct us first to summon—perhaps from the recesses of our brains or the backs of our business cards—our organization's (if not our own personal) mission statement. The leadership mantras of recent decades have indentured us to the mission statement, and not completely without merit. We craft the mission statement, publicize it, and weave it into our institutional fabric. We abide by that mission at nearly any cost. "This is what we do," we say. "Keep focused and don't get distracted."

There are fine reasons for this—focus is good for institutions, after all—but there are also major problems with this way of thinking. One has been brought to light in a hilarious YouTube meditation titled, appropriately, "How to Write a Mission Statement That Doesn't Suck," where Dan Heath describes the "soul-crushing" nature of many organizations' mission statements. That mission statements suck is no surprise, Heath observes, because the processes we use to come up with them is absurd. It's probably familiar to any of us who have endured (or perhaps even convened and led) a mission crafting process.

Heath offers the example of a pizza parlor in which a drafted mission statement reads as something to the effect of: "Our mission is to serve the tastiest damn pizza in Wake County." That's not bad, Heath suggests, and we agree. That is the kind of statement that is clear, concise, and concrete—easy to get excited about and in keeping with the mission statement mantra: "This is what we do. Keep focused." But, Heath observes, we usually can't leave "good enough" alone, so we host a group writing session in which we sit around a table and, inexplicably, wordsmith the statement into obscurity.

"Right in front of your eyes," he observes, "a transformation happens. All of these people who you like and respect suddenly become tenth-grade English teachers and begin to nitpick every word of this thing."

One says she likes the word *present* better than *serve*.

Another contests the use of the word *damn*.

Another asks why we've limited it to Wake County?

And yet another: "Guys, I know our pizza is good, but what about the calzones and salads? Why don't we just say 'highest-quality Italian food'?"

"Our Greek salad isn't Italian," chimes another, also noting the failure to mention the atmosphere for birthday parties.

And so then the mission morphs into finding "entertainment solutions."

"Yeah, *solution!*" says another.

For good measure, the quiet guy in the back reminds us that we haven't talked about integrity.

And who can argue with integrity?

And so, the mission to serve the tastiest damn pizza in Wake County is now nearly unrecognizable: "Our mission is to present with integrity the highest-quality entertainment solutions to families."[6]

Say what?

We can laugh at this because we've probably been there. And while it's possible that Heath overstates his case, his point is well taken: in a mission-crafting process, pedantry can lead to abstraction, abstraction to a wide chasm between mission and practice, and that wide chasm leads finally to a sense of mission that really means very little at all. If what we're committing to is presenting with integrity the highest quality entertainment solutions to families, then count us in agreement with Heath: what does that mean?

It's easy to imagine how we never get to why when we focus so much, like this, on the land. Forget ever looking up to find the stars.

Of course, some organizations focused on clarity of mission can send the pendulum too far in the other direction. They become too concrete, too specific, stifling possibilities in a way that can ultimately lead to an organization's demise.

Take the famous business school case study on railroads. As the nineteenth century neared a close, railroad corporations were among the biggest companies—of any industry—in the United States. Rail travel and shipment were on seemingly endless upward growth curves, and as that growth reached an apex near century's end, the railroad companies doubled down: new tracks, new crossties, new engines, new engineers.

"This is what we do. Keep focused and don't get distracted."

And just then, at the height of growth, the industry found itself upended when airplanes burst onto the scene, disrupting it all.

The big railroad companies, once mighty and invincible, saw customers flee in droves when they were invited to "come fly the friendly skies" or to board "the proud bird with golden tail." After all, this newfangled flying seemed like the height of human achievement, something we'd always dreamed of doing. Rail travel suddenly wasn't that exciting, and in time, with fewer passengers, the big companies went out of business. Their failure was that they neglected to understand themselves as anything other than railroad companies.

"This is what we do."

The business school textbooks teach this as a cautionary tale: had the railroad companies viewed themselves as being in the mass transportation business, rather than just the railroad business, things might have fared differently, we learn.[7]

But alas.

This is a good lesson, of course, but it's a lesson that can be improved. Both these examples, the pizza and the railroads, point to the two directions one might fall from the tightrope of mission "properly understood" by the purveyors of mission statement mantras: too much abstraction leads to an unclear understanding of what we actually do; too much specificity leads to missing opportunities for growth or innovation. Walking this tightrope is no easy task.

But we need ask if we should we be on this tightrope in the first place.

In other words, if we're clear on our why, then suddenly the what becomes a secondary concern. To be sure, what we do matters—it requires our attention, and it's important for institutions across sectors to develop clarity. But "what" can be malleable. What should always be malleable. Indeed, we are free to be much more innovative with our what if we start with, and hold to, our why.

The railroad example is sure to seem relevant to many of us in this age of disruption. As we'll discuss in the next chapter, the perpetual threats of disruption can leave us perplexed and feeling like we have to keep focused on the mission. But if we're clear about our why, we're much freer to adapt when forces beyond our control inevitably disrupt the what and how of what we do.

Undoubtedly, some leaders and institutions are able to lift their gazes above the everyday stuff (the what) and begin to think about other things. Often, if and when they do, they'll turn their focus to the "where." They cast vision for where the organization is going, often by developing what Jim Collins and Jerry I. Porras called BHAGs (pronounced BEE-hags), short for "Big, Hairy, Audacious Goals," which, according to Collins and Porras, the "inspired companies" can translate into short statements of vision.[8] As Graham Kenny describes them in the *Harvard Business Review*, vision statements typically say something about where the organization wishes to be in some years' time, usually drafted by senior management in an effort to take the thinking beyond the day-to-day activity in a clear, memorable way.[9]

Sometimes these are compelling; sometimes they are so general as to lose impact.

McDonald's wants to provide "the best quick-service restaurant experience."

The Mayo Clinic strives to be "the most trusted partner for health care."

Ericsson would like to become "the prime driver in an all-communicating world."

Southwest Airlines aims toward being "the world's most loved, most flown, and most profitable airline."

American Express aspires to be "the world's most respected service brand."

Stanford University says it is "a place for learning, discovery, innovation, expression, and discourse."[10]

All these are good and worthwhile goals perhaps. All these tell stakeholders that "this is where we hope to go." But notice something: in every case, the vision is about *us*. *We* will be *x*. *We* will be *y*. *We* will be known/loved/revered/respected. In essence, *we* will profit and all shall be well.

But what about everyone else?

Certainly, there is merit to a good vision statement or tagline and a clear sense of where an institution is heading. As John P. Kotter has argued, good vision serves three important functions. First, by clarifying the general direction—by saying the organizational equivalent of "we need to be south of here in a few years instead of where we are today"—it can simplify hundreds or thousands of more detailed decisions: the vision of McDonald's to be the best quick-service restaurant takes off the table the possibility of a foray into fine dining or selling auto parts or helping customers plan for retirement. Second, good vision can motivate people to take action in the right direction: no need for the corporate chefs at McDonald's to experiment with seven-course dinners or investment strategies for Roth IRAs. Third, good vision can help coordinate the actions of all the stakeholders in a fast and efficient way.[11]

Check, check, and check. But it's easy to imagine waking up one day, saying "here we are—we did it! They love us! We're the best!" But chances are, even with good BHAGs, we might still find ourselves asking why. Is this kind of vision good enough? Is being known/loved/revered/respected worth all that much at the end of the day? What, really, is the point? What's the purpose?

Strategy, of course, is another important consideration—the how to our what and where. For many leaders, strategy is the bread and butter. This is what consumes time and energy and thought—and certainly for justifiable reasons.

Take our McDonald's example. If McDonald's is moving toward the BHAG of providing the best quick-service restaurant experience, then a million possible strategies come into view, and a savvy company like McDonald's will have teams of strategists devoted to implementing the right ones—usually with something like a five-point plan, and usually the result of a rousing strategic planning process.

We'll be the best because of taste. That requires quality beef, great potatoes, and as much uniformity as possible. Ready, set, go!

We'll be the best because of quickness. That requires sharp employees, specialized information systems, and efficient restaurant design. Let's make a plan!

We'll be the best because of hospitality. That requires friendly employees, congenial environments, and sparkling facilities. Dial up all the franchisers and tell them what to do!

You get the idea. Strategy moves from what and where to how, and developing as a strategist is an art form all its own—an important one, sure. And the problem isn't so much that we devote good time and energy to strategy; we should. The problem is that we're often not that good at connecting how to why.

A. G. Lafley and Roger Martin note that if we don't begin with an aspiration, we tend to reduce our trajectory to incremental change, long-term fixed plans, and short-term techniques. We miss the important questions of strategy that focus on our aspirations and drive us toward richer and more iterative processes for moving our institutions out into the wilder seas fruitfully, faithfully, and effectively.[12]

Such strategic work that focuses initially on purpose, the why, points to the importance of practicing traditioned innovation. It points us toward the End, and it also compels us to look deeper at our traditions and all that has borne us faithfully and fruitfully into the present. As Winston Churchill famously observed, "The longer you can look back, the farther you can look forward."

Focusing on mission, vision, and strategy—what, where, and how—are all important. And sometimes mission, vision, and strategy are interwoven with a sense of the why—the purpose—in ways that bring them to life quite powerfully.

Unfortunately, too often the why is missing. And if we neglect the why, then chances are that we're unfulfilled by the results of even the best-laid plans. We get in the car to go to the grocery store, for example (where—vision). We know what to do: adjust the mirror, buckle up, press the gas, signal a turn, press the brakes, park the car, walk up and down the aisles (what—mission). We develop a strategy, perhaps even a sophisticated strategic plan: *It's 5:00, so there will be gridlock on the 405. Maybe I'll take surface streets. "Siri, what's the fastest way to Whole Foods?"* We might even drive with great principles and values, letting harried drivers over into our lane while we drive our fuel-conscious Prius to Whole Foods— Whole Foods, for crying out loud!

And then we get there.

And we don't know why we're there.

Was it to buy for a dinner party? Was it weekly grocery shopping? Was it habit? For the fun of it? Do I even need any of this stuff?

When we focus on mission, vision, and strategy unmoored from a more compelling and transcendent purpose, we begin to suffer from something Richard Gunderman has called "inspirational deficit disorder." We align all our focus on making sure we achieve the mission, for example, but we become prone to miss the more inspirational and aspirational purposes that ought to drive our work.

Gunderman uses philanthropic organizations as one example of where we're prone to suffer this disorder. Many foundations and nonprofits are taught to develop "dashboards," collections of metrics and gauges to evaluate the organization's performance and effectiveness. They begin to measure the things the IRS loves to collect on its Form 990: revenue, expenses, fundraising and administrative costs, working capital ratios, and so on. These dashboard gauges perhaps even measure good and important things: how many patients we treated, how many meals we served, or how many tickets we sold. Did we pay our employees fairly and equitably?

There's nothing wrong with measuring these things. But as Gunderman notes, something has gone terribly wrong when "we begin driving with our eyes glued to the instrument panel." Inspiration and aspiration go into deficit because Form 990 doesn't capture those.[13]

It's not just philanthropic organizations that are guilty, of course.

School systems do it. They focus on the efficient use of resources. They focus on graduation rates and test scores and state ratings. These are good things, perhaps, and in some cases *very* good things. But they miss something important about why.

Businesses do it, too. They focus on profit for shareholders and investors. They focus on producing quality goods and even "solutions . . . with integrity." They are known/loved/revered/respected—good things all, perhaps. But why?

Universities, too. They focus on research outputs and R1 status, retention and four-year graduation rates. They make sound strategic plans that encourage the support of donors and prestigious grantmakers. They compare themselves to peer institutions as well as aspirant ones. Good things? Sure. But why?

These days, even churches and other Christian institutions do it, too. We focus on quantifiable metrics as signs of health to the exclusion of a clear answer to why. What distinguishes a congregation from a Rotary Club? A Christian college from a state university? A Christian nonprofit from the United Way? We have learned from painful conversations that, too often, congregations and other Christian institutions cannot offer a very compelling story of their distinctiveness—their answer to why.

Indeed, many Christian institutions suffer mission drift as they seek to become more like other institutions and describe themselves generically. This is sometimes driven by regulation such as accreditation or tax laws, sometimes by an institution's own successes in reaching increasingly broad constituencies, and sometimes by well-intentioned short-term thinking that loses connection both to the riches of the past and the promise of the future that are rooted in clear thinking about purpose. We forget to ask why.[14]

The truth is, we all do this. We focus on doing good and being good. We focus on efficiency and non-maleficence, perhaps even ethics. We focus on knowing what we do and not getting distracted. We focus, maybe, on where we're going. We even devise good strategies for how to get there.

These are good things. Surely, they are. But we suffer a halting case of inspirational deficit disorder when we neglect to align these to a transcendent purpose. We end up lost when we never even look for the stars.

There is an old story, with unknown origins and many variations, about a traveling man in medieval Europe who came upon a construction site, where three different men laid stone. To each worker the traveler asked, "What are you doing?" The first replied, "I am a stonemason. I am laying bricks." The second answered differently, "I am building a wall," he said, raising the stakes. The third, hard at work on the same apparent task and confronted with the same question, looked up beaming, his eyes heavenward, and exclaimed, "We are building the cathedral!"

He was a small part of a project designed to give honor and glory to God, and the architecture as well as the construction were done with God in mind. His why was rooted in a vision of God's Reign, the role of the church in the community, and long traditions of cultivating beauty (along with truth and goodness) as ways of giving honor and glory to God. With a clear sense of purpose, he knew what to do, where to do it, how he was contributing—because he knew why the project was so important.

Why do we do what we do? Why are we going where we're going? Why is this how we're doing it? Why?

After they bought the small house with a caving-in back room, Susan Cowley and her friends set up shop. Unsure of what to do, they knew why they were there: to "love people into life" because they had experienced God's love so powerfully in their own lives. Their why is rooted in a rich sense of what love looks like when its deepest meaning is found in the love of God expressed in Jesus, and learned and lived as part of embodying the biblical story. They were content to lead with that purpose and then figure out the rest for their nascent organization, which they were clear was a church.

At first, their mission and strategies weren't terribly sophisticated or elaborate—enough repairs to make the house habitable, followed by a long eight-year season of what came to be called "The Ministry of Hanging Out." As committed as they were in principle to the virtue of love, Susan and her friends knew it wouldn't naturally flow two ways with their neighbors, not under the circumstances that drew them to the neighborhood, and not with the barriers of race, economics, access, and opportunity. And so, Marsha, by then CrossTies' full-time pastor, would come to the house during the day, settle visibly on the porch, or walk the neighborhoods, and shoot the breeze with anyone and everyone. They knew they needed to love their neighbors enough to learn from them.

Early on, Susan remembers with a smile, a rumor swirled in the neighborhood that these strange ladies, doing unconventional things in an unconventional way, were "lesbian witches." They had anticipated obstacles, but not that one. Children, fortunately, were the first to debunk it. Kids would come by on the way home from school, backpacks in tow, utterly perplexed when asked to show off the day's artwork. Pulling items from their bags, Marsha and her colleagues would effuse, heaping praise on these children for their macaroni necklaces or Popsicle-stick snowflakes, as though Van Gogh himself had traded oil-on-canvas for crafting supplies to produce these originals. Pretty soon, the neighborhood kids' artwork took over the drug-house refrigerator and found its way onto kitchen walls.

This hadn't been the strategy, per se. And it's a good thing Susan and her friends, having named themselves CrossTies Ecumenical Church by that point, hadn't felt compelled to develop a strategic plan and pledge themselves to keep focused early on. If they had, it's doubtful that they would have included "hanging out" or creating a kids' art gallery among the important first priorities. In fact, they might have seen such things as distractions. And they would have missed out.

But their unyielding sense of purpose was to love neighbors into life, to learn from them, and to be so committed to their flourishing that the "what" seemed secondary. They wanted to lead with love, and that meant they had to learn how to do that well, because love is a virtue that requires much more than desire. As learned and lived as part of a vibrant Christian journey, love requires commitment, steadfastness, patience, and hope. And when abiding within another culture, CrossTies also learned, "it means getting your own therapy so that you 'do no harm.'" Love is the virtue that perfects, orients, and orders all the others. It requires what Pope Benedict XVI called "a heart which sees." This kind of heart "sees where love is needed and acts accordingly."[15]

Such an insightful love began to help Susan and her friends recognize a phenomenon they'd previously only read about—that children were being swept up into the forces of their neighborhood, suspended from school early and far too often, picked up at first for petty offenses, and sometimes for drugs, eventually for things even far more serious. What had previously only been a textbook social phenomenon with a terrible, alarming name—the "school-to-prison pipeline"—began to develop a face. It was Marquise, the boy whose handprint Thanksgiving turkey was on the fridge. It was DeAndre, with that infectious personality, who could hold court on the front porch for as long as anyone would listen. Then came the year when CrossTies buried more teenagers than they saw graduate from their one pocket of poverty. Three burials to one baccalaureate—that was the tipping point.

This was a crisis—not an abstract crisis or some "issue" to care about or "injustice" to fight. It wasn't a political battle so much as it was a tragedy for their friends, for people they knew and saw and loved. That might demand social or political action, of course, but that can be a long slog, with mixed results. To advocate is important. To innovate is perhaps more vital, especially when the focus is on shifting the equilibrium so advocacy and service become less necessary. So Susan and her friends began with something much more incarnational than advocacy or service.

Susan, Marsha, and Sherry, by that time, had been joined by new CrossTies members: Kim Jamison and Carol Salvesen. In the language of CrossTies, it was Kim who "sounded the call." Carol, an Occupational Therapist, responded with a clear "yes." Susan and Marsha "came alongside" the new "Mission Group." Initially, the four thought they'd start a school, some place that would give hope and support to the kids in the neighborhood, since, theoretically, they were already in the pipeline. A school, they thought, might re-route the pipes. So they met with their neighborhood's local elementary school administrator to seek advice—someone who had a pulse on what these kids needed, and someone likely to confirm their inclination to start a school. The four women posed their first question, and it would be their last: "What is the number one problem you have with entering kindergarteners from this neighborhood?" They were stunned by the administrator's immediate response.

"By the time they're here for kindergarten," she reported, "their mental health is already shot and they can't learn."

Susan and her friends were heartsick and deeply moved—and more than a little surprised. Expecting this trusted source to confirm their impulse to start a school, she instead hinted that it might do little good—too little, too late. Susan and her friends left and reconvened on the school's front steps. They looked at each other with one burning question, "Now what?"

Having no expertise in mental health, much less the mental health of kindergartners, they were nevertheless committed to finding approaches and experiments where they could make the biggest difference. Love drove them to look for leverage—a love that is patterned in Christ, who always wanted the best for "the least of these" (Matthew 25:40, NIV). As Maggy Barankitse, the Aurora Prize-winning Burundian humanitarian and social innovator, is fond of saying, "love made them inventors."[16]

Carol set up a meeting with a friend who was a child psychologist. The psychologist was not at all surprised by the school administrator's realization. His advice to them was clear: "Start a mental health, therapeutic nursery and don't let anyone tell you to start at two or three. Begin at birth!"

In retrospect, it's easy to look back and think: of course—why not? But it's important to note that at the time, nothing like that existed anywhere in Texas. There were no models close by, nothing to replicate. As best they could tell, there were only a few such facilities anywhere, clustered in New England and often in major medical centers. It was a far-fetched idea for four women without that kind of training. They had full-time jobs and full-time lives; they were just there to love their neighbors, after all.

But as it turns out, a deep love, a "heart which sees," and an abiding commitment to flourishing can drive people to do creative and courageous things that have deep wisdom on which to draw. They were practicing traditioned innovation, as they cultivated new relationships across sectors.

Convinced that starting a therapeutic nursery was the right intervention and determined to make it happen, the CrossTies women set out to learn what it would take to start one. It would take money, they learned. It would take facilities and equipment. It would take experts—all sorts of them. It would take teachers who were creative and flexible enough to learn new methods and new interventions and who were risk-tolerant enough to join a start-up. Since they had none of those things, it would certainly take vision and courage and more than a little gumption. Love and purpose fueled all these.

In 2003, after a few years of hustle, Susan and the CrossTies' Talitha Koum Mission group of four women opened their new therapeutic nursery at the site of an old Boys & Girls Club complete with a World War II airplane hangar as its gym, purchased with the generous support of a local foundation. They called it Talitha Koum Institute (TKI), drawn from an Aramaic phrase that Jesus used, which translates as "My child, rise up!" They were innovative in developing a new organization that was deeply rooted in their sense of purpose, drawing on the riches of their Christian faith as well as insights gleaned from others. It wasn't just any old preschool; it was something powerfully new.

Deep poverty, they had learned in their correspondence with too many experts to count, produces traumatic effects on a child's cognitive development and mental health, leading toward outcomes, by kindergarten, that had been so vividly described by the heartbroken school administrator years earlier. Inspired by that influence, Talitha Koum set out with a vision to send their children into public kindergarten with a brain organized for learning, emotional strength to self-regulate, skills for problem-solving, and deep compassion for others. It's a vision they were learning from their faith about what it means to be human, yet they were implementing it in fresh ways.

Many preschools admirably start work on similar goals with two-, three-, and four-year-olds, often with modest success. But Talitha Koum wasn't a preschool; it was a therapeutic nursery that existed to love people into life. It was doing something different, willing to risk a new approach for the sake of its larger purposes. Its founders had learned from researchers that for kids afflicted by the trauma of extreme poverty, age two or three can be much too late to make a difference in their lives. They began their programs, then, with children at eight weeks of age, since those early months present the greatest window of opportunity for brain development.

Since opening in 2003, Talitha Koum has developed in impressive ways. Starting at infancy, the children at Talitha Koum receive individualized cognitive plans and sensory integration "diets" that are regularly reviewed by a team comprising the institute's clinical directors, the child's teacher, and a psychology doctoral candidate (through a partnership with Baylor University). The teachers—one for every three children—then "loop" with the children, moving into successive classrooms with them through the first three years of life. This continued, unbroken relationship creates attachment and bonding between teacher and child and minimizes dysregulation. It also has the profoundly deep effect of building relationships and deep trust between Talitha Koum and the children's parents. None of this was on their radar in the 1980s or 1990s. Now this is all Susan can talk about—a successful marketing career seems a distant memory these days.

In the earliest days of operation, Talitha Koum was so focused on the children that the parent dynamic caught them off guard. But a purpose-first approach left them nimble enough to adapt when parents expressed needs too, and, in many ways, working with parents has become central to the mission. After all, to promote the flourishing of neighbors can mean looking beyond the crawling age.

"It's hard to resist being loved and respected," Susan told us one day in her office, just after we'd observed a busy classroom, where one child spun rapidly in a sophisticated swing that hung from the ceiling and another pushed heavy blocks so they collided with the wall, grinning at us every time they crashed. This was all part of their sensory diets, we learned.

"At first," Susan told us, "many parents wonder: 'What is this—this way you're treating me and my child? Is it a middle-class thing? Is it a white thing?'"

The latter of these theories gets put to rest just as soon as parents see the diversity of Talitha Koum's staff. Still, Susan explains to parents that it's neither of these things.

"It's love. Our purpose is loving everyone, every time, and after that, you just put into place all the best practices and research you can find."

The mission and the strategy—the what and the how—start to evolve with the circumstances and needs. Love of this sort leads to trust—not every day, of course, but over time. And because there is trust, kids and parents "never leave."

"Once a Talitha Koum parent," Susan is fond of telling them, "always a Talitha Koum parent." And with that, new and interesting conversations begin to develop, often over pastries supplied to teachers and parents every morning, courtesy of the local Panera Bread.

"Do you think I can get my GED?" one parent will finally muster the courage to ask Susan during a Tuesday evening parenting meeting.

"Yes!" the she resounds. "And we'll help."

A few years later, "Do you think I can get my CNA [Certified Nurse's Assistant degree]?"

"Yes!" And more of the same—with the help often coming after everyone has clocked out for the day.

When asked to describe their philosophy about working with families (not just kids), Susan will often tell donors and other partners (who often ask questions such as "What do you make the parents do?") that it's really quite simple. "You really can't make someone do anything. We love and respect our parents; that's the greatest power in the universe. They don't come to the weekly parenting meeting because it's a requirement or a demand. They come because it's hard to resist being loved."

If you spend any time walking the halls of Talitha Koum Institute, it's easy to see that love is tangible, and "loving people into life" isn't just some purpose in the abstract. It's found in simple things, like the vocabulary, where Talitha Koum refuses to use words like *agency* and *client*, for example. ("These are parents and children and teachers," Susan says. "'Agency' and 'client' are way too bureaucratic, and bureaucracy is not about love, it's about rules.") They trade the title "Board of Directors" for "Covenant Partners"—signaling something even deeper than fiduciary responsibility—and govern by consensus rather than majority will. There is a culture of love among the staff as well, where their own flourishing is prized by Talitha Koum's leaders. Every week, teachers and administrators set aside intentional time to look into how "pass-along trauma" is affecting them and to share ideas on the self-care needed for remaining healthy themselves and being safe adults for the children in their care. It's also not uncommon to find Susan, now the full-time executive director (having retired early from her marketing firm), working in the laundry room, watering and weeding the flower beds, sorting hand-me-down clothes—and other things that most would think well below her pay grade.

An abiding commitment to flourishing means this as well: Talitha Koum Institute doesn't relinquish care of their kids once they've passed successfully into the public school system—the place TKI originally imagined as the finish line. A mission to "run a good therapeutic nursery" might suggest that they should. But "once a part of Talitha Koum, always a part of Talitha Koum."[17]

It is an admirable vision of a Christian ministry practicing traditioned innovation. Children and families aren't called "graduates" of Talitha Koum, because they remain part of the family. The children head off to public kindergarten alongside a mentor, a long-term relationship with a local individual, couple, or family, vetted and matched and supported by Talitha Koum. "Kindergarten to College or Career," says the brochure of this major personal commitment. This wasn't part of the original strategy, but parents began to discover that the care their family received from Talitha Koum was far superior to anything the public schools and other social supports could give. And they wanted more of it. So, Talitha Koum evolved its mission and strategy because the purpose to promote flourishing led them to do so.

This works. Just ask Kelle, a member of Talitha Koum's first class of toddlers and the first Talitha Koum alum to go all the way through the mentoring program, with two mentors contributing to her future. She and her family stuck with Talitha Koum through high school, even— perhaps especially—when times were difficult.

"There were a lot of money issues, not having enough," Kelle says. "My mom would struggle with not having enough to eat, paying bills, or she just struggled. She lost us once to [Child Protective Services]. Talitha Koum really helped her with getting us back, me and my sister, and helping us just be stable."

Kelle played in the high school orchestra and good grades, always eager to share her successes with her mentors and the team at Talitha Koum. Just prior to graduating, Kelle learned that she was among the five hundred students in America, out of forty thousand applicants, to become a Dell Scholar, which provided a $20,000 scholarship—and a laptop, of course. Kelle spoke at Talitha Koum's annual fundraiser, Rise Up! Waco, reading a portion of her Dell application letter. She had barely finished the passage before hundreds rose to their feet to applaud the success of this bashful senior. No matter her major, Kelle says she wants to be that person who can offer the same kind of mentoring and encouragement she has felt fortunate to receive.[18]

On March 8, 1960, Dave Packard—best known from the second half of his company's name, a little group called Hewlett-Packard—waltzed into a company training of middle managers at Palo Alto headquarters, bringing remarks to the participants, ostensibly to reflect on how each employee might do his work more efficiently as the company itself sought growth through efficiency. In all of it, Packard wanted to help the company maintain its character. It sounded, at first, like a rousing *This is what we do* speech. But Packard threw a curveball.

Setting the gaze beyond the efficiency of middle management, Packard instead determined to expound on why a company exists in the first place. It was not, he was quick to point out, simply to make money. Rather, it was incumbent upon every institution to do something worthwhile, to do work that would "accomplish something collectively" that exceeded the sum of individual parts. And while some within the company might give the appearance that they only want to make money, Packard was convinced that, for everyone, "underlying drives" are rooted in "a desire to do . . . something which is of value."

As Packard saw it, that deeper "something" is a guiding purpose that outlives any one of us. "Purpose," he believed, should last at least a century, but it "should not be confused with specific goals or business strategies (which should change many times in 100 years)." While a company might achieve a goal, deliver on a promise, or complete a strategy, purpose is something altogether different. "You cannot fulfill a purpose; it's like a guiding star on the horizon—forever pursued but never reached. Yet although purpose itself does not change, it does inspire change. The very fact that purpose can never fully be realized means that an organization can never stop stimulating change and progress."[19]

How, then, might we begin to "forever pursue" a "guiding star on the horizon," one that is more reliable than "dashboards" and "instrument panels," profit motives and mission statements? It starts by naming it, by believing, with Packard, that we can do "something worthwhile," that we can "accomplish something collectively" that we "could not accomplish separately." It means committing ourselves, and our institutions, to the well-being of others and giving ourselves over to it. It means joining Richard Gunderman in espousing that perhaps "the greatest gifts any human being could ever share with us, or any of us could share with another, is assistance in becoming the best persons, families, and communities we are capable of being."[20]

Paradoxically—indeed, surprisingly—devoting ourselves to purpose, to cultivating the flourishing of others, leads also to our own flourishing. A Christian imagination calls us to focus less on ourselves, indeed to "deny" ourselves, to forget ourselves, and focus attention on others and especially on God. Jesus's call to discipleship invites us to find our true vocation in service to God and others, and thereby discover the fullness of life to which we are called.

We need not become "chumps and doormats," as Adam Grant's nuanced research on "givers and takers" has demonstrated. As Grant has discovered, we underestimate the success of "givers"—those who are other-focused and prefer to give more than they get. Because we're sometimes surrounded by "takers"—those who prefer to take more than they give or see the world as inherently competitive—we tend to think givers will just get run over. But it's not an either/or, Grant has found. By maintaining a clear sense of purpose and ambition for our own flourishing while being willing to give of ourselves to others more than we receive from them—Grant calls this being "otherish"—we turn out to be both surprisingly successful and deeply fulfilled. "Otherish" givers are less prone to burnout than everyone around them, and they're positioned to flourish alongside the ones to whom they give.[21]

This is as true for institutions as it is for people. We are called to a clear sense of purpose that leads us to want to be the best we can be, while maintaining an orientation toward others.

Otherish behavior has deep resonance with a Christian imagination. Twice in scripture—in Philippians 2 and James 3—we are enjoined to put away "selfish ambition." The adjective "selfish" suggests there is an ambition we need not put away, and actually cultivate. We might call it "Gospel ambition"—a clear sense of purpose that is focused on serving and empowering others, and our institutions, to cultivate life that really is life.

This view reinforces William Damon's findings on people with other-centered purpose. Damon has observed and concluded three important and closely related things that support Grant's findings and the importance of a gospel-shaped ambition:

1. Only a positive, pro-social purpose can inspire and maintain a purposeful life. The primary reason, he says, is hard-wired into our biology: We're programmed to experience "moral elevation" when we behave benevolently and empathically toward others.

2. In a related manner, ignoble purposes burn out, "either slowly in growing doubt and uncertainty, or suddenly in self-destructive activity." Again, our species is programmed this way: we experience "moral disgust"—not immediately and not with regularity, perhaps, but eventually and unavoidably—when we pursue our own interests primarily.

3. The purposes we find "noble" and fulfilling over time are always the ones that promote the well-being of others and are pursued through means that conform to moral standards. They are accomplished in a spirit marked more by humility and service than self-aggrandizement.[22]

Damon goes on to note that purpose can be noble without being "heroic" or requiring daring, life-endangering adventures. One need not be Susan Cowley or Mother Teresa, in other words. "But noble purposes," Damon writes, "also may be found in the day-to-day fabric of ordinary existence. A mother caring for her child, a teacher instructing students, a doctor treating patients, a citizen campaigning for a candidate for the sake of improving the community, all are pursuing noble purposes." Each of these examples involves promoting the flourishing of another, and when we couple this with ambition about our own flourishing and those of the institutions and communities of which we are a part, we are deeply fulfilled.[23]

In short, giving for the betterment of others is more powerful and less dangerous than most of us suppose. As Juliet said to Romeo, "My bounty is as boundless as the sea. The more I give to thee, the more I have."[24] Sociologists Christian Smith and Hilary Davidson have found that this paradox proves true: the "paradox of generosity," they have shown, is that it's good for those who practice it and good for others as well.[25]

And when it works, when givers succeed, Grant has found that giving and flourishing become contagious, spreading and cascading. Philosopher Christian Miller has written that we can see something that is "so powerful in its goodness" that it has the powerful capacity to "make us care."[26] People start to root for givers and support them, and their success actually *creates* value, Grant notes, rather than claims it, developing virtuous cycles and collective benefits.[27]

The upshot is this: we all stand to benefit when we start with why, when our purpose is to promote the flourishing for which we all yearn—in our own lives, in our relationships and institutions, in our communities, and in the world at large. Starting with the End, flourishing, and holding to that purpose, deepens and sustains our commitments and enables us to be open to a more hopeful future. And this is crucial for institutions as well as in our own personal lives.

Starting with why also allows us the freedom and nimbleness to innovate. We're freed from the rigidity that stifles too many institutions when their focus is on the rigid beliefs and practices that say "this is what we do, this is where we're going, and this is how we get there." As Talitha Koum teaches us, a purpose that precedes and transcends mission, vision, and strategy, weaving all of it together, can enable the sort of evolution that engenders trust, sustains commitment, and achieves lasting impact. We practice traditioned innovation and discover opportunities to start new institutions, renew existing ones, and develop synergies across sectors.

Perhaps most important, when we start with and hold to a commitment to human flourishing at the heart of our purpose, we help other people develop what Gunderman calls "larger, more complete conceptions of themselves as human beings."[28] And we develop institutions that bear witness to such conceptions and practices. We discover the life that really is life.

Chapter 3
Bewilderment

To venture on wilder seas
Where storms will show your mastery

—Sir Francis Drake

"Finding the stars" is key to navigating these wilder seas. Yet as Sir Francis was well aware, on the seas come storms and fog that usually mean disorientation, confusion, paralysis, and bewilderment. These things can blind us from seeing the navigational stars at all. Those storms and fog include the bewilderments that come from massive disruptions such as a global pandemic that disorients all of us and threatens to fracture our communities and world in ever-new ways.

We currently live in a world that resembles the stormy, foggy seas of the Drake poem. This world can confound us, and, even when we start with the End and commit to flourishing as a guide to where we're going, it's easy to lose sight of that purpose because of the storms and the fog and our own instability. It's impossible to stay focused when we're so bewildered.

Sometimes this happens because the world is changing so quickly, and we feel ill-equipped to adapt. Other times it's because the problems we encounter, or the contexts in which we seek to address them, are so wicked and complex. For most of us, it's some combination of both these factors, along with an enduring mystification about human nature—the ways we are able to be good to one another, yet also so corrupt, self-interested, or prone to let suffering abide, so long as it's not our own. Whatever the case, there's a lurking sense that things are shifting, and we have to figure out ways to account for our nature and respond to these shifts, even though we find ourselves bewildered.

As Charles P. Pierce has written—in *Sports Illustrated* of all places, signaling just how prevalent our bewilderments have become—"We are in some sort of unstable period right now. Nothing seems solid. Nothing seems permanent. The tectonic plates of our institutions—all of our institutions—seem to be grinding loose, and all the questions begin, 'How can you still . . . ?' How can you still . . . believe in politics, go to that church, or trust your money to that bank?" Pierce has diagnosed well, it seems. We trust less, and we're unsure of where to turn. This era is indeed profoundly disorienting.[1]

Too often, our bewilderment compels us toward one of two responses: toward ill-advised *traditionalism* on the one hand, where we double down, attempting to do as we've always done out of habit, nostalgia, fear, or resistance to the idea of doing anything else; or toward *futurism* on the other, rushing simply to disrupt, disrupt, disrupt, since unfettered faith in "progress" seems the prevailing zeitgeist, the game our culture plays. We mistakenly sense that what we've done in the good times will be sufficient for us now, or we panic and simply mimic the storm, as though effort and ingenuity will be enough to combat such big forces. We start to long either for the comforts of returning to shore, where, at best, "our dreams come true because we dream too little" (to borrow from Sir Francis), or we continue to venture recklessly onward, suspecting that our technological ingenuity and innovation alone (the "abundance of things we possess") will provide all we need to master the seas.

Neither of these impulses is sufficient, and neither alone is wise in this era that is so confounding that it's earned ominous labels that feel spot on: an "age of acceleration," a "VUCA" (volatile, uncertain, complex, and ambiguous) era, a "time of distrust." And now, in the wake of the pandemic, all of those labels together.

A lot is at stake, and the fact that the flourishing for which we yearn is always under threat—from deep and complex forces outside our control, from technological advancements that present questions about what it means to be human, from those parts of human nature that perpetuate suffering and evil—means that we ought to think earnestly about how to navigate this bewildering world and the complex, unpredictable future toward which we're headed. And we don't have a lot of time to do so.[2]

In this chapter, we offer both diagnosis and prognosis. As we're quick to acknowledge, our era is certainly not the first to experience turbulence. People throughout history have experienced challenges, changes, tumult, even pandemics, as change is inevitable and often disorienting. We're not historically alone in facing a set of complex navigational challenges.

Yet we can't minimize what makes our era distinctive. There are times in history when the fog is denser and the storms are stronger, and there are eras when the changes and challenges are more profound than others. We live in such an era. And because of that, believing that this is just another set of changes and challenges can lead to misjudgments that are as problematic as ignoring the storms altogether. We need diagnoses that take us to the heart of our bewilderments so that our prognoses and strategies for dealing with them will be as fruitful as possible.

In this chapter, we begin to examine the world in its bewildering state, our tendencies to respond impulsively, and the potential hazards of continuing these impulses. In doing this, we also want to suggest how traditioned innovation might begin to spark a different imagination for our lives and institutions, a new way of seeing how to navigate the future.

We introduced you in chapter 1 to Sergio, whose compelling migration from deep suffering to healthy flourishing provides a glimpse of what's possible when people and institutions commit, like Father G and

Homeboy Industries, to the yearning we all share for flourishing lives, institutions, and communities. Of course, in our initial rendering, we blew past some of the important details, presenting the story as if there were a sort of inevitability to Sergio's journey. Let us be clear: there most certainly was not.

Indeed, part of what makes Sergio's story so compelling is that it came about in an unlikely way, through the love and ingenuity of a priest-turned-entrepreneur who partnered with a Hollywood bigwig—not something you hear every day. Sergio's rebirth and reformation weren't simply fated, and Homeboy Industries didn't just happen: it wasn't destined to come into being, to remain afloat, to innovate and succeed in rehabilitating thousands of people in situations like Sergio's, let alone set them on a path toward flourishing.

One version of Father G's and Sergio's shared story starts in 1925, long before either of them was born, when the Catholic priests of LA's St. Mary's Parish established Dolores Mission, a church to serve economically poor neighbors in "the Flats" of Boyle Heights in East LA. An effort that was right in line with Catholic social teachings to serve those on society's edges, Dolores Mission focused its resources and attention on immigrant neighbors who struggled to make it in the United States and lacked opportunity for economic success. In those early years, Dolores started the area's first Catholic school, which served children in the neighborhood for decades.

Then hard times fell on Dolores Mission in the 1980s. The neighborhood's poverty was compounded with violence as drugs and gangs took over the neighborhood, and parishioners lived in fear. The nuns who had always run the school dwindled in number, and when there were too few of them to keep the school open—and too few active parishioners to justify the church's continued operation—Dolores Mission faced a harrowing set of choices. In a last-ditch effort, the presiding cardinal turned to the Jesuits, members of the religious order called the Society of Jesus who, for five hundred years, have sought to live out the vision of their founder, St. Ignatius of Loyola, to "find God in all things" by caring "for the whole person: body, mind, and soul." This often took them into difficult situations, where they worked undaunted. Asked to take over at Dolores in the 1980s, the Jesuits soon called one of their own, a newly ordained priest named Gregory Boyle, to serve as parish priest.

In 1986, Boyle (not yet known as Father G) arrived at Dolores Mission—which happened to be near where he grew up—from a stint serving in Bolivia, where he'd worked alongside a needy but vibrant community. When he returned to East LA, Boyle found the situation dire, and there seemed no clear way forward. In addition to the dwindling prospects of the Dolores Mission school and parish, the neighborhood presented immense difficulty. Boyle Heights, population one hundred thousand, had more gang members per capita than any other place in the United States, and eight warring gangs held far more sway over the neighborhood than any Catholic church could. "If Los Angeles was the gang capital of the world," Father G has since recounted about his arrival, then "our little postage-stamp-size area on the map was the gang capital of LA."[3]

Perched between two large public housing projects, Dolores Mission was the poorest Catholic church in the city, and it was not a pleasant place to be. It was quite dangerous, in fact, with gangs known to fight and shoot indiscriminately. Boyle Heights had become the kind of place most people only wanted to escape.

In those early years at Dolores Mission under Boyle's leadership, a few possible futures began to come into view, and there were plenty of opinions given by parishioners and the church hierarchy. One was for the congregation to fortify—to cloister, hole up, and self-protect. According to this reasoning, the context had clearly changed since the original priests founded Dolores Mission with such hope and goodwill. Why not go back to shore, then, and return to a simpler time by simply closing?

No one could blame Father G if he opted to seal off from the chaos of the Flats by accepting this way of thinking. If this new context is not our fault, then why should we adapt to it? But if you know anything about Father G, you know this: he was unimpressed with these kinds of ideas.

Another option was to try to neutralize the chaos—to broker peace and figure out ways to keep warring gangs from shooting at one another, so that the neighborhood could go on living and the church wouldn't find itself in the cross fire. According to this reasoning, if we're living in chaos, then let's just stop the chaos. Then we can go about our business, and keep doing what we do.

This held considerable, logical appeal, and Father G tried it. But as you might guess, it succeeded only modestly and temporarily. The deep forces of poverty, violence, drugs, racial strife, inequality, failing schools, and a general feeling of hopelessness were far too potent and complex to be held at bay by a priest brokering a peace deal—no matter how capable the priest and how compelling the peace. Attempts to neutralize wouldn't be enough. It was like trying to neutralize a thunderstorm or fog.

So Father G began to envision something better. This thinking involved connecting past, present, and future, and investing in institutions. It was guided by an infectious hope and a belief that the flourishing we yearn for is always worth striving for, even when the circumstances are difficult or complex. It went something like the following: *What if we recapture the animating vision that brought Dolores Mission into being six or seven decades ago, adapt it to our current context, and improvise a new way forward? What if we draw wisdom from the past while we renew this institution with a pioneering focus on a better future? What if we stop trying to hide or neutralize and instead wade into an uncertain and chaotic future, animated by a life-giving purpose to promote the flourishing of everyone in our reach?*

The thoughts weren't quite this crystalized when Father G pushed Dolores Mission out onto these wilder seas in the early 1990s. But the instincts were there, the commitment was strong, and Father G drew from a deep well of wisdom and tradition. As Father G knew well, the wisdom of the past can help illumine the path toward flourishing in the future. It wouldn't be a straight or easy path, but Father G and his parishioners were willing to follow it.

❖ ❖ ❖ ❖ ❖ ❖

Not all of us confront gang members in the streets of East LA, where deep forces of violence and poverty are the prevailing threats to flourishing. But we do all share the reality that big forces beyond our control threaten our capacity for flourishing. We inhabit a rapidly changing and chaotic world where bewildering forces present fundamental questions for us as individuals, for the institutions we lead and serve, and for our communities and society at large. Whether our context is business, education, health care, churches, or government—all locales that face a complex and unpredictable future in one way or another—it's easy to find ourselves confused and confounded by problems that are wicked and interrelated.

While there are a lot of ways to dissect the changes and complexities we encounter, at least three things are clear: change is happening, flourishing is vulnerable, and most of us aren't sure how to navigate this reality in our lives, in our institutions, or in the world. We owe ourselves a little grace, of course. Evidence has mounted suggesting that the problems that threaten our flourishing are growing more complex than they've ever been, a reality compounded by the fact that they're also coming at us faster than they ever have before.

We can tease from the malaise a few contributing factors shared across contexts, some broad and macro-level; others a little closer to home. Looking macroscopically, things like business model disruption, mounting power disparities, and demographic shifts swirl overhead much like an advancing thunderstorm, menacing as we try to navigate things down here in our own lives and institutions. We glimpse in that storm the uncertainty faced in business, social, and political institutions when the old business models are not so reliable anymore because technology and artificial intelligence are upending even the most stable industries. Add to that a blurring, and in some cases an expansion, of industry boundaries, giving immense power to tech companies or financial institutions and leaving most of us uneasy over concentrations of power in the hands of people we don't know and don't have a reason to trust. Then, amid demographic changes—such as aging populations in developed countries and exploding young populations in the majority world—we glimpse the pressures these factors can put on climate, land use, food supply, and other domains where mass-scale conflict seems inevitable because we don't trust one another.

All of this has been intensified and accelerated by COVID-19. The pandemic has caused disruptions to health care and the economy and intensified political fracturing. It has accelerated some trends (such as the importance of technology) while stopping other trends (such as globalization) in their tracks.[4]

These significant macro-pressures that swirl around us all the time and influence our lives and institutions even more than we realize give us deep unease. We are aware of them, and forward-thinking leaders and institutions attempt to account for them. But the reality is that most leaders feel a sense of helplessness about these big, brewing storms; we have enough on our minds as it is. That is, there's so much fog down here surrounding our own boats—more immediate concerns that are amply disorienting—that we can hardly pay attention to the storms brewing on the horizon.

What are those immediate concerns? Admittedly, the range and diversity of our problems are distinctive for each of us. Yet it's safe to assume that three important forces cut across our contexts and influence our pursuit of flourishing, so we'd do well to examine and account for them. They are acceleration, declining trust, and the sneaky prevalence of market forces.

It's difficult to grasp just how quickly changes are coming at us. As Ray Kurzweil, director of engineering at Google, has observed, "We're entering an age of acceleration. The models underlying society at every level, which are largely based on a linear model of change, are going to have to be redefined." On the one hand, Kurzweil's observation sounds like a stock response to technological development: *the world's changing; get ready*. But the immensity of what he's suggesting is hard to absorb. This "age of acceleration" means that technological growth is happening exponentially with no signs of slowing. And because of the explosive power of exponential growth, "the twenty-first century will be equivalent to 20,000 years of progress at today's rate of progress." The result? "Organizations have to be able to redefine themselves at a faster and faster pace."[5]

So taken was *New York Times* columnist Thomas Friedman with the phrase "age of acceleration" that he borrowed it for the subtitle of his 2016 book, which aims to help us understand the big forces of our age. In Friedman's view, simultaneous accelerations in technology, globalization, and climate change are interacting with one another to marshal an entire age that is defined not just by change, but by a drastic acceleration in the pace of change.[6] In the past, for example, companies took years to build, and industries took decades or even centuries to develop. Today, high-flying tech start-ups, known in the industry as "unicorns," can win billion-dollar valuations within a year or two of entering existence, a reality that fundamentally shifts the ways even the world's biggest and steadiest companies and institutions operate.[7]

This is no small development. It is more than just a threat to business-as-usual lurking around every corner—an Airbnb to upend my hotel chain, an Uber to negate my taxi service, or a University of Phoenix to siphon off students who would otherwise enroll at my university. What's at stake is also more than the sort of angst over the tech platform *du jour* that causes some old-school executives to pop antacids—*are the young people using Snapchat now? I thought it was Instagram. And how is it that Facebook is already obsolete?* These things are important, of course, but they're only a small part. Take, for example, the fact that "Moore's law"—the once outlandish, but still-coming-true expectation that microchips double in power every two years—has expanded its reach across multiple technology platforms and shows no signs of slowing.

Take also what Geoff Colvin has called the "mind-bending progress" of machine learning and artificial intelligence, which comprise, at once, some people's wildest dreams and others' darkest nightmares. We're either boundlessly optimistic if we find ourselves privileged as producers on the cutting edge, or we are becoming more and more depressed about technology and robotics dominating our lives and making us increasingly irrelevant. There are driverless cars and story-writing computers. Watson, the personified IBM computer and *Jeopardy!* champion, is even designing new dishes as a chef. What's next?[8]

These forces, and many others like them, keep us operating at a frenetic pace. We are continually told that everything is changing, and to a certain extent it is. Senior leaders often feel like they can't keep up. Emerging leaders grow frustrated because institutions won't change fast enough. All of us sense that we need to fundamentally adjust just to keep up with the acceleration. And, to some extent, we do.

Meanwhile, our trust in institutions—from governments to businesses to religious bodies—is taking a nosedive. As we touched on in chapter 1, even our most cherished institutions find themselves on the defensive. From 2014 to 2017, Americans polled by Gallup reported that the single most important problem facing their nation was the government itself—not war, not economic fragility, not terrorism, but the very institutions put in place by the people to achieve the public good. The same sentiment holds true across Europe. The pandemic has intensified the awareness that our institutions are far more dysfunctional and broken than we even thought.

Polls show that trust in mass media has fared just as poorly. While, for much of American history, most Americans trusted the media to do the important work of informing the public, today fewer than a third do, fueled by political leaders who call the press—in contradiction of its very mission and purpose—"the enemy of the people."

Or take financial institutions, where Europeans and Americans experience declining confidence in banks and brokerage houses that, based on experience, are capable of bringing down entire economies. Across a variety of business and social sectors there is a crisis of trust in institutions.

Religious institutions have not been immune, either. Many, in fact, stand at the vanguard of this trust decline, where a host of factors is at play, from general secularization to a rash of sex abuse scandals and cover-ups, disillusioning people from institutions that once held more sway than any other in Western cultures.[9]

At the same time, confidence in higher education is waning. While there is a long tradition in the United States of undying allegiance to one's alma mater, it turns out we don't actually trust them to have a positive effect on the way things are going in the world. While those on the political left often see colleges and universities as bastions of patriarchy and racism, those on the political right see them as citadels of untrustworthy progressivism that is cancerous to society. Whatever the case, only about half of Americans see colleges and universities as positively influencing the direction of society.[10] And the viability of higher education as an industry is in doubt in the wake of the pandemic.

In combination, these factors have led to what Gallup has called "hope and trust" deficits across the United States and Europe, where, depending on the country, between a quarter and a half of people—an astounding number—describe themselves as "disaffected and discouraged," in a state of disillusionment and not hopeful about the prospects of emerging.[11] They're all asking, with Charles Pierce of *Sports Illustrated*, "How can you still . . ."

This is problematic—full stop. Indeed, institutions across society bear responsibility for this decline in trust, and many of the reasons we mistrust are justified. But institutions can't be abandoned—and certainly not at the pace at which we're abandoning them today. The biggest threats we face and the most important problems we need to address throughout society cannot effectively be solved by individuals working in isolation. The work of flourishing is not the work of lone geniuses, and disruption is only sometimes helpful. The building and maintenance of healthy, vibrant institutions is vital to flourishing lives, communities, and societies.

In addition, as change accelerates and trust diminishes, something subtler is also contributing to our malaise and bewilderment. We operate increasingly in a context in which almost every sphere of life is penetrated and influenced by markets—forces that are almost entirely out of our individual or institutional control, but which affect us profoundly. Almost everything from how we manage our organizations and our lives, to how we make decisions at work and at home, and even how we think about ourselves, is deeply shaped by markets and market-based thinking. Even our best impulses to do good in the world, to orient our lives toward human flourishing, happen in the context of market forces. We compete: my university, hospital, business, church, or nonprofit wants the same students, patients, customers, members, or donors as yours. Or: we'll be the best quick-service restaurant experience, the most trusted partner for health care, the prime driver in an all-communicating world, the most loved, most flown, most profitable, most respected.

Competition is healthy so long as it is nurtured by a broader vision of flourishing. Too often, though, our institutions and lives have become connected by forces that don't foster the mindsets that lead to flourishing. We can't "fix" that reality—the markets are strong and perhaps even endemic to human social interaction, as philosophers have long observed—but that doesn't change the fact that the prevalence of market forces can cause angst and discomfort when we yearn for flourishing that seems inconsistent with the mindsets and behaviors that unconstrained markets compel.

To be sure, markets are valuable. Markets—usually in concert with technological progress and sound governance—have helped lift billions of people from grinding, abject poverty; have created the very idea of a middle class; and, yes, have made a lot of people rich. Yet we need markets also to be connected to broader purposes to maximize their positive impact and minimize their risks and damage.[12]

So let's recap: Macro-forces, like business model upheavals and seismic demographic shifts are swirling all around us like a brewing thunderstorm, making us feel uneasy and helpless. Meanwhile, we encounter a fog of breakneck technological change, rapid declines in trust, and stealthy market forces that shape nearly all facets of our lives. It's no surprise that leaders are bewildered, if not anguished and distressed.

We encounter a unique context, marked by "VUCA"—volatility, uncertainty, complexity, and ambiguity. We are confounded by the age of acceleration. We are aggrieved by the era of distrust. We feel vulnerable, not unlike the parishioners at Dolores Mission, who were threatened in the cross fire of warring gangs.

It's not surprising, then, that leaders across sectors are increasingly reporting their disorientation. In 2013, Duke Corporate Education studied CEOs around the globe, asking them to describe the evolving contexts in which they're attempting to lead. What quickly became clear was the near-universal feeling of bewilderment. The study reached a compelling set of conclusions about what it means to navigate toward the future. In short, leaders across industries agreed that:

- it's increasingly challenging to foresee problems,

- the problems leaders do identify are more multidimensional than ever before,

- the solutions to these problems are more complex,

- the shelf life of information is short,

- the interconnection of information resources is complex,

- access to information is uncontrollable,

- and the source of differentiation—of making yourself or your institution distinct—lies in figuring things out as opposed to finding things out.

Whether or not these things are actually true is beside the point. The important takeaway is that this is a widespread perspective among leaders of institutions and the general population: we are disoriented, confused, mystified, uncertain. In short, we feel bewildered.

Because change has accelerated like never before, unpredictability has become a fact of life, and complexity is the new norm. Whereas leaders once could rely on certain patterns, rules, and predictability about who makes the rules, such constants have evaporated. As one CEO in the study described it, "It used to be that we could rely on models. We now have to release ourselves from these and think differently," devising more complex approaches to solve even those problems that seem, at face value, like familiar ones.

As the challenges themselves have become less predictable, so too have the nature and reliability of what we "know." Because of the explosion in information technology, access to knowledge is increasingly universal and virtually uncontrollable, and our knowledge bases are continually expanding, thus leading to what the Duke Corporate Education study called a "shorter shelf life for information." As a result, the most important type of knowledge is not *what* is, but *why* it is. It's also more important to consider how to think than what to think.[13]

As Friedman has written, experiencing accelerations such as these has opened a wide gap between the pace of change on the one hand, and the ability of people to adapt to and manage change on the other. Many people are feeling a loss of control and are desperate for navigational help.[14]

That part—the need for navigational help in the face of bewildering circumstances—isn't new, of course. As Avivah Gottlieb Zornberg notes in *Bewilderments*, her book about the Israelites' wilderness wandering centuries ago, when you're bewildered and have lost a sense of where you're going, the risk is that, at best, you're paralyzed. For the Israelites, though, it was actually worse. They became so disoriented that they only wanted to return to slavery in Egypt, which means, as Zornberg characterizes it, they suffered something worse than death: it was the death of their imagination.[15]

When we're bewildered, we often hunker down. Perhaps we panic. We grow paralyzed. We need others, yet we isolate ourselves. Perhaps, like the Israelites, we suffer something worse than death with the loss of imagination. We sense that the future isn't what it used to be, so why bother? Why care about someone else's flourishing when I feel threatened myself?

With all of this in mind, it matters how we orient ourselves and respond in our bewilderment. We can't simply trust that the world will continue to be the way it has been or that the institutions we have relied on will endure and function in the ways we have grown accustomed.

This VUCA world is confounding, and we now have less time than we used to have to address the bewilderment. Mirroring our VUCA world, we, too, find ourselves confounded.

Even if we don't always know what to do, much less how or why to do it, there's a growing awareness these days that many older models and practices are increasingly dysfunctional for addressing our current challenges. At times we're not sure we're even asking the right questions, much less working on the right problems or cultivating the best approaches and institutions that will move us toward the sort of flourishing we like to imagine.

It's increasingly the case that senior institutional leaders, many of whom have given their professional lives to institutions, feel a heavy burden as they look to the future, worried that they're ineffective or ill-equipped and that their institutions might not survive, much less flourish, amid the storms and the fog on these wilder seas. Younger people often feel that the institutions they're supposed to inhabit are ineffective, untrustworthy, or otherwise dissolving—*How can you still.* They're not sure what to do about it or what to develop instead. People of all ages worry that we don't have sufficient language or frameworks to navigate the future.

If we take a step back—release our paralysis in the face of bewilderment for a moment—it's helpful to realize that every person and institution shares a dilemma that is endemic to humanity and to the created order of time: we must reckon with multiple tenses. The past is always increasing, while the future, in all its vastness, is always right in front of us. A question we must perpetually face, then, is how should we live in the present toward the future in light of the past—which, as William

Faulkner famously observed in *Requiem for a Nun*, "is never dead. It's not even past."

As we mentioned earlier, we seem prone toward two main impulses in response to that question, particularly when the present is so bewildering: One is *traditionalism*, the impulse to maintain a tight grip on the past, to return to it, or, even worse, to return to a fictionalized and nostalgic imagination of it, ignoring or denying the ways we need to adapt to the future; another is indiscriminate *futurism*, which is a rush toward the future in a race away from the past. Some of us are far more inclined toward one than the other, but it's likely that most of us exhibit both of these, depending on the circumstance. Let's consider how they manifest themselves.

Traditionalism involves, at its core, what John W. Gardner has called an "incapacity for self-renewal," where we settle into rigid and fixed views and set ways of doing things. When we do this, we progressively narrow the scope and variety of our lives, and thus our imagination for the future. Whether or not we say it this way, we adopt the mindset that we ought to keep doing things the way we've always done them.[16]

Søren Kierkegaard observed the paradox that although life must be lived forward, we can really only understand it backward. Most of us find far more comfort in the things we understand or have experienced than in those we don't, which creates a natural tendency to preserve the past because we know it—whatever its merits.

Following the lead of Jaroslav Pelikan, a former Yale historian, we want to steadfastly distinguish traditional*ism* from tradition. "It is traditionalism," Pelikan argued, "that gives tradition such a bad name." Tradition, Pelikan instructs, is "the living faith of the dead" (more on that in due course), while, by contrast, "traditionalism is the dead faith of the living."[17] To state that differently, if a little less cleverly, traditionalism connotes a maintenance of the past to the exclusion, sometimes ardently, of change in any form.

Beyond the fear that animated the Israelites' "Back to Egypt" mentality in the face of bewilderment, four other drivers of traditionalism—pathologies, we might call them—are prevalent:

- nostalgia,

- unexamined habits and assumptions,

- perceived lack of imagination, and

- outright obstinance—resistance to change because it's change.

Each of these is related, of course, and sometimes they mix potently together to keep us rooted in the past and ill-equipped to navigate the future.

The first of these, nostalgia, might seem the least pernicious because there's something universal, almost deeply human, about sentimental longing for the past. For all of us, there are moments or feelings or places in our past that spark wistful affection—playing in the creek as the sun set on a summer day in our childhood, the smell and softness of our children when they were babies, a memorable vacation with dear friends or family. There is, in its pure form, nothing wrong with this feeling—in many respects, nostalgia can feel, and perhaps even *be*, deeply right.

It becomes problematic, however, when we begin to develop an orthodoxy of nostalgia, where we normalize, nurture, and even formally validate a regular longing for past glory. Johannes Hofer, the Swiss medical student who in 1688 coined the term "nostalgia" in an attempt to diagnose what he thought to be a clinical condition, would probably be baffled that we would make such a condition "orthodox." Hofer thought the listlessness, longing, and homesickness of Swiss mercenaries, who had descended the majestic Alps to fight enemies in foreign lowlands, were products of a mental disorder born of ear and brain damage from the incessant ringing of cowbells the soldiers had heard on alpine hillsides throughout their youth. He thought nostalgia required clinical treatment; maybe he was on to something.[18]

Literary greats have done their best to caution us, with characters mired in nostalgia frequently becoming the subject of tragedy. Take F. Scott Fitzgerald's Jay Gatsby, whose only wish seemed to be a return to the past, to a life with his beloved (and idealized) Daisy. Gatsby's ambition and wealth accumulation were simply efforts to retrieve a romanticized past, a yearning "to recover something, some idea of himself perhaps," an effort that ultimately proved elusive, hollow, and tragic when he found himself alone and sad. The lesson—the tragedy—was that the ideals Daisy was supposed to have embodied were romanticized rather than real, and even if they had been real, they would have remained elusive—something we all can learn from. Fitzgerald was resolute: "You can't repeat the past," he said. Like Gatsby, it's always "just out of the reach of [our] hand." The greatest lesson of *The Great Gatsby*, for Fitzgerald, seemed to be that Gatsby is all of us: "We beat on, boats against the current, borne back ceaselessly into the past."[19]

There's a measure of truth in this, inasmuch as we tend to remember the past in a way that idealizes it, and sometimes that sends us on an errand to recapture something that never quite existed. Throughout this book we're interested in how the past might help us navigate the future, how we might draw wisdom from the past or carry forward habits and mindsets and virtues that embolden and inform the ways we encounter uncertainty. But to draw from and to carry forward are not the same as to romanticize, idealize, or attempt to recover that which never quite existed in the ways our nostalgia tends to remember it.

This kind of orthodox nostalgia can be subtle: *Remember when John was in charge? Oh, those were the days!* Or perhaps we start to suppose (often from the stories of our predecessors) that, *Once upon a time, they had it right around here. Why can't we get it right like they did?*

In much the same way, habit, like nostalgia, can become a gateway to traditionalism. Habit is universal and deeply human, of course, and it is crucial to character and flourishing: it is by habituation we become virtuous, wrote Aristotle in the *Nicomachean Ethics*. But often, habits signify the less-than-virtuous behaviors we maintain without any deliberation or intentionality. We are creatures of many habits, and, over time, our un-considered habits become unexamined assumptions that guide our insti-tutions and our lives. More often than not, our unexamined habits and as-sumptions lead us down paths of least resistance, not paths of flourishing.

That's because habit formation is subtle. As social scientists have ob-served, we tend to think that we are making decisions all throughout our days—and all throughout our lives—when in fact, more than 40 percent of our daily actions are a direct result of habits. At some point they started as a decision, perhaps, or maybe even a series of decisions, but, eventually, they became rote, unnoticed, and unquestioned. Charles Duhigg, in his book *The Power of Habit*, has distilled the complex and growing scientific literature on habits by writing that something called a "habit loop" takes shape to dictate this 40 percent of things we do. The habit loop forms in three basic steps, which he calls *cue*, *routine*, and *reward*: a cue is a trigger that tells your brain which habit to use and puts your brain into automatic mode; a routine acts out the habit—physically, mentally, or emotionally; and we embrace these routines typically because a reward follows, rein-forcing the habit, closing the loop until the cue triggers it all again, and helping the brain figure out if this particular loop is worth keeping for use in the future.[20]

Experiments on rats in mazes have demonstrated much of what we in-tuit from our own experience: with enough routine, our brains can go into autopilot even as we do some pretty complex things. Think about driving out of your neighborhood this morning. Actually, maybe you can't, and that's the point. You had to start the car, back out of the driveway, adjust the temperature, turn into traffic, tune the radio or remember the plot of your now-playing audio book, signal a turn and execute it, check your hair in the mirror, and start to run through your morning work to-do list, all while making sure the other morning commuters didn't plow you over as they did the same. Now think back to the clunky, perhaps death-defying process of learning how to drive a car. Could your fifteen-year-old self have imagined doing all those things without even realizing it?

You get the point. Certain habits and assumptions emerge because our brains crave the efficiencies of routine. Our brains like to go into autopilot, and, because they're such remarkable organs, they can do that even when we execute complex tasks or processes that once required our deliberate attention and perhaps even represented our best thinking. These habits and assumptions become unnoticed—routinized. They become comfortable. And suddenly, sometimes unconsciously, we develop patterns of unchecked assumptions and start to believe—consciously or otherwise—that the way we're operating is the only way to operate. This is a traditionalism born of unexamined assumptions: the belief that we should do things the way we've "always" done them, nurtured simply because we do things as we are used to doing them.

Sometimes, of course, habits lull us into a belief that we lack the imagination to do things differently, which is another pathology of traditionalists. We resort to what we know, and we do the things we've "always" done because we simply can't imagine a way to do them differently—or so we think. In reality—and the research is clear—it's often just that we fear trying. We fear the doctor more than the disease.

These destructive myths about imagination and creativity can lead to the state that Zornberg described as being worse than death for the bewildered Israelites. In our lives and institutions, that state often manifests itself in a belief that imagination and creativity are fixed traits, perhaps genetic, reserved for those who have them, out of grasp for those (like me, we often think) who don't.

Tom and David Kelley, who run the design consultancy IDEO, which is responsible for an amazing array of new ideas and innovations, have diagnosed this myth as a persistent and socially nurtured deficit in what they call "creative confidence." We are afraid to fail, afraid that we don't have enough of that magic creativity gene, and afraid of shame or embarrassment if we try new, hard things that don't succeed.[21]

It turns out this deficit is curable, and perhaps the most important part of the cure is to recognize and name our fears, and to adopt what psychologist Carol Dweck has now famously termed a "growth mindset." It's easy to see, though, in the absence of creative confidence and growth mindsets, how our perceived lack of imagination leads to stagnant traditionalism.[22]

We, and the institutions we inhabit, would do well to foster a culture that encourages failures that result from creative experimentation. At Stanford's Hasso Plattner Institute of Design, better known as "the d.school," any failure of this sort is marked by the fail-er exclaiming, like a proud magician, "ta da!" Not a bad idea. As venture capitalist Randy Komisar is fond of saying, what distinguishes pockets of entrepreneurship like Silicon Valley is not their successes but the ways they deal with failure. Cultures that encourage successful innovation are the ones that appreciate and understand "failing forward," or what Komisar calls "constructive failure."[23]

Of course, some of us are just stubborn. Some of us—all of us, sometimes—just don't want to change. Take the example of Dutch chess grandmaster Jan Hein Donner. As Erik Brynjolfsson and Andrew McAfee have described him, Donner simply doesn't plan to adjust to the new way we think about chess mastery, which has started to pit humanity's best minds against IBM's best computers (in a contest that seems almost a bit too perfect as a symbol of past against future). Many of us have seen Watson shred the competition on *Jeopardy!*, but less known is IBM's Deep Blue, the opponent of the future for any chess grandmaster. Donner, confronted with the impending prospect of facing Deep Blue, said he'd already planned a strategy to match wits, if someone ever forced him to play the computer. What's his plan? "I would bring a hammer."[24]

If one of our very best minds is prone to resort to an ancient tool that would simply destroy the prospect of facing a technologically enhanced opponent, then surely we must be in good company when we're inclined to retreat from the prospects of a future that intimidates us. But do we see this tendency in ourselves?

It bears mentioning that these patterns and pathologies of traditionalism—nostalgia, habits, fear, and stubbornness—are not unique to us here and now. Anthropologists have observed empirically, across time and space, that adherence to tradition is a social glue that brings cohesiveness to a clan or tribe, and people tend to be myopic about their own shared customs, practices, and ways of thinking. Over and over, anthropologists have been told, "That is the way we have always done it," even when they know, in fact, that a specific custom has recent origins. This probably sounds familiar to many of us. We humans are good, as it turns out, at believing that we should continue to do things the way we've "always" done them.[25]

Traditionalism endures because it's comfortable. It keeps us pointed toward our past, and Kierkegaard was right that we're better equipped to understand backward than forward. So our nostalgia gives temporary solace amid storms and bewilderment. Routines are easy. Imagination and creativity might leave us vulnerable to shame. And sometimes we just decide that we won't change because we don't like change.

But cultivating these patterns, while easy, is no way to navigate the future. Traditionalist responses lead us to become bitter, insular, and stagnant—the bitterness born of our frustrations when the illusions of the past become elusive in the present. There is a surprisingly slippery quality to the past, after all, primarily because the circumstances of the past always differ from the circumstances of the present. Heraclitus of Ephesus said as much twenty-five hundred years ago: "No man ever steps in the same river twice, for it's not the same river, and he's not the same man." That frustrates us.

And often, when we're irritated and bitter, or if we're simply after an elusive past, we close the circle. We become insular or tribal in deeply detrimental ways. Trying to do things the way we used to do them, once upon a romanticized time, we start to marginalize those whose connection to our past is tenuous or strained. Employers forget how the business once held women back. Universities forget that they once barred Black students. Hospitals forget the ways they stigmatized mental illness. We do this at the expense of trust, collaboration, friendship, and future hope. We end up fostering us-versus-them mentalities that fester. We begin to tell self-justifying stories of our past that become less and less truthful.

And one way or another, by fostering traditionalist mentalities, we inevitably stagnate or regress. John Gardner observed this in 1964, and is worth quoting at length:

> When organizations and societies are young, they are flexible, fluid, not yet paralyzed by rigid specialization and willing to try anything once. As the organization or society ages, vitality diminishes, flexibility gives way to rigidity, creativity fades and there is a loss of capacity to meet challenges from unexpected directions. Call to mind the adaptability of youth, and the way in which that adaptability diminishes with the years. Call to mind the vigor . . . of some new organizations and societies—our own frontier settlements, for example—and reflect on how frequently these qualities are buried under the weight of tradition and history.[26]

In our better moments, our disorientation in the storm inspires resolve, courage, and some form of forward movement that resists the urges of traditionalism. Yet this kind of orientation, without guardrails, can be hazardous. Sometimes it starts to manifest as a form of futurism that is boundless but unchecked, optimistic but naive. Terms such as *change*, *progress*, *innovation*, *advancement*, and *disruption* start to form a shared language across a range of our institutions and industries. We become so surrounded by change, by so much fascination with change, by so much addiction to change, that we can't help adopting the mentality that everything must change.

Many of us start to believe this and practice it in the face of our bewilderments, even if we're wise enough not to say it that way. The impulse shows up throughout our culture, and it becomes our own as we are inundated with new methods, technologies, patterns of thought, and techniques. We are promised that innovation will fix everything, so we start to promise that to ourselves.

The impulse isn't all bad, of course, because innovation is vital to ongoing flourishing. Such an impulse leads us to experiment, and it is guided by an admirable optimism. It's also right in line with our uniquely human disposition to be future-oriented, prospective beings, as we'll discuss in the next chapter.

But even as there is something very positive about this willingness to experiment and to be hopeful about where it might lead, there is also something fragile about many of our approaches and our beliefs about what innovation will achieve. We start to think that we are masters of the sea, and we don't adequately account for the storms and the fog or our own fallibility. The danger in viewing innovation this way is that we start to view methods and innovations as cure-alls for that which ails us—whatever "that" is.

On their own, many of the prevailing methods and fixes—such as design thinking, hack-a-thons, technological faith, faith in progress, and strategic plans—become the intellectual equivalent of 5-Hour Energy shots: They create bursts of energy that are ultimately short-term fixes, and when misaligned, misapplied, or misunderstood, they can actually cause harm. Many of these approaches are fruitful when they jog our imaginations and orient us to the importance of intentionality and innovation for the future. But when we miscalculate what they can achieve, fail to account adequately for the vagaries and complexities of the storms, we find ourselves frenetic and flailing, unsure why they're not working. We instinctively start to fight disruption with more disruption.

John Gardner warned us of this, too, even long before our age of accelerations, noting that so many people have a decidedly undiscriminating view of change: "They think it is, without qualification, a good thing," Gardner says. But guess what: "Death is a form of change. So is deterioration."[27] With our undiscriminating view of change, we start to imagine that everything "new" is "improved." And in an effort to keep up, we tend to want to cast out everything from the past.

The follies of haphazard or aimless futurism are different from those presented by traditionalism but are equally as stark. One is that we start to think that it is our job, always, to lead change, as though we can always conceive which changes are best for an unknown future. When we think this way, we demonstrate hubris that is at best unwise and at worst deeply harmful to ourselves, our institutions, and the world. We also isolate ourselves, merging into the market forces guiding us to think we have to be right, that our innovation has to win. This leads to destruction rather than to flourishing.

It's also true that our faith in "progress" is sometimes literally killing us. As Richard A. Swenson, a physician, has observed, the relationship between progress and pain can best be seen not by looking at large global trends, but by looking much closer, at the people who sit on his examining table: "I worry about the deteriorating statistics," he writes, "but numbers don't feel pain." What concerns him most is that "patients are stressed, depressed, and exhausted. Some are desperate. Their jobs are insecure. Their marriages are in trouble. They worry about the cultural forces nipping at the heels of their children because the promise of progress has too often soured into personal and relational pain."[28] This is perhaps counterintuitive. What we think will save us can actually cause us angst and harm.

Indeed, the problem with a boundless futurism is that it fails to account for the depth of wisdom that can be mined in both our past and present. There is wisdom in tradition and in people—both the ancient sources and those more immediate. There is wisdom in experience, including our tried attempts at innovation. And as we will suggest in chapter 6, there is wisdom in what we learn from one another, through unlikely friendships, vibrant institutions, and entrepreneurial collaborations that help us see possibilities we can't see on our own. These things, not futurism, are more likely to lead us toward flourishing.

❖ ❖ ❖ ❖ ❖ ❖

So, what about Father G?

Leading a long-running organization in a complex environment, Father G found himself presented with three possibilities for Dolores Mission: retreat and fortify, following a traditionalist impulse; attempt to neutralize, which he knew wouldn't last; or figure out a better way forward, toward a more hopeful future that leads to flourishing. Father G chose the latter, but not with a callow futurism. As someone working in the midst of systemic oppression, he was aware that the deeper problem he needed to confront was despair that any future is possible. How do you inspire hope in the midst of so much suffering and oppression?

The first steps were modest. Because there were so many gang-involved kids being kicked out of public schools, the members of Dolores Mission decided to start an alternative school for the neighborhood kids booted by public schools. Doing this shifted the entire mindset of Father G and his parishioners.

Soon enough, gang members began to "kick it" at the church—the garage became a makeshift weight room, and several young people would regularly gather by the Dolores bell tower to hang out and smoke, which the church allowed. It wasn't sophisticated, and certainly these activities weren't rerouting kids out of gangs, but it wasn't nothing: at least if they were there, Father G reasoned, they weren't out on the street. At least here they were more likely to glimpse a different possibility.

Yet, when the forces of neighborhood violence and poverty were so strong, this wasn't enough, and Father G knew it. When he started to meet and know these guys—that is, when he began to see that they were far more than just gang members; when he realized their genius to survive in the face of impossible odds; when he understood that most of them faced unimaginable childhood traumas that compelled them to escape *somewhere*; when he saw that the gangbanger was usually just a tough-guy facade for most of them, that they were human beings capable of love and life and tenderness and flourishing—when he saw these things, Father G wanted desperately to point these guys toward something better, toward that "life that really is life."

Father G didn't invent this idea or this way of awed, compassionate thinking, of course. Instead, he drew it from a rich history and tradition, including the experiences of Ignatius of Loyola, who started Father G's Jesuit order. Long before Father G, the Jesuits had persisted on a commitment to promote "the good of all humanity." They saw themselves as "contemplatives in action," which had long led them to work on behalf of reconciliation and peace and to promote dialogue and good work on immigration, economic, criminal, juvenile, and environmental justice. They had built networks by collaborating and cooperating with many diverse people of goodwill, and with these friends and partners, they had long committed to "reach out to a broadly diverse world because that's where God is." They had long held that "meaning, value, and divine purpose can be discovered 'in all things.'" Father G had spent his adult life steeped in this kind of thinking.

Likewise, Dolores Mission itself had been animated by similar purposes. From its inception in 1925, it had committed itself to the neighborhood and to the people nearby who struggled to make ends meet. It had started a school—twice—out of a commitment to see neighbors flourish. It had been steadfast, remaining in the neighborhood despite temptations to flee, even when threats of violence and despair took root right outside the doors. It was rooted in the hope of the gospel.[29]

Steeped in and steadied by these traditions, Father G began to navigate a way forward toward flourishing that drew from the traditions' best proclivities and offered new ways through the malaise of a neighborhood where flourishing was always under threat. As he retells it, Father G began to envision a way for gang members to "jettison their gang past for lives more full in freedom, love, and a bright reimagining of a future for themselves."[30]

In 1988, along with several friends from his parish, Father G founded "Jobs for a Future," a new organization through which gang members could be placed in jobs at a variety of businesses and nonprofits while, scraping together everything they could, Jobs for a Future paid their salaries. They adopted a motto that "the best way to stop a bullet is with a job," and although Father G has since traded that statement for more hopeful words, in those initial days, it usually rang true.

The program showed early promise. Then, in a surprising way, its progress accelerated when LA erupted into mayhem in 1992 following the brutal police beating of Rodney King. Amid looting and riots all over town, Boyle Heights, to nearly everyone's surprise, stayed relatively calm. In a *Los Angeles Times* article, Father G attributed that miracle to the fact that gang members with jobs now had a stake in their neighborhood. They didn't want it to erupt in violence. Also, the jobs gave them a better way to use their time—and a clearer vision of what they could achieve in life without resorting to looting and riots.

Ray Stark, a wealthy and successful Hollywood agent and producer—whose film credits included *West Side Story*, *Annie*, and *Steel Magnolias*—read those comments and wanted to help. Father G was glad to let him. This made for an unlikely friendship and an innovative collaboration between a priest and a Hollywood bigwig. They were good for each other.

The first thing Father G did was to convince Stark of the merits of something outlandish: buy the old closed-up bakery across from Dolores Mission—you know, in the gang capital of the gang capital, sandwiched between two housing projects. In this less-than-desirable business location, which had already produced at least one failed bakery, the priest would open a new one. Not only that, it would employ—on purpose, mind you—the members of rival gangs. "And we'll call it," Father G said with a flourish, "The Homeboy Bakery!"

Stark was electrified, and before he could blink, they'd also commandeered a tortilla machine from the Grand Central Market, leading the duo to create two start-ups that employed gang members and sworn enemies looking for an exit ramp toward a better future. For many of them, this was it—this was the ramp.

Soon there were more businesses, and, with a full fleet up and running, Jobs for a Future rebranded as Homeboy Industries in 1992. This is how Father G met Sergio, who came looking for a job fresh out of prison some years later. It was Homeboy that offered Sergio a new imagination for flourishing, a new set of skills he could take to the job market, a reliable reference who could vouch for him, and a set of tools to manage the anger and recover from the suffering inflicted by an abusive mother and a life on the streets.

All this came from an unlikely team in an unlikely place. Father G's approach was unique: a refusal to give in to a traditionalist impulse—to do things as they've always been done—while still drawing from a rich tradition as a source of innovation. The unlikely friendship and entrepreneurial collaboration developed with Ray Stark led to the creation of a vibrant institution willing to try new things in the face of difficult circumstances that presented all sorts of complexities. Surely there are lessons we can draw in our own bewildered states.

Homeboy is now home to many social enterprises. For employees, they also provide tattoo removal (to help reduce stigma for future job interviews), workforce development, education, legal services, and mental health services. They even cover tuition if someone wants to enroll in a local solar panel installation training program.

But Homeboy, for many people, is also a whole lot more—like for Danny, a now-former gang member whom Father G has known since Danny was thirteen. "He was a knucklehead," Father G recalls, "and was allergic to walking through my doors [at Homeboy]. He just wasn't going to do it. I knew him on the streets and in the juvenile hall and in probation camp. Then he went to prison, and got out at 20."

And then, just as he got out, Danny discovered that his mom had cancer, with six months to live.

"So he spent time with her daily," Father G recalls, "kind of her hospice caregiver, never left her side. I saw him there; it was very tender. Then she died. A week later, I buried her, and a week after that, he walks into my office for the first time." His mother's death had broken him.

Hopeful about what this might mean, Father G put Danny in the eighteen-month program. Danny was deep into the forces of his neighborhood, deep into a gang life that made him lots of enemies. It wasn't a sure bet. But his mother's death had altered something.

"He'd only been with us four months, and I watched him working with enemies," remembers Father G. "In recovery, they say it takes what it takes—the birth of a son or the death of a friend, taking care of a mother who's dying of cancer. Who knows what it takes? But I watched Danny come alive."

So in walked Danny to Father G's office one day, just four months in, and he said, "What happened to me yesterday on the way home has never happened to me in my life."

Danny had been on the Gold Line, the train from Pasadena to the east side. He wore a sweatshirt that said, "Homeboy Industries—Jobs Not Jails" across his chest. He was in the car, and it was packed, but he was able to get a seat. Right in front of him, hanging onto the pole, was an older guy—a homie, Danny assumed, because of his tattoos—who was a little bit drunk. Danny didn't know him.

Looking down at Danny's shirt, the drunk man asked, "You work there?"

"Yeah," Danny said.

"Is it any good?"

"Well, it's helped me," Danny reported. "In fact, I don't think I'm going to go back to prison because of this place."

Then Danny stood, reached in his pocket, and found a paper and pen. He wrote the address of Homeboy Industries and handed it to the man, who studied it. "Come see us," Danny said. "We'll help you."

The man thanked him and got off at the next stop.

Sitting in Father G's office retelling this story, Danny filled with emotion.

"What happened next has never happened to me in my life," he said. "Everyone on the train was looking at me. Everyone on the train was nodding at me. Everyone on the train was smiling at me."

Then he could barely speak. He said, "For the first time in my life, I felt admired."

And then, sitting in Father G's office, he cried. "And I cried," Father G recalls. "It's like any biblical story where somebody is experiencing sight after not having it, or liberty from whatever place they felt captive. And I didn't do that to that kid, but boy do I feel grateful to witness that it happened."

Homeboy Industries has become the largest gang intervention, rehab, and reentry program in the world. Gang members arrive at Homeboy, often fresh out of prison, to build marketable skills and a work history—things they'll parlay after a short stint with Homeboy into jobs with private companies all over the city.

But at Homeboy, many people find so much more. Amid chaos, deep forces, and bewildering circumstances, they find, like Sergio and Danny, a vision for life that really is life. All because a priest discovered that tradition can inform innovation. We don't have to choose one or the other.[31]

So if *traditionalism* risks bitterness, insularity, and stagnation, and if indiscriminate *futurism* leads to instability, hubris, isolation, and recklessness, then surely, as Father G shows us, there has to be a better way.

Whether our context is one borne of a rich heritage and privilege, or whether we are seeking to cultivate hope in the midst of suffering and systemic injustice, or some combination of the above, there are significant opportunities to cultivate a better way. In Washington, D.C., an organization called "The House DC" emerged out of relationships among two groups of Christian men: one African American and one Anglo. They came together to support an initiative within Anacostia, an under-resourced and predominantly African American neighborhood in the Washington, D.C., community that has suffered from decades of systemic racism and injustice. The House DC emerged as an organization to come alongside young people to address their understandable despair and provide them with opportunities to flourish. They draw on a rich Christian tradition of flourishing, the wisdom of their communities across time, and a wholistic understanding of achievement. They do this partly by helping kids with their studies. And much like Father G at Homeboy, they also do this by pointing to new alternatives that encourage under-resourced young people to find life that really is life. Their success rate is remarkably high. They instill hope rather than perpetuating despair or selling cheap "futurism."

The better way that Homeboy and The House DC and many others have found is to draw on complex traditions of the past in order to discover a more hopeful future. Such hope, we suggest, is very different from either futurism or traditionalism. It is hope that helps stimulate imagination in the face of bewilderments.

Delivering the 1983 Jefferson Lecture in the Humanities, Jaroslav Pelikan offered ideas that might help us today, providing a foundation upon which we build throughout this book. Using the term *insight* in much the way we are using *innovation*, he employed a sport metaphor, and returns us to the images of "the dead faith of the living" and "the living faith of the dead." Pelikan argued:

> The dichotomy between tradition and insight breaks down under the weight of history itself. A "leap of progress" is not a standing broad jump, which begins at the line of where we are now; it is a running broad jump through where we have been to where we go next. The growth of insight . . . has not come through progressively sloughing off more and more of tradition, as though insight would be purest and deepest when it has finally freed itself of the dead past. It simply has not worked that way in the history of the tradition, and it does not work that way now.

Instead, Pelikan wrote, "By including the dead in the circle of discourse, we enrich the quality of the conversation. Of course we do not listen only to the dead, nor are we a tape recording of the tradition. That really would be the dead faith of the living, not the living faith of the dead. But we do acquire the 'insight' . . . when we learn to interact creatively with the 'tradition.'"[32]

Heeding Pelikan's advice, our opportunity is to develop ways to consider how, in the present, to live toward the future in light of the past—to perform a running broad jump rather than a standing one. We can begin to think of ways to hold together past and future, rather than choose between them. We can navigate both continuity and change, acknowledging, as Steven Johnson notes, that what is possible is vast, but for now, there is only an "adjacent possible," connected to what we know or have heretofore achieved.[33]

These realities are timeless. We could have argued these same points in the eighth century or could argue them again in the twenty-eighth. But it's also the case that these realities are particularly urgent and pressing now. In turbulent times, when change happens so fast that our hard-earned knowledge and expertise can feel obsolete with every passing disruption, it's vital to consider how we might hold together past and future so that our work and institutions maintain relevance, meaning, and purpose.

So we ask: How do we navigate through the bewilderments? In our movement toward the future, how might we continue to "find the stars" and maintain a path toward flourishing, carrying forward those things that help us see new possibilities for a future that is sure to be different from the past and even the present?

One vital way to do that is to practice traditioned innovation, a different way of seeing that invites us not to choose past *or* future, tradition *or* change. Rather, as Father G's experience with Homeboy shows us, traditioned innovation is a mindset, habit, and way of seeing that holds past and future together in creative tension, animated by both wisdom and improvisation, aimed toward the cultivation of human and institutional flourishing. Requiring both a deep fidelity to certain patterns of the past that have borne us to the present and a radical openness to the changes that will carry us forward toward the future, traditioned innovation can help guide a vision for institutions and leaders as they advance flourishing and look for an array of creative possibilities to achieve it in the future.

Traditioned innovation is neither a quick fix nor something we do just once. It requires sustained attention to what to preserve and what to cast off, as well as what and how to innovate. That means we ought to equip ourselves with dynamic ways of approaching the future and bringing forward the past—a running broad jump, not a standing one. It requires us to look toward the future with hope, curiosity, awe, and humility, even as we carry forward the past with gratitude and discernment.

Storms bewilder us. But there are reasons to hope as we navigate the future.

Chapter 4
Imagining

We ask You to push back
The horizons of our hopes

—Sir Francis Drake

The field of psychology is undergoing a quiet revolution. Throughout its history, it's been guided by what Martin Seligman has called a "120-year obsession" with the past and the present. Take psychoanalysts: they've long practiced on the belief that treating patients is a matter of exhuming the past and confronting it—think of lying on the therapist's couch and talking about childhood. Or take cognitive psychologists: their work has focused in large proportion on phenomena such as memory and perception—in other words, the ways we encounter our past and present. This is how we've tended to explain human behavior and motivation.[1]

There's just one problem: a recent (and fascinating) study by social psychologist Roy Baumeister involved, for a sustained period, a group of five hundred Chicagoans with cell phones. Like a swarm of pesky gnats, Baumeister and his research team repeatedly pinged the cell phone subjects at random points throughout their days and asked them a simple question: What are you thinking about, right now, at this exact moment? If they weren't involved in a specific task, which kept them focused on the here and now, the subjects' thinking revealed a bit of a surprise: Baumeister found that they were likely to be thinking about the future—to the tune of three-to-one future-to-past. Think about that: three-to-one, they were imagining events and emotions that, technically, weren't real. These were things that hadn't yet happened—and, of course, might not happen at all.

In line with these findings, there's a growing body of evidence beginning to make clear that people spend inordinate amounts of energy thinking imaginatively about the future. As Steven Johnson neatly summarized these findings, "Human beings seem to spend a remarkable amount of time thinking about events that are by definition not real, that are figments of our imagination—because they haven't happened yet." As Martin Seligman artfully put it, "Our minds brim with futures. This is not to be fought. The future is our nature. We are creatures who are drawn to the future."[2]

In chapter 2, we started with the End. We argued that anchoring to purpose, both as leaders and as institutions, compels us through our work to promote human flourishing, to orient our actions toward taking hold of and fostering in others life that really is life. In chapter 3, we acknowledged that flourishing is always under threat—that forces big and small can confound and bewilder us in ways that imperil the flourishing for which we yearn. Echoing Avivah Gottlieb Zornberg, we're also convinced that to remain mired in our bewilderment is to experience something worse than physical death: death of the imagination.

So, to move beyond that bewilderment, in this chapter we want to return to the End and suggest that our imaginative natures and capabilities play an important role in our ability to promote flourishing and navigate the future. It's by cultivating a rich imagination that we're able to give shape to, and discover new possibilities for, the sort of flourishing for which we're designed and for which we yearn.

While imagination is inherent and native to us as human beings, cultivating a rich imagination for flourishing is not an automatic occurrence, nor does it happen in isolation. It is, instead, a running broad jump, not a standing one, and results as the product of our abilities to learn for wisdom, to take stock of our limited abilities, and to cultivate a hopeful posture toward future possibilities. So, as we discuss and explore imagination in this chapter, as we consider the ways in which our imaginative abilities might lead to new insights and new opportunities, we do so with knowledge that the richest possibilities for imagining occur in the flow of our traditions and in concert with others.

The next two chapters take up those topics specifically. This one focuses on what it means to look forward with imagination past the bewilderment; to join with Sir Francis in a quest to "push back/The horizons of our hopes" so that we might better discover and clarify the many pathways that might lead toward flourishing. We lead with imagining because traditioned innovation comes alive most fully when we are oriented by the End.

This is a chapter in two movements. The first explores the nature of our prospective, imaginative abilities and the ways in which ongoing imagining can orient us to new possibilities beyond the bewilderment of our present circumstance. The second considers how we become people, institutions, and communities that are better equipped to imagine richly toward these ends by cultivating the virtues of curiosity, humility, and hope. Woven throughout are stories of people and organizations who excel in the art of imagining better futures.

In all of this, the invitation is to a richer, fuller, more purposefully cultivated imagination, one that helps us see vividly the possibilities ahead as we orient toward flourishing and navigate a turbulent future. Too often, our sense of purpose and our capacity for imagination are stifled by bureaucracy. We find ourselves searching for survival skills rather than being stirred by an imaginative and hopeful future, caught up in the bewilderments of our world, our institutions, and our own lives.

When this happens, organizations and institutions settle for incremental thinking. "Strategic planning" becomes a term for trying to improve a bit on existing reality, rather than envisioning a bold and transformative future toward which we might move. We put together focus groups and strategic planning processes that leave us with a vision of faster horses, rather than the possibilities of an automobile. Our invitation is to practice traditioned innovation by imagining the future in ways that point toward the life that really is life, the life that the God of Jesus Christ calls us to discover and live.

Let's start with the story of Alan Barnhart.

A Memphis native and the son of small business owners, Barnhart left home for Knoxville in the early 1980s to study engineering at the University of Tennessee. His plan was to return home after graduation and work in the family business, the global headquarters of which was "the back two bedrooms" of the family home. It was a self-styled "mom-and-pop" business with about ten employees whose enterprise was "to pick up and move heavy things."

As he neared his college graduation, Barnhart found himself wrestling with a call to ministry, to give over his life in service to others and the church. Friends encouraged him in that direction, but over and over he felt that his gifts really were in business and engineering, not in preaching or teaching. Although vocational ministry didn't seem like the right path for Barnhart, what did seem clear was that he felt drawn toward a life of significance and service. So, after graduation, he returned home to Memphis, joined the family company, and grappled with what it might mean to live with purpose in the "moving heavy things" industry. He also met Kathy, and when they married, they began to think a lot about the future, to dream about and imagine what they wanted their lives to be.

About two years in, in 1986, Barnhart's parents decided they were ready to leave the business, and they gave Alan a choice. One was that they'd sell the company, and Alan would be free to pursue whatever life he wanted, free of any obligation to carry on the family legacy. The other was that they'd give it to Alan and his brother Eric, and they could run it together. Alan and Eric were savvy in business and competent in engineering, so the Barnhart brothers felt like they could run it successfully, a prospect that sounded enjoyable. There was just one problem.

All of Alan Barnhart's Bible reading—his steeping himself in his tradition as he considered a life in full-time ministry—led him toward a sober view of money; a fear of it, in fact.

"The love of money is a root of all kinds of evil."

"Do not lay up for yourselves treasures on earth."

"It is harder for a rich man to enter the kingdom of heaven."

"Keep your lives free from the love of money."[3]

These biblical sayings daunted him, and although he felt more and more drawn toward the possibility of running the family business with his brother, although he knew he wanted it to succeed—and that it could succeed—Barnhart had been formed by his Christian faith and tradition in a way that made him wary of regular business success. And it was that wariness, interestingly, that pointed him toward an alternative imagination.

As Alan and Eric Barnhart took over the company, they did it with three creative commitments and safeguards. First, they said, *this is God's company. God owns it. It's not ours. We're just stewards.* Second, they would set what they called a "lifestyle finish line." They'd cap their income squarely in the middle class, and they'd give away anything beyond that. And third, they'd tell others in the company what that commitment entailed in order to establish accountability and foster buy-in. The fruits of your labor, they promised, won't go toward increasing our lifestyles. Those fruits will go to do good in the world. This was the kind of imagination that set Barnhart Crane & Rigging down a fascinating path—and certainly not a path one would expect of an engineering company.

In the first year, it wasn't even clear that the company would make it. But make it they did, and at the end of the year, there was some money left to pour back into the business for growth, plus an additional $50,000 to use with discretion—more than Alan's take-home salary, and typically an amount that a company's owners would keep for themselves. Not the Barnharts. Instead, they assembled a group of six employees and met to decide what to do with the money, which, ultimately, they gave to charitable purposes around the world.

As time passed, it turned out that the Barnhart brothers were indeed pretty good at business, and their success started to increase. The second year, the company grew more, and they had an excess $150,000, which they gave away once again in partnership with employees. Then it grew more the next year. And the next. And the next. And over the course of the next twenty-three years, Barnhart Crane & Rigging grew an astounding 25 percent *each year*. To do that math is to realize that, twenty-five years in, the company was more than one hundred times its original size. What had been a very small company with ten employees in Memphis became a national company with more than one thousand. And each year, *making* more money meant *giving* more money. By the early part of the new millennium, they reached the $1 million mark in annual giving, and a particularly eager salesman in the company prodded them toward more, suggesting a goal of $1 million a month. Significant national growth in nuclear power translated into a lot of heavy, important materials that needed moving, so between 2005 and 2008, Barnhart grew from a $50 million company to a $250 million company. And since then, they have in fact been able to give away more than $1 million each month.

Alan Barnhart's salary? About $140,000 a year.[4]

In practice, about 50 percent of all company earnings are donated immediately to charity. The other 50 percent is reinvested to grow the business, a practice that has been in place since the beginning. Just as remarkable, the Barnharts still don't dictate the giving process. That belongs now to a group of fifty-five employees and spouses, who fully oversee about half of the company's giving and help foster a rich company-wide culture of generosity. Each employee in the group develops a relationship with one or two potential grant recipients, performing due diligence to understand that organization's effectiveness and to vet its grant requests. "Small" grants, under $100,000, go before a six-member subcommittee for approval. Larger ones, those above the $100,000 threshold, go to a twelve-member board that meets quarterly. Most of the money goes overseas, though some stays in Memphis, aimed at helping young people in blighted neighborhoods find a pathway out.

As Alan Barnhart tells it, this commitment to a modest lifestyle, even when presented with such huge material gain, is a gift to him and his family. "It's a great benefit to my children," he says curiously, "to not have to grow up as rich kids and to learn the word 'no.'" They get to practice what Barnhart calls "Rolling Stones theology," the idea that, as the song goes, "you can't always get what you want."[5]

But beyond this, they have learned what Barnhart describes as the great "alternative to 'no,'" which is the joy of giving. This has led to enriching, transformational relationships for the family around the world, and a resounding affirmation of what sociologists Christian Smith and Hilary Davidson call "the paradox of generosity." As Smith and Davidson have found,

> generosity is paradoxical. Those who give, receive back in turn. By spending ourselves for others' well-being, we enhance our own standing. In letting go of some of what we own, we better secure our own lives. By giving ourselves away, we ourselves move toward flourishing. This is not only a philosophical or religious teaching; it is a sociological fact.[6]

Alan Barnhart and his family agree, and have certainly affirmed this sociological paradox. "The alternative and the trade-off has been wonderful," Barnhart reports. "This is not a sacrificial life. We take our skills and gifts, put them to use, work hard, try to be as good as we can at what we do, and then not get caught up in the stuff, the toys."[7] They also provide good wages and an honest living to more than a thousand workers and their families, while establishing in the industry a well-earned reputation for fairness, innovation, and quality. In all this, Alan Barnhart and his family live a life that is deeply fulfilling—far more fulfilling, they're quick to point out, than any material riches would provide, and all because they dared to imagine a richer sort of flourishing for themselves and the world.

It wasn't all that surprising of a leap, then, when in 2006, the Barnharts' imaginative thinking led them to give the company away. They didn't sell it or divest it. They gave it—right in the midst of its fastest period of growth.

It's not uncommon, of course, for successful business owners to leave their private companies to their own established foundations when they die. That's not what the Barnharts did. They were still in their forties, still running the company, and still very much invested in its growth and success and the fate of its workers. So they worked with the IRS on a highly unusual arrangement to put 99 percent of their business ownership interests, in the form of nonvoting stock, into a charitable trust under the National Christian Foundation (NCF). In 2012, they weren't finished, electing to give the remaining 1 percent to a second charitable trust that gives NCF the beneficial interest and ultimate ownership, but allows the family to retain operating control of the company by serving as trustee.[8]

To hear Alan Barnhart talk is to hear a man who is deeply joyful, more so than probably any CEO of a massive company. It appears, too, that the company has realized the power of imagination, just as Barnhart has. The company slogan, in fact, is, "minds over matter," and the website is splashed with a formative conviction: "At Barnhart, we never stop asking 'what if?'"—a commitment, in a field that is unmistakably functional, that seems to have made all the difference. "There is no magic formula for innovation," they state, "no mathematical equation for creativity. At Barnhart, we have the confidence and the experience to find solutions that others might not see. For us, innovation isn't just a word. It's at the core of what we do . . . a product of the way we think."[9]

While Alan Barnhart had no way of knowing in 1986 that it would all play out this way, what's clear is that his imagination, coupled with a deep conviction about the wisdom of his tradition and a commitment to serving others, set him down a path that availed him to a life far richer and more fulfilling than most, a life that really is life. Alan Barnhart dared to cultivate a bold imagination, and he dared to live it out in a way that not only surprises, but appeals and fosters buy-in from the people who work with him. And the world, undoubtedly, is better because of Alan Barnhart's imagination.

We humans are peculiar, it turns out. A group of leading scholars, including Baumeister and Seligman, has begun to make the case that not only are we more oriented toward the future than we've previously realized, it's actually the case that our imaginative, future orientation is what distinguishes us as a species. Unlike the other animals, we seem to be guided by imagining alternatives that stretch before us. In fact, these scholars have gone so far as to claim that this is such a distinctive feature of our species that we've misnamed ourselves: *Homo sapiens*, they say, should instead be *homo prospectus*.[10]

We like to look ahead. Prospection is the mental process of projecting and evaluating future possibilities and then using these projections to guide thought and action. That's a dry description, and not all that complicated, but it's immensely powerful. Think of an old-time prospector searching for gold: like a gold prospector, we devote considerable mental energy to mapping and imagining both the landscape lying ahead of us and the array of possible pathways that will enable us to pass through that landscape.[11] We imagine futures, daydream what-ifs, turn possible scenarios over and over and upside down. The past isn't insignificant, of course. But rather than the past defining or compelling us, it's more like we metabolize it to create possible futures.[12]

Imaginative prospection is a fundamental human capability. We thrive, psychologists are beginning to understand, by considering our prospects and by looking into the future in both our conscious and unconscious states. This is largely because, unlike experience, which stretches from the present back into the past, action can only stretch forward in time, from the present toward the future. That's less complicated than it sounds: it simply means that we can't do anything about the past because only the future is malleable, and we humans are drawn to that reality in a profound, essential way.

Imagination also creates order and incentive. Along with Peter Railton and Chandra Sripada, Seligman and Baumeister have demonstrated in a compelling set of studies that our prospective ability actually orients our behavior, because our minds develop motivational systems that shape the way we experience the present and move toward the future. In other words, we're not always guided animalistically, by immediate desires or urges that have been conditioned or that emerge from some magnetic attraction to a thing that is immediately tempting—like sugar or alcohol or sex. While those forces are real and can be strong, it's also the case that we've drastically underestimated the ways in which we're moved by images of possibilities that aren't real—not yet, anyway. To say that differently, we're tangibly motivated by the images we create and the imagination we cultivate. Imagining our beach body or a future without a heart attack might be a strong factor to inspire our turning down the donut next time.[13]

The same is true for the more creative possibilities we might imagine if we allow ourselves to entertain them. If our imaginative, prospective abilities enable us, in any given moment, not only to contemplate a new behavior, but to motivate that behavior through an imagined future reward, then our status as *homo prospectus* proves vital to our ability to promote flourishing and navigate the future. A prospecting mind enables us to see and feel and simulate future possibilities, sometimes really creative ones that the world around us needs in order to flourish, such as turning an engineering firm into the fuel for global humanitarian work.

Our brains are able to find motivation to act toward the futures we mentally construct, enabling us, even in bewilderment, to move beyond the "death that is worse than physical death." As Railton phrased it, we "*want* to take an action because we like the *idea* of what that action might yield, even if that is remote in time or novel in character." In that way, it seems we're *drawn* toward future possibilities more than we're *pushed* by the past. And while that's a subtle distinction, it's also an important one, because it's this capacity that underwrites our human faculty for innovation.[14]

So why not, even in the midst of our bewilderments, cultivate a richer imagination that enables us to strive toward the future flourishing toward which we're drawn? Why not be more intentional to imagine better ways to flourish, in our lives, institutions, communities, and in the larger world? If our prospective abilities enable us to be drawn forward toward the future, rather than pushed forward by the past, then we humans are quite capable of charting pathways that help us navigate the future pointed toward our most important purposes.

That sounds easy enough. But for most honest people, the word *imagination* is a word that strikes fear—even if it shouldn't. If words like *imagination* and *creativity* intimidate us, it's because we've too often misappropriated them to the exclusive provenance of artists, "creatives," or geniuses—Mozart or Beyoncé, Spike Lee or Van Gogh, Dostoyevsky or Maya Angelou or Steve Jobs. But as anthropologist Agustín Fuentes points out, we should work to demystify these terms because imagination, as his anthropological research makes clear, is "everywhere in the human experience . . . central to the extraordinary story of human evolution."[15] In reality, imagination is a universal human capability—something we all possess, and have possessed forever.

In fact, imagination is partly about guiding and intentionally directing what our minds already possess. Imagination is actually built on the interconnections of ideas, experiences, and the prospective nature already part of our make-up,[16] an "ability to tap into our [existing] mental pool of resources—knowledge, insight, information, inspiration, and all the fragments populating our minds," as Maria Popova eloquently put it.[17] Of course, it also requires a little bit of effort and intentionality if we want it to yield something fruitful.

Because sophisticated neuroscience has begun to illumine fresh new understandings of how our imaginations work, Stephen T. Asma actually argues that we're better served to think not of imagina*tion* (a single mental faculty that we either possess or don't or have in limited supply)—but of imagin*ing* (the process, the action, the verb). The science seems to demonstrate that our imaginative powers grow out of general intelligence capabilities and emerge from a network of interconnecting systems and bodies of knowledge. The stuff we already know, in other words, constitutes the raw materials of what we can begin to imagine.

Take Einstein, who famously claimed that "I have no special talent. I am only passionately curious." Neuroscientists might concur, and Einstein's practice bore that out. As he saw it, imaginative breakthroughs were often the result of what he called "combinatory play" or "associative play." He'd take things from one body of knowledge, playfully associate across domains, and develop new insights and possibilities, which he'd explore to great effect. This is because the process of imagining, as Einstein seemed keenly aware, is more associational than computational, linking ideas together instead of simply deriving, inferring, or divining them.

There is no muse or magic creativity gene.

We see this play out across industries and sectors. Jeff Dyer, Hal Gregersen, and Clayton M. Christensen discovered in their studies on particularly effective innovators, in fact, that industry disruptors rarely, if ever, invent something entirely new out of nothing. Instead, they associate, question, observe, and experiment in ways that simply "recombine the ideas they had [already] collected in new ways," leading to new insights for new purposes or new contexts.[18] Think of, say, a savvy engineer and businessman who grapples with a call to ministry, and begins to imagine how his knowledge and skills in the business of engineering might function as ministry creatively redesigned.

This surely translates. If we think of imagination this way—as something we all possess, as something we naturally practice as part of the human experience, and as a product of things we already know—then we begin to realize that imagination is not just something for "creatives." Imagining new possibilities, in this way, is a potential we probably underestimate and underutilize in ourselves and our own contexts—in business or healthcare, education or church work, law or government or the social sector. And we do this to our own detriment.

A few simple practices might serve as first steps for those of us less inclined to embrace this human capability. One accessible way to consider cultivating an imagination for flourishing is to consider alternative ways of using and applying what we already know, and directing that toward a better future. So, for example:

- How might my medical school understanding of the spread of infectious disease help us rethink the culture of bureaucratic resistance that prevents us from giving the best care to our patients in this hospital system?

- How might my nuanced legal understanding of judicial scrutiny help us reimagine personnel policies within the nonprofit where I serve on the board?

- How might our college draw on the best of our founding impulses to offer a Christian imagination for the education and formation people need in order to flourish in the future?

- How might my technical understanding of inertia apply beyond physics—to my understanding of individuals, systems, and organizations, which also tend to want to minimize the use of energy or resources?

- How might my knowledge and skill in the garden help me better cultivate the conditions that help my children or students grow, thrive, and flourish?

These limited examples aren't all. While applying what we know to new contexts is one important form of imagination, it is just the start. After all, it's not as though simply "knowing things" is enough. As Einstein believed, imagination is far more important than knowledge, because "Knowledge is limited. Imagination encircles the world."

In fact, the great potential of imagining, echoing Einstein, is that it's virtually limitless, an idea confirmed by Harvard psychiatrist Arnold H.

Modell. Modell notes that our minds have the remarkable capacity to create what he calls a "second universe"—an internal environment of possibilities, the limits of which we decide and construct ourselves, which exist simultaneous to the real physical world, but without all its stubborn laws of nature. The problem is that, for one reason or another, we too often neglect to adequately construct or explore this "second universe." We're either intimidated or find it impractical. We don't want to push beyond the limits we already know.

Too often we then settle for tweaking what is, rather than imagining the future to which God is calling us and discovering fresh possibilities for the future. This is critical for our own lives and vocations as well as for the communities and institutions of which we are part. We can't afford to settle for the status quo, much less to long for a past that never was.

And yet, if imagining is to be more than just some passive process in which we're spectators of images that drift into our minds, and instead is to become something fruitful whereby we actively construct new possibilities and new behavioral options, then we have a little bit of work to do. Our ability to move back and forth between the realms of *what is* and *what could be* is how we discover new possibilities and new imagination for flourishing.[19]

This is a concept at the heart of design thinking, an approach to innovation that encourages people to tap into their inherent creativity and apply it meaningfully to the world. Built on core values such as radical collaboration, rapid experimentation, and creative risk, design thinking also attempts to guide problem-solvers through the complexities of their challenges by nurturing imagination. While the approach is not a panacea, it can be incredibly useful as a means to spark creative thinking and to help people move nimbly toward breakthrough ideas and solutions.

In brief, design thinking is built on five key components:

- **Empathizing** with the end user as a way to ensure that any ideas or innovations are in fact what people actually need.

- **Defining** our problems or challenges accurately, and doing so in an ongoing way as our challenges evolve, so that our action is in fact addressing the right things.

- **Ideating**, producing as many ideas as possible, no matter how outlandish or "bad" they might seem at the outset.

- **Prototyping** and rapidly **testing** our ideas or innovations so that we can quickly change the things that don't work and improve our ideas to better suit the needs of our end users.

What's often most useful about design thinking is its speed, the fact that no one has to come up with the genius idea that will lead to the ultimate breakthrough. Instead, it invites people to collaborate around producing as many ideas as they can, as quickly as they can, knowing that most of the ideas will be bad, and maybe a few will be good enough to explore. This mindset seems to liberate people and invite them into a fun process that unleashes creativity because no one has to impress anyone. When the understanding is that everyone will produce some bad ideas, people let their guard down a little and find themselves willing to generate ideas more creatively because they don't have to worry that they'll look bad.

The most fruitful part of design thinking for imagination is ideation. Ideation sessions are easy and fun and can take place anytime a group of two or three people can gather for five or six minutes. One way is to play "yes, and": simply stand by a blank wall, hand everyone a pad of sticky notes and a marker, pose a "how might we" question about a specific challenge, and set a timer for two minutes. Some great questions are:

- How might we structure our appointments so our patients feel like they're being cared for holistically?

- How might we address food insecurity in ways that look both upstream and downstream, addressing both causes and symptoms?

- How might we create better classroom environments so our students retain what they learn?

- How might we organize our college so that we optimize opportunities for collaboration and equip our students with the capacities for imagining what they will need in the future?

- How might we direct our work as an engineering firm toward the larger purposes of human flourishing?

Everyone scribbles as quickly as possible any idea they can come up with, typically by adding to the last idea by saying "yes, and," and slapping their sticky note quickly on the wall. The purpose is to generate as many ideas as possible for two minutes before then adding a constraint, something like: "Now every idea must cost at least a million dollars" or "Now every idea must involve fantasy or magic." Even if you don't have a million dollars or a magic wand, these kinds of constraints force thinkers to get outlandish and creative and to think big. And even if a million-dollar or magic idea isn't itself reasonably attainable, there might be a nugget of insight in the idea that can lead down a path you otherwise weren't exploring.

The value of an ideation session is that the bad ideas only live for a minute or two. Once you've slapped dozens of ideas on the wall, all you have to do is pull down the bad ones and throw them in the recycle bin. Hang on to the good ones and consider what's worth exploring, which ideas contain insights or ambitions that merit longer considerations or additional strategy sessions. Embedding this kind of operating mode in an organization can prove revolutionary, inviting people always to push and explore and think imaginatively.

This willingness to engage and expand our imaginations—whether in serial ideation sessions or otherwise—seems essential to moving beyond our bewilderment, and doing so in ways that lead toward flourishing. We must be willing and able to think creatively as we consider the future, to imagine what flourishing means for our contexts, and come up with innovative ways to move in those directions—remembering that imagination empowers new ideas and, more important, the construction of new pathways to help us achieve them.

Peter Railton tells a useful story, which we'll modify slightly, about a primitive man in search of food. Having hunted for much of his life with erratic and sometimes unpredictable success, the man began to discover during cold winters that animals were sparse, his snares turned up increasingly empty, and he became increasingly hungry. *How might I find a better way to fill my belly in the winters?* he wondered.

Fish, he realized one night, while sitting by the fire in his hut, could be the answer. *Getting fish*, he thought, *could keep me full throughout the winter. Now*, he pondered, *how to get my hands on some fish.*

Just as he turned to race toward the lake, he remembered it was frozen. He also realized that wandering out onto the frozen lake with no resources—hoping to find a hole in ice that is nonetheless solid enough to stand on, or trying to lure and catch a fish by dangling his hands in the freezing water—would be unwise, because he himself might freeze. Simply knowing that there were fish, and that he'd like to eat them was not enough. It was a good idea, but insufficient on its own. Before venturing out into the cold, while still warm in his hut, he began imaginatively to explore the pathways toward getting a fish in his belly the next day.

First, he contemplated a way to get beneath the ice, imagining various processes that would require him to break it. In imagining how he'd do so, he thought of something hard and strong, like a pounding stone, something very much within his grasp—*right there, by the fire, that might work!*

Then he imagined what would need to happen if he got access to the water beneath the ice. From experience, he knew that fish wouldn't likely come jumping out, so he began to consider how he might bait them. *Beetles*, he thought, *like the ones I saw them snag from atop the water last summer!*

But baiting the fish wouldn't alone do the trick—he'd need, he imagined, some mechanism to grab, spear, or hook them. *A sharp stone! Or a sharp stick! Or a sharp stone on the end of a sharp stick!*

And with that, our hungry man, through his imaginative abilities, became an innovator, and a very practical one to boot. His imagination gave structure to the future, made actions and outcomes possible that otherwise would have been unavailable had he just wandered out into the cold because he was hungry and wanted some fish. His mind created a "second universe," which he would then go inhabit the next day after preparing his imagined fishing tackle. In so doing, having used his imagination to envision a future in which he wasn't hungry, the man found a beetle, repurposed a firestone, and made a fishing spear out of rocks and sticks. Imagination, toward very practical ends, made him an innovator. And probably kept him alive.

Railton rather technically sums it up like this: "Intelligent action over time involves not only taking choices in light of a causal model of possibilities, but *creating* possibilities—'working backwards' from distant goals to the proximate actions that are preconditions for them, and 'working forward' by conceiving and acting upon ideas and ideals that will sustain new ways of acting in the future."[20]

To put that in simpler terms: we humans can imagine desirable futures, often even highly creative ones if we allow ourselves to; as we strive for ways to attain them, we can begin to create new, creative pathways. Those pathways and possibilities then guide our actions, enabling us to jump back from the "second universe" of our imaginations to the "first universe" of the present, where we can "work forward," prototyping and testing, improvising and innovating toward all sorts of desired outcomes.[21]

We can apply this, surely. If our unique capacity for prospective imagination is indeed foundational to human activity, to innovation, and perhaps also to flourishing, then we should look for better ways to utilize it toward those ends. The present is often bewildering, we know. The future is complex and unpredictable. And yet, as we orient toward the future, drawn forward by our purpose to promote flourishing, imagining is a foundational part of what can help us navigate these complexities and uncertainties. Imagining is what helps us envision a flourishing reality, even as it's also what helps us map the best ways to get there, just as it helped Alan Barnhart grow an engineering firm into the fuel for global humanitarian work. As Asma put it, "Dreaming our ideals helps us organize our daily lives and institutions to bring about those ideals."[22]

So how do we do it? How might we tap into our immense imaginative potential?

Matryoshka Haus is a London-based collective of entrepreneurs, freelancers, creatives, and friends who spend their days working, as they describe, toward a world transformed by hope, justice, and restoration. One way of putting it is that they want to create more people and organizations like Alan Barnhart and Barnhart Crane & Rigging. This takes many forms, clustered in three main areas. First, they start their own projects and companies, which, to date, have included more than a dozen of their own initiatives, such as a social enterprise training women in homelessness to repurpose jewelry, and the creation of impact measurement processes that help organizations across sectors design and evaluate their work. Second, Matryoshka Haus helps people develop their own initiatives and ventures, assisting throughout the process from idea to launch, and sometimes beyond. And third, they work with organizations across sectors, helping them design solutions for their issues related to innovation and impact.

Much of how Matryoshka Haus has evolved since its inception in 2004, they are quick to admit, has been instinctive, informed by their beliefs, experiences, and skills, more than some predetermined master plan. One thing has become clear, however, as they've paused recently to reflect on their successes and failures: even though their processes and their successes haven't been linear, every good thing has been born out of a willingness to cultivate what they call an "alternative imagination."

"Every project, enterprise or idea we act on," they note, "begins with a period of reflection, reading, research and conversation" that sometimes takes weeks, sometimes years. They add, "The aim of this phase is to get a new imagination compared to the status quo, to believe that things could and should be different." In this, their hope is always to "start to enthuse others" who can be part of designing the way forward.[23]

For Matryoshka Haus, much like Alan Barnhart, this way of being and of seeking alternatives is borne out of the traditions of their Christian faith, which, as they see it, offer a compelling invitation to find the contrast between "the way things are" in the world and "the way things could be." As Mark Sampson, one of the principal movers at Matryoshka Haus, puts it, this is about "a way of seeing how a richer story of the human struggle for justice challenges and provokes our dominant cultural narratives. Seeing with [these eyes] changes how we create art, justice initiatives, and business plans," as just three examples of the diversity in the Matryoshka Haus portfolio.[24]

At the heart of the work is an alternative economic imagination, not entirely unlike what Alan Barnhart has developed. Most of us walk around, Sampson argues convincingly, with a default setting that is steeped in the status quo. For example, those of us in the United States or the United Kingdom tend to abide in the captivity of our economic imaginations, where we have one tool to fix all problems—namely, the logic and practices of the market, as defined and shaped by supply, demand, and our self-interested efforts to maximize utility. While there are many advantages to what mainstream economic markets can do—and Matryoshka Haus is not out to disparage those possibilities—there are some problematic assumptions that undercut what they see as the more important work of human flourishing.

Specifically, they see as a fundamental flaw in the logic of markets that we are typically forced to enter the marketplace as self-interested individuals, there to compete with others in a world of scarcity. This sort of configuration can be essentially antisocial, based on a kind of self-interest that runs counter to other important, even more foundational, goods, such as mutuality, friendship, collaboration, abundance, or generosity. Self-interest, often assumed to be the heartbeat of a market economy, usually leaves little room for alternative possibilities.

In the dominant cultural narrative, and in mainstream economic activity, the word *resources* is code for "money," argues Sampson. Since just about everything in our society has a price—and if it doesn't, we develop sophisticated equations and accounting schemes to monetize anything from expertise to time—we tend to walk around thinking that to make our ideas a reality, we simply need enough money. This spawns a cultural fear of scarcity—that, in effect, there's not enough money to go around, so we are all in a constant state of competition. Add to this the powerful cultural myth of the lone genius entrepreneur, the Steve Jobs or Bill Gates out in the garage, and you have what Matryoshka Haus calls "a toxic mix of competition and individualism."[25]

A marketplace based only on competition, by its very nature, limits possibility for collaboration and connection, while one based on transaction leaves little room for transformation. An alternative economic imagination is therefore required, believe the folks at Matryoshka Haus, if we indeed want to be about the kinds of things that lead to flourishing. Matryoshka Haus attempts to imagine possibilities that are alternatives to the status quo, and they do so by prizing and uplifting the roles of gift, reciprocity, and collaboration—not as opposed to entrepreneurship, social enterprise, and participation in the marketplace, but as core components of them. So what does that mean?

One example involves a business accelerator Matryoshka Haus runs in the United States or the United Kingdom called "Make Good," which takes entrepreneurs from an initial idea about a product or service that might have a social impact to being ready for launch. The course culminates with the participants pitching their ideas to potential investors, and for a while, as Matryoshka Haus is a little embarrassed to point out, that took the sort of form we've grown accustomed to seeing in the prevailing conventions of the marketplace: a pitch event resembling the TV show

Shark Tank. In its early form, entrepreneurs at Make Good stood in front of potential investors and had three minutes to pitch, followed by the investors' questions, challenges, and possible investment. This high-stress, high-stakes environment, it turned out, seemed to transfigure everyone, taking social investors—some really good people, in this case—and turning them into "sharks," while the entrepreneurial do-gooders turned into fierce competitors, all trying to outswim the others. Some received financial investment, and some walked away empty-handed. It was just like the self-interested markets of mainstream economics.

Just as soon as the folks at Matryoshka Haus realized this, they knew their structures had to change—"no more equating money with voice and influence," Sampson remembers. He adds, "The offer to the participants could no longer be just the possibility of financial investment. We needed to move from competition to collaboration, from transaction to gift."[26] To do this, to move forward with this alternative imagination, they redesigned the pitch event into a "Pitch and Pledge." Now, everyone in the room—participants, guests, and investors alike—is given a stack of blank cards in multiple colors, each representing a different type of contribution. Some represent a monetary contribution, our traditional understanding of what we mean when we think of contributing "resources" as investors. But beyond that, anyone in the room can become an "investor" by offering cards of other colors—connections, support, time, skills, influence. This works against the fierce individualism and self-interest of the traditional marketplace, and it leads toward collaboration, celebration, gift, and mutuality.

Partly by virtue of these experiences, by having learned that the marketplace can yield good, but that it often won't do so with an acceptance of the standard modus operandi, Matryoshka Haus began building alternative pathways through an alternative economic imagination, something that has become the heart of its work. Matryoshka Haus believes that we need new tools, language, and concepts in order to build resilient organizations that make a difference in the world. While our broader culture and society tends to lean on one tool to fix all problems—the logic and practices of the market—Matryoshka Haus has experimented with many ways of resourcing projects, from the creative understanding of resources at Make Good, as just one example, to bartering, donating, grant funding, and selling. Not only do they encourage these things in the organizations they support, they live this imagination themselves. "Our sustainability to date," they note, is "marked by our ability to manage this mixed economy of resource."[27]

At Matryoshka Haus, they believe that many of our problems of "business as usual" stem from a faulty economic imagination. They don't claim to have all the answers, but they're curious enough to look for better ones. They're willing to admit when they fail, adjust when they can, and experiment on the belief that "everything we do contains the seeds of an alternative economic imagination—where money is a means, not an end; where we expect more of people, not less; and where markets and enterprise are humanizing, not demoralizing." There are no grand illusions that their way will become the only way, or that competitive markets will one day fully cede to collaboration. But Matryoshka Haus proceeds on the steadying hope that alternative ways of imagining the world will invite others to join the work of human flourishing. And often, they're right.[28]

If imaginative abilities are universal, then why does it often feel as though the right kinds of imagination are in short supply? Based on evidence found partly in people like Alan Barnhart and organizations like Matryoshka Haus, we'd like to make the case that the quality of our imagining derives, to a significant degree, from our character formed in particular kinds of communities. The cultivation of a richer imagination for human flourishing is not so much a matter of technique (though certainly some techniques, such as design thinking, can help break the logjam). It is rather a matter of becoming people who are better able to see new possibilities. That requires deep work on our part.

This happens, or is at least far more likely to happen, we'd contend, if we become people who are curious, humble, and hopeful. If the science tells us that imagination emerges from what we know and what we do with what we know, then cultivating the kind of imagination that sees new possibilities to promote flourishing involves, fundamentally, an assessment of who we are and how we see the world around us.

So that's where we want to start, here in this second major movement of the chapter. Specifically, we believe that cultivating a rich imagination for human and institutional flourishing involves cultivating the virtues of *curiosity*, *hope*, and *humility*. If it's the virtue of love that anchors us to purpose, then curiosity, hope, and humility can expand, guide, and sustain our imaginations, respectively, toward those ends.

David Brooks tells an instructive story about the behavior of little gobiid fish, which live in shallow ocean water. When the tide goes out, the gobiid habitat transforms drastically from the vast, untamed sea to small puddles and tide pools. As this change occurs, the gobiid fish do something remarkable: they jump accurately over rocks and ridges from tide pool to tide pool. It's quite a surreal sight, actually: they're small fish, so they can't see above these barriers to see exactly where they're jumping, yet they always land in another pool. Put them somewhere else, though, say in an aquarium next to other aquariums, even ones they can see, and they won't jump at all. Why?

It's because, during high tide, gobiid fish wander around absorbing their environment, storing maps of the rocks and ridges in their brains. Then, when the tide goes out, they have a mental map of the landscape, enabling them to know instinctively what ridges will be dry at low tide and what hollows will form pools. With enough time, exploration, and absorption of the landscape, gobiid fish know where to jump during low tide, regardless of what they can actually see. This is how they know how to land in another pool.

This "wanderer's knowledge," as Brooks calls it, provides a useful model for us humans, as we develop the kinds of imagining that will help us navigate ever-changing environments. We develop insight, a richer imagination, and a refined ability to navigate new circumstances with better ideas when we're perceptive enough to "wander and absorb." And this requires a sense of deep curiosity—but not, we'll quickly note, just any kind of curiosity.[29]

What we need, to develop a kind of curiosity that helps guide our imaginations toward flourishing, is a curiosity that goes beyond knowledge or information and instead seeks wisdom. A curiosity oriented toward wisdom is what enables us to jump over rocks and ridges—perhaps ones that are different from those at the last low tide—and still land in another tide pool.

As Michel Foucault observed, that kind of curiosity requires more than being an "infovore," or someone who seeks after mere knowledge or trivia. "Curiosity evokes 'care,'" Foucault once wrote. "It evokes the care one takes of what exists and what might exist; a sharpened sense of reality, but one that is never immobilized before it; a readiness to find what surrounds us strange and odd; a certain determination to throw off familiar ways of thought and to look at the same things in a different way."[30]

Our ability to see in a different way, to hone a curiosity that leads past information to wisdom, depends significantly on how we orient our curiosity. Prevalent in the literature on innovation is a construct called the "T-Shaped Person," which describes one useful way to shape our curiosity. First made famous by McKinsey & Company, the concept describes someone who continually attends to a breadth of knowledge across many fields, accompanied by a depth of knowledge in one—shallow and wide horizontal knowledge, deep and singular vertical expertise, the shape of the letter *T*.

In many ways, this construct is not all that new. It evokes, for instance, a 1953 essay by philosopher Isaiah Berlin, called "The Hedgehog and the Fox," where Berlin pointed to a concept from ancient Greek poetry in his description of Leo Tolstoy's imaginative way of seeing the world. Observing these two animals twenty-seven hundred years ago, Archilochus, the

Greek poet, noted that "a fox knows many things, but a hedgehog one important thing."

Berlin observed that most of us tend toward fox or hedgehog, one or the other—in our worst tendencies either dilettantish and unfocused or fixated and myopic. But some people, like Tolstoy, can escape categorization into one of these two groups by cultivating both types of curiosity. According to Berlin, Tolstoy was by nature a fox but by conviction a hedgehog. This led to a sort of wisdom that is similar to what Brooks called the "wanderer's knowledge" of gobiid fish. According to Berlin, such a state of clear thought and feeling emerges "not by a specific inquiry and discovery, but by an awareness, not necessarily explicit or conscious, of certain characteristics of human life and experience. . . . [It] is not scientific knowledge, but a special sensitiveness to the contours of the circumstances in which we happen to be placed."[31]

This ability to toggle between the "many things" and the "one important thing" is certainly a refined type of curiosity. Even though it's difficult in practice, it's a key to developing new insights and a new imagination for human flourishing. The type of curiosity that leads to wisdom involves being hedgehog *and* fox *and* gobiid. It means cultivating curiosity along both dimensions of the *T*, while being able to "wander and absorb." It means being a bit like Leonardo da Vinci, who described himself, aptly and somewhat defiantly to the experts around him, as a "disciple of experience."[32]

The advantage to this way of being stems from the fact that most of the world's great and imaginative ideas don't start out as flashes of insight. Even though bursts of ideation and "yes, and" can help us push past particular challenges or think beyond the status quo, they are not, as we said before, sufficient. They might produce an insight, but that is only part of the battle.

In fact, we usually overestimate the importance of eureka moments or instant insights, because it turns out that the most important ideas have to evolve over time, in much subtler, quieter, and more gradual ways—

ways in which the "wanderer's knowledge" proves beneficial. Sometimes eurekas happen to us, but often they are the product of something that builds over time, because the best imaginative ideas take shape in partial, inchoate form. Often, as we wander and absorb, our brains become seedbeds for ideas or hunches that might someday germinate into something profound. But usually, we have to walk around with these ideas for a while before they mean something. Most likely, we also have to bump into people who are doing the same thing.[33]

When this happens, partial ideas can start to connect over time. Sometimes this happens internally by a process that Dyer, Gregersen, and Christensen attribute to T-shaped people, because their imaginations take shape through their ability to make surprising connections across areas of knowledge. This might happen in two ways: (1) when they import an idea from a different field or domain into an area of deep knowledge, or (2) when they export an idea from an area of expertise into one of the broad fields in which their knowledge is shallower.[34]

In the best networks (which we'll discuss later), ideas, insights, and what Steven Johnson calls "slow hunches,"[35] can start to complete one another. Most of the imaginative ideas and hunches that "break through" to be of any consequence in the light of day have to endure a period of wandering or germination. They might begin, as Johnson describes, as "a vague, hard-to-describe sense that there's an interesting solution to a problem that hasn't yet been proposed."[36] And these senses manage to linger in the shadows of our minds for a while—sometimes for decades—where they assemble new connections and gain strength. "And then one day they are transformed into something more substantial: sometimes jolted out by some newly discovered trove of information, or by another hunch lingering in another mind, or by internal association that finally completes the thought."[37] It's like Einstein with his associative play, or Barnhart with his insight that "lifting and moving heavy things"[38] was just a means to a larger end.

Most of the time, our ideas never last long enough to flower into this sort of insight, because they pass in and out of consciousness and memory quickly. Something occurs to us and we never write it down. Or we host one ideation session, gather a few good ideas, and never carry them through or connect them to the ideas generated somewhere else. We go to a conference, get inspired, but fail to develop the networks that would actually shift our mindsets and habits toward the idea. By the time we get back home, entrenched habits and mindsets of survival take over.

Or perhaps we get a feeling there's something interesting, something worth exploring, or a problem that might one day lead us down a promising new direction, such as:

A bakery run by gang members?

A renovated crack house in South Waco?

A belief that money is not the only resource in a market-based economy?

Johnson notes that we ought to be more intentional about sustaining these thoughts over time. "Sustaining the slow hunch," he says, "is less a matter of perspiration than of cultivation. You give the hunch enough nourishment to keep it growing, and plant it in fertile soil, where its roots can make new connections. And then you give it time to bloom."[39]

This is why curiosity matters. Our imaginations develop to a significant degree through our willingness to cultivate and sustain curiosity—by wandering and absorbing; by reading incessantly across multiple fields and genres; by making unlikely friends in unlikely places; by jotting ideas, however half-baked;[40] by opening ourselves to new experiences that will enable us to learn new things and make new connections; by giving our half-formed ideas the time, space, and daylight they need to germinate; by practicing design thinking; and by looking to our traditions for the wisdom that delivered us to here and now.

This kind of curiosity, the kind that leads to wisdom, is born of knowledge, experience, and patience. It is rooted in traditions. This kind of curiosity is the wellspring of imagining that leads past bewilderment, toward flourishing.

Curiosity is only part of the story, of course. Just because we're curious, and just because our curiosity can produce imaginative ideas, doesn't mean that we can trust that our ideas are as good as we think they are, or that they'll work as well as we think they will. Imagining is usually optimistic, if not idealistic. And while that's generally a good thing, sometimes it's also wise to dampen our ideals, to acknowledge that the world is too complex and we are too limited to achieve all we imagine.

Edmund Burke, the eighteenth-century philosopher and British politician, advanced this way of thinking in 1790 while reflecting on the revolution in France, which had been guided by an idealistic sense that all would be made well when the king was replaced by the will of the people. In his masterful *Reflections on the Revolution in France*, Burke argued that political decisions, which are both complex and consequential (a safe assumption about many of the decisions we make in our own lives and professions outside politics), should be guided by the accumulated wisdom of the ages. This was because, in essence, none of us is smart or capable enough to shape the world toward the outcomes we desire.

Each person's private stock of reason and knowledge is small, Burke argued. So even though imagination is one of our greatest human faculties, even though it can paint new possibilities that are well worth our striving, it's still limited in what it can achieve. We might imagine vividly, but when we do, when we stop there, we often fail to take full account of the complexity that awaits us in a future that won't be exactly like the present.[41] Even the best-laid plans, right?

This isn't just good philosophy; empirical research in psychology has demonstrated this sort of wisdom. As Nobel laureate Daniel Kahneman reports,

Most of us view the world as more benign than it really is, our own attributes as more favorable than they truly are, and the goals we adopt as more achievable than they are likely to be. We also tend to exaggerate our ability to forecast the future, which fosters optimistic overconfidence. In terms of its consequences for our decisions, the optimistic bias may well be the most significant of the cognitive biases. Because optimistic bias can be both a blessing and a risk, you should be both happy and wary if you are temperamentally optimistic.[42]

So while the world always needs to change for the better—it isn't as it should be, and would probably be a whole lot better if it matched our imaginations—we ought to be careful, guided by a *humility* that says that we're not as capable as we might think. As Burke believed, in a manner similar to what we called the folly of futurism in the last chapter, there is something inherently unwise about pure revolution or untethered innovation. Instead, a better approach to the future, and thus to the shape of our imaginations, is humility, which Simone Weil once defined—similar to how Michel Foucault and Steven Johnson described curiosity—as "attentive patience."[43]

While philosophers have categorized many types of humility—on a spectrum from virtuous and wise to vicious perversions of honor—perhaps the best description of a properly ordered humility toward our imaginative abilities comes from David Brooks, when he revived in a 2009 *New York Times* column a concept from the Scottish Enlightenment and called it "epistemological modesty."[44] Epistemology is the study of how we know what we know, so epistemological modesty "is the knowledge of how little we know and can know." It's an attitude and an orientation toward life, toward leadership, toward institutions, and toward engagement with the future that seeks to take accurate stock of our finite ability to understand the future and shape it as we see fit.[45]

There is an alarming degree of overconfidence in many professional spaces, and that's not necessarily just a result of optimism. Studies in finance, for instance, have shown that CFOs of large corporations drastically overestimate their ability to predict the stock market. One study concluded that "financial officers of large corporations had no clue about the short-term future of the stock market; the correlation between their estimates and the true value was slightly less than zero!"[46] Perhaps more alarming, a study of patients who died in the ICU showed that physicians who were "completely certain" of their diagnoses antemortem were wrong 40 percent of the time. In both studies, these were highly competent, sometimes world-class, professionals who simply overestimated their abilities to diagnose and predict—sometimes with dire consequences. This sort of overconfidence, often optimistic in nature, endures in institutional contexts because, as Kahneman reports soberly, it is "highly valued, socially and in the market; people and firms reward the providers of dangerously misleading information more than they reward truth tellers."[47] As Kahneman has noted elsewhere, overconfidence is actually "a failure of imagination."[48]

Epistemological modesty starts with an awareness that we don't even know ourselves—that, as psychologists have increasingly discovered in recent decades, so much of what we think and believe lies below our consciousness. But even what is conscious is sometimes enigmatic. Our own minds are sometimes a tangled mess. Philosopher Jean Bethke Elshtain has argued that we humans are prone especially toward two vices—pride and forgetfulness—that are inimical to the humility-as-attentive-patience we ought to deploy. Pride and forgetfulness blind us to our limited abilities to truly know ourselves and each other. As Brooks said, "We are our own deepest mystery."[49]

Of course, not knowing ourselves, we also have trouble fully understanding other people. As Nathan Hill said in his novel, *The Nix*, "Seeing ourselves clearly is the project of a lifetime," and "sometimes we're so wrapped up in our own story that we don't see how we're [just] supporting characters in someone else's." The people around us are mysterious and unpredictable. Sometimes they delight, sometimes disappoint. Nearly always, they are fully capable of surprise.[50]

And so, not fully understanding ourselves, much less others, we can't presume to know fully the tangle of issues involved in any given circumstance. No issue, problem, or event can be understood in isolation from its geographic, historical, systemic, or interpersonal context. For all we know in any given circumstance, a million prior events, minute causes, and contextual factors affect that circumstance in visible and invisible ways. We live among "wicked" problems, those that are largely insoluble in the short-run:

- because they are complex,

- because our knowledge and appreciation of the problems is always incomplete,

- because the nature of the problems can appear contradictory,

- because they defy the boundaries of our sectors,

- because they lack any single cause,

- because they aren't likely to bend to the will of any single actor or institution,

- because any "solution" or "intervention" is a one-shot operation that can't be undone or redone,

- because there is no absolute test to measure the success of any one solution in isolation, and

- because the problems themselves are always changing.[51]

One set of policies won't end human trafficking, for example, no matter how imaginative or optimistic. A social welfare program can't end poverty, even if it's far-reaching, innovative, and full of promise. There's not a single cure-all for getting an equitable number of women into the C-suite, since it's not just a matter of creativity or will or optimism. And simply starting a school won't reroute an intransigent school-to-prison-pipeline; Talitha Koum taught us that.

In short, there's no one method for solving complex problems, and perhaps it's the case that our biggest problems are of such nature that "solving" is entirely the wrong paradigm. As Alan Watkins has stated, sometimes there is "no wisdom to match the wickedness of the problems we face."[52]

And sometimes—quite often, in fact—we're just wrong about what we "know" and can know.

One proven way to tame this in institutional contexts has been posited by psychologist Gary Klein, who proposes something called a pre-mortem. It's fairly simple. When an organization has almost come to an important decision but hasn't formally committed itself, Klein suggests gathering a group of people who are knowledgeable about the situation and the possible decision for a brief discussion. The discussion begins as follows: "Imagine that we are a year into the future. We implemented the plan as it now exists. The outcome was a disaster. Please take 5 to 10 minutes to write a brief history of that disaster." The exercise, and the discussion that often follows, seems to have three main advantages: it overcomes the groupthink that many teams seem to adapt once a decision has been made; it unleashes the imagination of knowledgeable people in a much-needed direction by encouraging even supporters of the decision to search for possible threats they had not considered earlier; and, perhaps most important, it legitimizes doubts.[53]

Imagination is a powerful thing, but it can't do everything. With this in mind, a kind of humility-as-epistemological-modesty becomes essential to the shape of our imaginations. If curiosity is the wellspring of imagination, humility might well be the guardrails. If curiosity helps grow our imagination, then humility helps guide it. And when that's the case, it's *hope* that can become the keystone.

Admittedly, this sort of humility can be depressing if left on its own. When confronted with the realities that the world is complex, and that we're not fully capable of bending it toward the outcomes we want, we can be prone to a mixture of pessimism, inaction, or despair. We can remain in our bewilderment with a dead imagination.

So let us be clear: humility is not the same thing as pessimism or passivity, and it ought not prevent us from acting. Humility is cultivated in a growing intimacy with God; the closer we are to God, the more aware we are that we are not God. This reminds us of how little we know, what a mystery the world is and we are to ourselves, and yet gives us confidence to act as those who are loved and blessed by God.

One could argue that humility provides precisely the right mindset and disposition for action, since it outfits us with a proper awareness of our ignorance and estimation of our abilities. It leads us to lean on our forebears more and the wisdom born out of our traditions. Equipping ourselves and our institutions with this wisdom, we can better design habits, systems, procedures, and networks to account, and perhaps compensate, for our own limitations, which can give us the right measure of confidence for wiser action.[54]

So what does this have to do with hope?

For St. Augustine, hope is a kind of love for, or devotion to, a future good that is desirable and possible to attain but is not yet present or possessed. Hope is a virtue that contains similarities to the idealism born of our imaginative curiosity and the sobriety that emerges from our measured humility and epistemological modesty. Hope combines the best of optimism and pessimism, while being much richer and more appealing than either. As Wendell Berry has said, "It's a bad move to get into a contest between optimism and pessimism. The steadying requirement is for hope."[55]

Optimists and pessimists have their merits. Empirical studies have demonstrated that optimists accomplish much more than pessimists, while pessimists typically have a more accurate understanding and interpretation of reality.[56] Both sound attractive. While optimists seem right to focus on the promising prospects of progress, especially when that motivates action, it's also the case that unfettered optimism is blind and unwise when it misunderstands reality or leads to presumption.

Hope is different from unfettered optimism. Even as it motivates action like optimism, it accounts for the brokenness, sin, and complexity that will undoubtedly disrupt our progress. Hope becomes something like optimism tempered by humility and a clarity of vision that sees the many ways our broken human nature can lead us (or others) astray. Michael Lamb has argued that hope's stable and enduring nature is what can help guide our unreliable passions with "right reason," enabling us to avoid the corresponding vices of presumption and recklessness, on the one hand, and despair and apathy on the other.[57]

Hope, in this regard, is a reconciling "both/and" of optimism and pessimism, presumption and despair. If presumption and despair are what Augustine called "two siren voices, each opposed to the other, but both dangerous, which lure people to destruction,"[58] then hope is a summons to rightly ordered imagining. It looks with optimism toward the future, even as it accounts realistically for the brokenness and limited capacity of human beings. It also draws on the wisdom of the past. It acknowledges that there is more than one way toward the better futures we imagine, even as it concedes that there will be obstacles no matter what. Hope recognizes the importance of human agency, just as it confesses belief in powers beyond our control. As psychologist Shane Lopez has noted, the most important thing to learn about hope, if we want to "make hope happen," is that flexible, creative thinking is important for achievement.[59]

Together, curiosity, humility, and hope are important keys to how we imagine and pursue human flourishing. Our bent is often to choose from among them, but wisdom comes through pursuing all three together. If curiosity grows our capacity for imagining, enabling us to live into our design as *homo prospectus*, and humility guides that imagining, calibrating our sense of what's prudent and possible, then hope enables us to sustain an evergreen sense of possibility without ever losing sight of all the challenges that surely will await as we navigate the future in light of the wisdom of the past.

The Minnesota Mining and Manufacturing company began in 1902 with a simple goal: to mine for corundum, a mineral they would use to make sandpaper and grinding wheels. Quickly, though, there was a problem: it turned out that what they thought was corundum was actually a low-grade mineral called anorthosite, not nearly as useful as corundum for the manufacture of these products. Undeterred, the folks at Minnesota Mining and Manufacturing reimagined what they might manufacture. Two decades later, this enabled them to stumble on a profitable little product called masking tape.

The Minnesota Mining and Manufacturing Company is now called 3M, and they make a lot more than tape and sandpaper. A fixture on the *Fortune* 500, 3M makes a staggering 60,000+ different products that are used in homes, businesses, schools, hospitals, and industries the world over. Just as astounding is the fact that over a third of their sales come from products invented in the last few years. They make everything from tape to streetlights to kitchen sponges to ballistic helmets for warzones.

In a world of corporate mergers and acquisitions, one might suspect 3M's breadth and diversity are a simple product of that tendency. Not so. The product list often hovers around an astonishing 1:1 product-to-employee ratio. Nearly everyone has helped to invent something.

The 3M corporate headquarters, located just outside St. Paul, is a five-hundred-acre landscape of laboratories, offices, grassy fields, and wooded parkland. It's not unusual to see employees out wandering through the greenspace, lying on a sofa catching sunlight, playing a game of pinball in the hallway, or doing all sorts of other things that don't look "productive." It's a bit surprising to see this at a company that is so successful in its growth. But everyone at 3M knows that this is actually the secret sauce.

Imaginative breakthroughs don't just happen if we keep doing business as usual.

Similar to Barnhart Crane & Rigging, 3M's website is splashed with questions that start with the phrase "what if?" It's the core DNA of the company to enable all employees to ask that question on a continual basis, something they can only do if they're given the time and space to explore, wander, and imagine. So while midday walks or pinball games might seem unproductive, it turns out to be some of the company's most productive time. In fact, 3M has adopted what it calls the "15% rule": every researcher can spend 15 percent of his or her workday pursuing speculative new ideas. The only requirement is that each must share these ideas with colleagues to help determine whether the ideas merit ongoing company time and investment. Some certainly do—hence, the company's ever-growing portfolio of new inventions.

"We're an unusual company," says Larry Wendling, a vice president who helps oversee research. He notes, "We have no niche or particular focus. Basically, all we do is come up with new things." The result is an astounding diversity of research and development and innovation. "I don't think there's another place that's trying to invent the next sticky tape *and* the next energy-efficient television screen *and* the next generation of vaccines," notes Wendling. "We're doing work in every scientific field."[60]

At 3M, much like Matryoshka Haus and Barnhart Crane & Rigging, the constant is a commitment to imagination. In all three places—though their work differs, their methods vary, and their outputs bear seemingly no resemblance—this commitment has made all the difference. We humans are imaginative, prospective beings, these organizations know, doing work and living lives that perpetually invite our imaginations to come alive. These three entities acknowledge this dimension of our nature, understand its great potential, and orient themselves to unleash it.

Like all three, we ought always to be asking questions like *what if?* or *how might we?* We should always be exploring new ideas and new possibilities. We ought to encourage those around us to do the same, and we should free space in our lives and our work that enables us to create and work toward the "second universes" of our imaginations and ideals. These aren't add-ons or things we should do just when there's time. There's never time. The time is now.

These are not recipes or checklists, something we do and then are done. They're principles, virtues, concepts, and commitments, things that require deep work on our part and an evaluation of who we are.

As James Clear has observed, our intentional habits shape our identity, and our identity shapes our habits. If we are to live into our capacity as imaginative beings, people whose commitment is to flourishing and to moving beyond the things that keep us mired in bewilderment, then we must decide the kinds of people we want to be and prove that we are those people by adopting the essential habits and behaviors that confirm this identity. This is true also for our organizations and institutions. To grow our capacities for imagining, we must be curious, always wandering and absorbing and cultivating both dimensions of the *T*. To guide our imagining, we must be humble, always checking our ambitions with epistemological modesty that takes account of how little we know and can know—and thus to lean into the wisdom of our traditions. In all of this, we must become people of hope, who know that much can be achieved even as much can impede us, and that the promotion of flourishing is always worth our striving.[61] We cultivate curiosity, humility, and hope as we stay focused on the God who calls us toward a future, the New Creation, that also points us back toward the past, to the beginning of all that is in Creation.

Our willingness to cultivate imagination will prove indispensable if we are to flourish as we navigate the future.

Chapter 5
Traditioning

Disturb us, Lord, when
We are too well pleased with ourselves

—*Sir Francis Drake*

One of the most dramatic scenes in all of literature occurs when Charles Dickens's Ebenezer Scrooge awakens on Christmas morning.

"Spirit!" he pleads, ". . . I am not the man I was. I will not be the man I must have been but for this intercourse!" It's the culmination of a wild night, a moment of clarity and strength for a character we've popularly come to know for his vices.

A Christmas Carol, published in 1843, abides in our collective consciousness, primarily because of Scrooge, the memorable curmudgeon whose miserly disposition loomed so large in the story that his name became shorthand for grumpy cheapskates. For most of us, *A Christmas Carol* is a story about the value of love and generosity, about compassion for Tiny Tim and the importance of charity over the bottom line. Most people think of Dickens's masterpiece as a cautionary tale about Scrooge, with a lesson resembling something like, "Reader beware: don't be a Scrooge." By that, we typically mean don't be a callous, petty, and selfish jerk.

That's good advice, to be sure, but there's another way of reading *A Christmas Carol* in which "Don't be a Scrooge" is exactly the wrong advice—in which the right advice might just be "Go on, be like Ebenezer Scrooge."

Scrooge, you see, was willing to see himself in a larger story, to see past, present, and future in a way that transformed his entire being and turned him into someone better suited to navigate the future in life-giving ways. "I will not be the man I must have been but for this intercourse," he proclaimed. And in this way, he has much to teach us.

As we noted in the last chapter, humans are imaginative, forward-looking creatures. We envision futures—usually better ones—and spend inordinate energy plotting ways to get to them. And while this is a marvelous feature of our existence, the reality is that our paths toward the future don't start today at "Go." Our lives and our institutional contexts don't have a reset button to give us a new start in which there are only present and future.

It's also the case that attempts to pursue a future unmoored from the past inevitably lead to drift. Just as we'd do well to apply dynamic metaphors (rather than mechanistic ones) to our perceptions of an unfolding future, it's also the case that organic metaphors prove instructive to our understandings of the institutions we inhabit. Organizations are much like organisms, in that they constantly evolve, adapt, die, and grow. Healthy institutions become aware of this inevitable change—whether it occurs by will or by external forces—and become adept at understanding themselves in context.

It's vital, therefore, to appreciate that while we are prospective by nature, we also carry forward a past. The past has real bearing on our futures, so it's important for us to develop a long view of time, not just prospective, but retrospective, too. We exist within larger stories, and we do well to find and situate ourselves there. If our lenses toward the future are truly to be marked by the curiosity, humility, and hope we've described, then our curiosity and humility and hope ought to compel us toward a continual evaluation of the past and learning from it.

Stories provide us with better vantage points and opportunities to see ourselves and the world, and they are instrumental in equipping us to navigate turbulent futures. A story can transform us, like it did Scrooge. So in this chapter, we're interested in a kind of storytelling that continually asks variations on four questions: What are we (and have we been) doing? What are we (and have we been) learning? Who are we (and have we been) becoming? And what do we carry forward that will compel, inform, and give shape to the life-giving futures we've imagined?

We call this process *traditioning*.

When we are confronted with a bewildering, complex world, we tend either to lurch back toward what we think we know or to try to disrupt our way to the future, downing a diet of faddish innovations, a bit like a toxic diet of "5-Hour Energy" shots. Neither tradition nor innovation is sufficient for navigating this complex future, even as both have something to teach us. Traditioned innovation, therefore, holds both together in creative tension, something that begins by anchoring to purpose and devoting ourselves to the promotion of flourishing lives and institutions. This sort of purpose encourages imagination and gives us a chance to look toward the future, something that evolves dynamically and organically.

Yet we are wise to note that we are not *only* prospective beings. Like Scrooge, we can, and should, resolve to live in past, present, and future, engaged in an ongoing process of traditioning. Earlier we distinguished the term "tradition" from "traditionalism" by echoing Jaroslav Pelikan's clever distinction between "the dead faith of the living" (traditionalism) and "the living faith of the dead" (tradition). The term "traditioning" follows suit; it's a bit like the process of keeping alive the faith of the "dead," even as it's also a good bit more.

Traditioning cultivates and requires the virtues of gratitude (for that which has come before) and discernment (about what to carry forward). It's a way of being that always takes stock of what we're learning and doing so we can properly assess who we're becoming and what to bring with us. The purpose of traditioning is to place ourselves within broader stories and to be transformed by those stories, enabling us to carry forward the wisdom of the past and to equip ourselves for the future. In some cases, like Scrooge, our stories enlighten a need for drastic change. In other cases, we come to appreciate and draw generously from the genius of those who got us here.

It's unorthodox, we'll say up front, to use "tradition" as a verb, when dictionaries tend not to list it that way. As a noun, tradition is *stuff*—content, information, beliefs, customs—the things we inherit or establish or hand down from one generation to another. Orlando O. Espín calls tradition the "time-bound and culture-molded attempts by one generation or community to witness to another generation or community what the first regards as 'our faith': what this faith has meant and why."[1]

Traditioning, the verb, certainly invokes the "stuff." It involves knowing and examining the content, the "faith," and the stories. It could be, in one sense, the dead faith of the living. But as verbing the noun might suggest, traditioning is much more dynamic, in that there is an action to traditioning that involves more than hearing and accepting—more than the content, the doctrines, or the customs. Traditioning is the process that births, defines, refines, and contextualizes the tradition. It forms us to be capable of wise imagination and innovation.

Traditioning is about placing ourselves within a story that extends backward and forward, beyond our present moment. It's a continual process of discovering the life-giving character of what has made whatever we are describing or narrating—ourselves, our people, our organization, our network, our culture—thrive (or not) over the years. It points us to what is most crucial to preserve as well as what most needs to be cast off, what we need to learn and what we need to unlearn. It helps to form and sustain identity—personal, communal, organizational, cultural, perhaps even cosmic—so that we can evolve our understandings of who we are, where we've been, where we're going, and who we aspire to be.

Peter Railton, whose work focuses mostly on looking forward, acknowledges the way our prospection is inseparably connected to memory. "The brain," he writes, "treats delving into the past and projecting into the future as a unified, ongoing task—because they are."[2] Seligman and Tierney make a similar point, extending that argument by suggesting that the whole point of memory is to improve our ability to understand the present and face the future. "To exploit the past," they note, "we metabolize it by extracting and recombining relevant information to fit novel situations."[3] In a similar way, Walter Brueggemann refers to a process he calls "imaginative remembering." This is an act in which the traditioning process "does not intend to linger over old happening, but intends to recreate a rooted, lively world of meaning that is marked by both coherence and surprise in which the listening generation, time after time, can situate its own life."[4]

Ebenezer Scrooge concurs. In the story he undergoes a remarkable and surprising conversion, perhaps as striking as any in English literature. And although fictional in key ways—most of us won't be visited by spirits and transported to see past and future—his example provides an insight into how seeing ourselves in bigger stories can fundamentally shape and reshape our trajectory.

So how, then, might we, like Scrooge, live in past, present, and future? How might we learn from the brokenness of the past that needs to be healed, and also to treasure and preserve the gifts of the past that enable our lives to be better than they might otherwise have been? How might traditioning inform and equip a better kind of action, or a wiser form of innovation, as we navigate the flourishing yet to come?[5]

One way is to tell stories—and in those stories to situate ourselves, to treat delving into the past and projecting into the future as what Railton called "a unified, ongoing task—because they are."[6]

❖ ❖ ❖ ❖ ❖ ❖

One way of retelling Western history, and US history in particular, is to recall what has long been a great experiment attempting to hold together people of different cultures, faiths, and politics—these people with different hopes, histories, languages, and customs; people with different stories and ways of being; people with different kinds of craft and industry; different ways of gathering for a meal and raising their children, of singing songs and worshiping God, of making music and playing games; different ways of growing up and growing old; different ways of celebrating a birth and burying the dead.

These strands of tradition that form us in indelible but sometimes subtle ways reside not in abstraction but in particularity: how a mother makes a sauce, or a father tells a story, or a child learns to pray, and how each watches and listens to and talks to the other. It's in the tiny but consequential details of communal life that we're formed as human beings. Who we are and who we are becoming result from tangible acts and the specific things we learn, inherit, internalize, and habituate.

For different peoples in the history of the West, and particularly in the United States, this has often involved having to live over against the oppression the larger culture (and other peoples) were inflicting on them. Even so, there was significant formation and traditioning occurring— indeed, it was often more powerful precisely because it required cultivating a counter-narrative to the dominant culture's story. That counter-narrative was bound up with the particularities of communal life.

This is the stuff of what philosopher Charles Taylor calls a person's "social imaginary"—the intuitive framework a person inhabits to navigate the world, human relationships, and a sense of self in relation to both.[7] We all inhabit these frameworks, probably to a much greater degree than we recognize or acknowledge, and they factor significantly in how we operate in the present and navigate toward the future.

At our best, people endeavor to create a world—or, at the very least, a society or community or set of relationships and institutions—where different stories, different ways of being human, might coexist within a social order, however fluid and loosely defined it might be. Americans, for instance, developed social structures that provided possibilities, usually voluntary, for education, financial opportunity, health care, governance, art, worship, and recreation, among others. The country developed as a "nation of joiners," to borrow Alexis de Tocqueville's durable phrase.

Social institutions were built and sustained by people of wisdom and ingenuity and through immense effort—schools and universities, businesses and banks, churches and libraries, hospitals and orphanages, museums and public parks, theaters and baseball diamonds. Over time these became, in the American case, the social institutions that shape culture and, in turn, shape the people who participate in and sustain them. They are the formative scaffolding of social and moral life, the social imaginary through which people imagine and participate in the world. They became the places where traditions were constructed, deposited, maintained, and passed on.

In many cases, and almost certainly in a macro sense, American social institutions have come to face a crisis of identity—not all of them, of course, but more than is healthy for a "nation of joiners." Because of various bewilderments, the center no longer seems to hold. And, in some sense, it has never held in the ways that a vision of God's Reign would suggest it should be held. The legacies of brokenness and systemic injustice continue to haunt us.

We have experienced—and perhaps continue to experience—an era in the human story in which so many previously dependable institutions and traditions face upheaval across cultures and communities. Sometimes this is a simple product of changed habits or practices: we log on to attend class; we do our Christmas shopping on Amazon, not at Sears; we might go to church in a bar; what was once our old stone church might now be a bar.

Changes in habits or practices like these are certainly not cause to fret, at least not on their own. Most of these changes entail just as many opportunities as they do challenges: we can flip classrooms or invite participation from the far corners of the globe, creating more dynamic learning environments; we can enter and enjoy unlikely communities through app-based ride-sharing or overnight hospitality. Altered practices, perhaps even when they produce crises of identity, are sometimes like healthy pruning and formative traditioning, affording opportunities to discern what needs to be left behind so that vibrant new life can grow.

But in our current cultural atmosphere, something more profound is taking shape than a changing set of habits or new ways of doing business. There is instead a general displeasure with the social and moral categories we have on hand to help us understand why institutions matter, what they do for society, and how people participate in them. Addicted to disruption, we forget or neglect the importance of what *is* and *has been*, and why it matters.

It's no stretch to say that we live in a time in which our understanding of, and appreciation for, the role of institutions in forming character and sustaining and contributing to a thriving society is drastically impoverished. It's assumed, too often, that institutions stifle people and undermine creativity. It is further assumed that powerful institutions are necessarily corrupt and so are their leaders. That is too often true, of course, and most of us have been wounded by bursting economic bubbles or senseless and harmful government shutdowns that stem from the unseemly or untrustworthy behavior of institutional leaders. Even churches and other social institutions too often betray their aspirations and convictions, leaving us with deep distrust and cynicism.

But when an "out with the old, in with the new" ethos becomes synonymous with anti-institutional sentiments that don't take seriously social institutions as cultural goods with immense value and which are crucial to forming healthy character, we risk losing something essential to flourishing. There is danger, notes Hugh Heclo, a political scientist, when we willfully develop amnesia about why institutions were created in the first place: ostensibly, to do good and provide contexts for traditioning. As

Tocqueville observed about the nearly incessant creation of institutions in the American context:

> Americans of all ages, all conditions, all minds constantly unite. . . . If it is a question of bringing to light a truth or developing a sentiment with the support of a great example, they associate. . . . As soon as several [people] have conceived a sentiment or an idea that they want to produce in the world, they seek each other out; and when they have found each other, they unite. From then on, they are no longer isolated [people], but a power one sees from afar, whose actions serve as an example; a power that speaks, and to which one listens.[8]

When our mistrust or suspicion of institutions results only in an impulse to eliminate them, we are deeply mistaken, perhaps gravely at risk, because there exists within institutions, in nearly every case, a kernel of Tocquevillian goodness or idealism. Indeed, institutions are part of the fabric of God's good Creation. They are neither optional nor merely necessary evils. They are necessary to the formation and sustenance of life that really is life. They tradition us in important and powerful ways.

That is why it is so problematic when we fall prey to cultural hand-wringing or, worse, to a general disdain for institutions. The solution to ailing institutions isn't their removal. It's creating better ones.

And the only way to create better ones is to value their potential and to understand the larger stories in which they're situated. To better understand what we want our institutions—and by direct connection, our*selves*—to become, we must first understand what has preceded us, what has enabled our oft-privileged position as inheritors. This invites what Heclo has memorably called "faithful reception"—a stance of being on the receiving end of things, admiring the excellences of what has been given to us. This requires us to be "mindful about time in a particular way," he says, stretching time tables from the past and into the future so they meet the present. In short, it requires a generous measure of gratitude.[9]

There are plenty of ways we might frame our traditioning stories. Sometimes we instinctively practice faithful reception by calling up heroes—Lincoln, or King, or Dorothy Day—and invite them to inform our present for the sake of our future. This is a valuable exercise that is commendable in so many ways. Psychologists have shown, in fact, that feelings of "elevation" emerge through admiration of "relevant and attainable" moral role models, and can substantially affect our own character development. Who we become can emerge from whom we admire.[10]

The problem is that we often place such people on a grand pedestal of achievement, to believe that they are in some way self-inventing or isolated in time. But human identity doesn't work that way. Even extraordinary people of tremendous influence inhabit and demonstrate rich moral imaginations only within the contexts of the relationships and institutions that formed their habits and cultivated their virtues—the things that inspired and enabled their incredible, sometimes miraculous-seeming, achievements. Stories of heroes usually miss the indispensable contextual and institutional factors that are often most important—specifically that those who led social progress had to dig deeper into their own traditions and institutions in order to imagine a way forward.

For example, there's no Abraham Lincoln without John Calvin's understanding of providence or the famous "team of rivals"; no Martin Luther King Jr. without groundwork laid by the NAACP or Howard University Law School's formation of Thurgood Marshall or the prophetic voice of the Black church shaped by scripture; no Dorothy Day without Teresa of Avila or Catholic social teaching. More than that, there is no accounting for the kinds of decisions Lincoln made, or the leadership King provided, or the bravery Day exuded without understanding how they were formed as human beings, without peeking into the kind of traditions and institutions they inhabited, which forged their moral imaginations and enabled them to see and respond to the world as well as lead it into new possibilities.

When we situate ourselves in a larger story on a longer time continuum, it's important for us to think beyond the heroes and to develop imaginations for the traditions and institutional contexts that summon forth great leaders and difference makers. Paying attention to the ways institutions help to "tradition" us for new life in the future is crucial. As Heclo argues, it is only through institutional attachments, not when we live unencumbered as individuals, that humans flourish.

Similarly, James Davison Hunter has observed (much like Tocqueville) that ideas are just ideas, however grand they might be, until institutions are established to "give form." "I have a dream" is just that, in the absence of the connections King made to the Student Nonviolent Coordinating Committee, the NAACP, and the faithful churches that organized "beloved communities" of resistance. To cultivate conditions that are conducive to the flourishing of all, Hunter contends, it's imperative that we get beyond ideas to institutions.[11]

Institutions, after all, are what give us what Gordon T. Smith calls "an opportunity and a mechanism, a means to invest in something much larger than ourselves and to make a contribution that we would never be able to make individually and on our own. We invest in something—a means, a system, an entity—that will outlast us."[12] As Yuval Levin puts it, institutions are "the durable forms of our common life."[13]

Institutions, in this way, are the means by which we plant trees under whose shade we do not expect to sit, even as they provide us with trees we did not plant, whose shade we very much enjoy. We inherit institutions. We tend institutions. We seek to remedy their faults and their tendencies toward bureaucracy and brokenness. We build and rebuild them.

By continually reclaiming their purposes, and aiming them toward hopeful futures, we position ourselves to go about the work to which we are ultimately called—as richly imaginative cultivators of character and human flourishing, now and in the future.

It's in this way that institutional thinking, however loose or highly structured the institutions themselves might be, helps order our stories and ground our traditions. This means keeping alive the stories of single institutions—telling them truthfully and hopefully, not neglecting their failures, yet situating them within their best aspirations.

It means also locating our institutions and ourselves in broader movements and contexts, where there is a rich well of traditions from which to draw as we place ourselves in the present and orient toward the future. It means we develop an understanding of, and an appreciation for, the many streams of tradition that converge into our particular time and place.

So, for example, in an educational context, that might mean tracing traditions to sources far upstream, like Plato and Aristotle and the Academy in Athens. It might mean positioning within the stream that flows through American education systems—public, private, religious, local, or land grant. It could summon us to explore the stories of our own institutions—the ways they were founded by people of goodwill seeking to be faithful to God and to nurture a Christian vision, on the hope and promise and imagination of a tree they'd plant but never see fully grown.

Perhaps we stand in the stream of our discipline's traditions, the way, say, social work has always connected to people on the ground, starting with Jane Addams's summons that "action is the sole medium of expression for ethics."[14] Or perhaps we summon those individual forebears, whose work in our own institutions we inherit—the great teachers or scholars who held our positions in previous generations, setting a standard for what we expect to achieve in ours.

When we invite ourselves to discover the life-giving character of the traditions that have formed the contexts we currently inhabit—as individuals, as parts of institutions, as parts of broader communities or cultures or movements—we nurture the practical wisdom that is indispensable for flourishing in the future. We become traditioned in ways that enable creative innovation.

How do we undertake traditioning? It involves an ongoing process of allowing our purpose and our imagining to help us interpret all that has gone before us that makes our lives possible. It also requires ongoing convictions, practices, and storytelling to immerse us in faithful reception of the past in ways that point us toward the future and illumine the present in dynamic interrelations.

At the broadest and most comprehensive level, our traditioning is into the story of God and God's love. We need to become immersed in the biblical story as an ongoing process of learning scripture as a "second first-language." This involves learning to think, feel, perceive, and live as a follower of Jesus. We are invited to see all that is, and all that we are, and all we are called to be and do, in the light of the story of God.

In a world filled with brokenness, distortions, and the ongoing temptations to self-deception, learning a practice of traditioning will require the cultivation of holy friends who help us unlearn destructive patterns and learn faithful ones. We will discuss this further in the next chapter. We also need ongoing patterns and practices of rehearsal to prepare us to be able to improvise into the future, as we will discuss in chapter 7.

Such friendships and rehearsals are part of what the early church understood by the term "catechesis," an extended process of apprenticeship to learn how to think, feel, perceive, and live as a Christian. This process lasted a minimum of two years, leading into a lifelong journey as a Christian toward holiness of heart and life.

Ongoing patterns of "traditioning" also involve ever-deeper immersion into the stories, experiments, convictions, and practices of those who have gone before us. We learn to think analogically as we discover examples of traditioned innovation by our close and distant forebears. It is only through traditioning that we discover patterns and practices that have too often become forgotten—of the early Christians founding the first hospitals, of medieval monks pioneering new patterns of agriculture and technology, of early modern Christians cultivating new approaches to mental health, of nineteenth-century African American Christians leading the way in insurance.

Traditioning is about immersion into the broad Christian story, and learning to see as God sees. It also involves learning the histories and life-giving traditions of the contexts in which we live, and the institutions of which we are a part. To be sure, like the Christian tradition as a whole, our contexts and institutions are complicated mixtures of traditionalisms and traditions. And we engage in ongoing arguments with others about what needs to be forgotten and unlearned as well as what needs to be remembered and learned.

Greg learned the importance of traditioning especially in his leadership of Duke Divinity School, beginning in 1997. An ecumenical Christian divinity school formally affiliated with The United Methodist Church, Duke has long focused on forming and educating students for wise Christian leadership—especially as pastors and scholars. He realized the power of traditioning to help equip people for innovative thinking and leadership as well, and he worked with colleagues to cultivate a robust approach to formation through traditioning.

He knew there was much to be unlearned and cast off. Duke Divinity School had a history of complex difficulties with issues of racism, sexism, and academic elitism that sometimes occluded its vision, even as there were also moments of keen insight, grace, and leadership along the journey. Leaning into the best of its traditions, and casting off traditionalisms, became an ongoing process of discernment.

When Greg was asked to serve again as dean in 2018, the dynamics of churches, the academy, and the broader cultures had all changed. The importance of traditioning had not changed, but a lot of circumstances had. This became especially true as The United Methodist Church became a more complicated institution to navigate in early 2019, and as broader perceptions of Christianity continued to be damaged by revelations of sexual abuse, partisan politics, and denominational infighting.

Greg drew on his long experience of working on traditioned innovation as an idea to connect the deepest form of traditioning—learning to live into God's story—with his understanding of the traditions of The United Methodist Church, Duke University (and the Divinity School in particular), as well as North Carolina and the American South. This has been particularly challenging given the turbulence on all of those fronts. What could be done?

Greg began to probe more deeply into his own traditioning, searching for stories that could offer insight and innovative leadership. He began to reflect on "the heart of Methodism" that could be distinguished from the bureaucratic morass of the structures of The United Methodist Church. He then realized that the heart of Methodism is an expression of the power of "Christianity's surprise" that occasioned such explosive growth in the early church. Greg learned that James B. Duke's indenture focused on churches, children, health care, and education in a way that closely aligns with the foci of the early Christians' institutional dynamism.

He also discovered that the heart of Methodism, as an expression of Christianity's surprise, offered strong resonance with the heart of social entrepreneurship as a burgeoning area of interest in the contemporary academy. And all of this is rooted in a vision of God, the future, and what it means to be human that can offer signs of renewal and hope to the contemporary academy, the church, and the broader culture.

In a process that is still unfolding, Greg realized that there were things he had taken for granted that now needed to be cast off: assumptions about semesters and courses and degrees in the institution of education; commitments to structures and funding sources that had become a dependency on an outdated denominational form called "United Methodism"; assumptions about the patterns of Western Christianity that carry too much Western, white-male criteria rather than a genuinely global and missionary gospel.

In articulating a vision of the heart of Methodism that expresses Christianity's surprise, Greg has discovered new insights from colleagues, new opportunities for engagements across the university, and new possibilities for missional and faithful witness. The innovations are emerging from a deeper immersion into the traditions of Duke, the traditions of the Wesleys and their heirs, and the traditions of Christians through the centuries and around the world.

Greg's experience and learning have cultivated new possibilities with colleagues and new growth for Duke Divinity School. And it has been dependent on ongoing traditioning that involves friendships, networks, and institutions collaborating together. This traditioning process has formed an imagination that enables us to see things we otherwise couldn't have seen, and to see them with a depth and clarity for which we all yearn.

To be sure, Greg has continued to fall prey to amnesia and traditionalism, even as he seeks to practice traditioned innovation. Even in the company of holy friends, broader networks, and partner institutions, our vision will continue to be a mix of insight and blindness, powerful possibilities and weak resignation.

Practices of traditioning help minimize blindness and resignation. Through traditioning we learn to see, think, feel, and live in ways that surprise others. And that traditioning enables new stories to be told and new patterns to emerge for unlearning brokenness and learning holiness.

Sometimes that happens at places like Duke; at other times it happens in contexts like Zambia.

In the African nation formerly called Northern Rhodesia, now Zambia, British colonists enforced an appalling array of racist laws from the time they colonized in 1911 until Zambians achieved independence in 1964. One particularly absurd law required Black residents, for the duration of colonial rule, to do all their commerce through shop windows. Not allowed to enter the stores, Black residents shopped from the street in a dehumanizing ritual: present money at store window, tell attendant what to retrieve, and have goods passed through the window after money changes hands.

There are many ways to change systems this broken—you can picket, protest, or provoke. You can foment insurrection, you can bomb, you can loot, and you can riot. As tensions grew in Northern Rhodesia over the racist structures and systems these shopping laws represented, and as Black residents began to consider a massive resistance against British colonization, Simon Kapwepwe and his friends hatched a better plan.

Kapwepwe bought a Land Rover.

The magic was in how he did it, and in the way the story trickled out through his vast networks. Kapwepwe had long been involved in networks and institutions forged from dissatisfaction with the colonial arrangement. He'd helped form the Northern Rhodesian African Congress and later the United National Independence Party, which the British deemed illegal. He'd been sent to prison for his affiliations and his possession of "subversive literature," but he had reentered society undeterred from his ideals. He'd been fortunate to earn an Indian Village Industrial Scholarship, which sent him to Bombay (now Mumbai) for study in 1950, where he became enamored with Mohandas Gandhi's ideals and nonviolent strategies. And this rich set of traditions and institutions led him to the Land Rover.

Kapwepwe saved his money, and, having done so, showed up at the dealership, waving his cash at the salesman through the window—the familiar shopping protocol. He pointed at the Land Rover he wanted, which sat inside, and requested, nonchalantly, that the salesman pass it through the slot in the window as the law required (much, perhaps, like a camel through the eye of a needle). The salesman guffawed, and told Kapwepwe he'd just bring the vehicle around back to the gate.

No, no, Kapwepwe insisted, channeling Gandhi. He said the law must be followed.

A crowd gathered, and because the salesman couldn't deliver the newly purchased Land Rover through the window as mandated and requested, Kapwepwe entered the building to retrieve it, bending the law a little, but only so he could follow it. He cranked the vehicle and, to the letter of the law, delivered it straight through the window himself—which meant crashing through the glass and taking down a wall in the process. The crowd was aghast—and they loved it!

Word of the stunt spread, and for a restless native population, it proved cathartic. What a clever, Zambian thing to do, many thought. These were a people who'd survived for a thousand years before the

135

colonists had arrived, and they were not interested in continuing the paternalistic arrangement of British rule. Kapwepwe's heroics, and the story about it that emerged and spread, helped to magnify and clarify an aged, ripened, and durable Zambian spirit, which existed on a time horizon that stretched backward and forward beyond the present moment. It helped to connect black Zambians to one another, psychically through the story itself and relationally through the institutional infrastructure in place. And it evoked a Zambian creative streak, compelling a vision for how to move toward the better future they imagined and deserved.

In a short time, a nonviolent uprising, known as the Cha Cha Cha, took root, the key element of which was noncooperation and demonstrations highlighting the irrationality and injustice of the colonial arrangement. While not all of the Cha Cha Cha uprising proved peaceful, many Zambians seemed to catch a glimpse of themselves in Simon Kapwepwe. There had been something brave and brilliant and a little playful in his nonviolent act—and many believed that such a spirit might just prove effective in an independence movement.

After several months of nonviolent noncooperation, the British Crown doubled down, choosing a new administrator for the colony who would enforce discipline and restore "proper" British order. Fair enough, thought Julia Chickamonenga, a strong, rabble-rousing Zambian who'd been inspired by Kapwepwe. She decided to organize a "welcome party" for this new administrator, gathering a group of women to greet him with welcome songs on arrival at the Lusaka airport. These weren't just any women, of course. These were the biggest Zambian women she could find. She assembled them and explained the plan.

When the new administrator arrived, he stepped off the plane to the sound of beautiful singing. He looked across a sea of harmonizing Zambian women, and he realized quickly that these weren't just any women. They were huge and strong. And every last one of them, pleasantly singing their songs of greeting, stood completely naked—intentionally, deviously, defiantly—from head to toe.

Once he lifted his jaw from the floor, the administrator stepped straight back onto the plane—petrified, apparently—and ordered the pilot directly back to London.

Within weeks, Zambia was an independent nation. And Simon Kapwepwe became its vice president.[15]

The story of Simon Kapwepwe, as carried forward by his successors and network of resisters, is instructive in many ways. Just as there's good reason to think that the way people understand themselves is by telling their own stories, there's also perhaps better reason to suspect that we can gather, discern, and carry forward the instructive wisdom of traditions when we are story *listeners*—much like Julia Chickamonenga. Because traditioning depends on our capacity to hold past, present, and future together in coherent stories, and because it's the communal and institutional traditions that prove themselves to be richest, the importance of listening is difficult to overstate.

Philosopher Alasdair MacIntyre notes in *After Virtue* that any vibrant tradition exists as an ongoing argument about how best to tell the story of that tradition. Gary Riebe-Estrella calls it, in much the same way, a "conversation." The tradition, in this respect, is always malleable, always subject to reinterpretation, meaning it's crucial to develop the skills, dispositions, and habits that enable us to listen to one another. This helps to challenge and improve our own partial and biased understandings, even as it also enriches our capacities to tell the stories well ourselves. It also enlarges our imaginations.[16]

Jewish families and communities engage in a traditioning ritual every Passover, when the youngest child begins the Seder by asking, "Why is this night different from all other nights?" That question prompts the host into a story that is at once well worn and new, incorporating everyone present as characters in a story that stretches far beyond the present moment. It tells who they have been, who they are, and where they are going—as a people and as communal inheritors of the tradition. That night is then typically linked, among Jewish children, to the future—toward preparation for a bar mitzvah or bat mitzvah, signaling a transition from childhood to adulthood and maturity as a member of the community.

There are ongoing arguments within the Jewish tradition of what the Passover story conveys. And it is by being inducted into that tradition that children learn how to argue well, even amid deep differences about what the future of being Jewish might and should mean.[17]

As Jean Bethke Elshtain has argued, no complex tradition ever gets exhausted.[18] The problem is that *we* do. John Gardner, who has plenty to say about our individual, institutional, and even societal tendencies toward deterioration and renewal, notes that for those of us who carry forward complex traditions and attempt to adapt them for the future, "the need for endless learning and trying is a way of living, a way of thinking, a way of being awake and ready. Life," he continues, "isn't a train ride where you choose your destination, pay your fare and settle back for a nap. It's a cycle ride over uncertain terrain, with you in the driver's seat, constantly correcting your balance and determining the direction of progress."[19]

This is why all healthy organisms, including institutions, communities, cultures, and societies, have embedded in their stories ongoing arguments about the heart of the traditioning process. They continually interpret and reinterpret the key questions about who they are and hope to become in the wake of what they've done, what they've learned, and what might prove most instructive in the discerning process about what to carry forward to compel, inform, and give shape to the life-giving futures they've imagined.

This is perhaps what is most instructive about the traditioning that occurred in the stories of the Cha Cha Cha. The stories of Daniel Kapwepwe and the Land Rover became stories that, once activated in the context of networks and institutions, could at once clarify, connect, and compel.

❖ ❖ ❖ ❖ ❖ ❖

As a means of clarifying, Kapwepwe's story illumined several important things. For one, it highlighted the absurdity of the inherited situation and the injustice of this particularly injurious form of colonization. In addition, it elucidated a character among a community and a people who were permitted, through humor especially, to see anew who they were, who they'd become, and who they wished to be. They'd always been a strong and capable people—with a playful or mischievous streak as well. But absurd circumstances had squelched and repressed the mighty potential of that spirit. Kapwepwe sparked a conversation that summoned this spirit and asked whether it might still be relevant for today and tomorrow.

Traditioning in this way involves telling the stories that serve as light to help us see ourselves and the ways our past and present influence our trajectory for the future. But this is not always as easy as it sounds—when the spaces we inhabit grow cloudy, when certain memories fall by the wayside, when path-dependence or habits deeply ingrained leave us in ruts with no clear way out, or perhaps when we just neglect the work it takes to find the right memories and stories to clarify what is at stake in the present.

Novelist Wiley Cash, who teaches creative writing, always tells his students on the first day of class that their lives are worth literature—that, in effect, mining their own experiences can produce the insights to craft something full of meaning and beauty. Many are skeptical, Cash says, including a student who raised his hand one semester and said that he was "just a hick from Mount Airy," and that everyone in the room could tell by his thick accent. Cash pushed back, and remembers it this way: "He did not sound like a hick. He sounded like someone who was from somewhere and that he should rely on his knowledge of the place he is from when writing because you never know what you will come to understand about yourself when you scour your past and investigate the places you call home and the people you knew there."

To hammer home the point, Cash's first assignment of each new semester requires students to write a personal essay portraying the places they call home and considering the ways that their understandings of these places and the people they knew there have changed over time. Part of the assignment requires them to draw a map of their neighborhood and label the places that meant something to them. He presents questions such as, Where did their friends live? Where did they play? Where were the places that scared them? Where were the places where they did something brave or got hurt or had their hearts broken?

Cash himself joins in the assignment, no matter how many times he's taught the course, and as he traces the map, he always seems to access a new memory. One time, while mapping his grandparents' neighborhood instead of his own, he discovered a memory of goats behind the neighbor's garage, something he hadn't thought of in years, which prompted other deeply buried memories. "Where had this memory been for so many years?" he wondered, and he used his goat story to frame the next class meeting. He asked the students to consider how they would use voice and the perspective of time to tell stories. Would they limit their perspectives on a memory to the perspective they held as a four-or ten-or fifteen-year-old, or would they move beyond that perspective and tell the story from the contemporary moment of being a college student or adult? As Cash himself plumbed the memory of the goats, it led him to memories of a father's comfort when a grandparent died, which led him to a more recent memory of the comfort he provided to his own daughters as his father died. A link, and a new story, was born.

"These memories have been locked inside me from anywhere from two to 36 years," Cash notes, "and they are layered and resonant and difficult to describe." And even though these kinds of memories are difficult to describe, and perhaps even more difficult sometimes to develop into something coherent or meaningful, Cash believes that something poignant occurs if we make a point to access them, to allow the passage of time to change our understandings of them, and to retell them so that our new vantage points lead to richer *clarity* about ourselves, our past, and our movement toward the future.[20]

Perhaps just as important as clarity is connection. The stories of Simon Kapwepwe and the Land Rover created connection—a way for a people to draw together around a shared understanding of the past and a hopeful vision about the future. Stories, after all, help people form friendships, networks, and communities. They are the best lenses we have for glimpsing the experience and perspective of someone else and for understanding what we share—whether that's a past history, a present circumstance, or a shared interest in working toward the future. Stories come in many formats, in written or visual form, in books or on screens. But stories that come directly from another human being, like the ones we tell in our institutional contexts, do something remarkable to us.

When stories are told in person, a speaker's and a listener's brains can begin to align. As hearers, we not only experience the story, we and the storyteller begin to have the same experience, even physiologically, as though we are in the stories ourselves—sweating, breathing faster, laughing, or crying, right along with the storyteller. Researchers call this "neural coupling," where the same parts of the brain are energized in the teller and hearer—not just those parts controlling speech and language, but also, remarkably, those parts that discern another person's beliefs, desires, and goals. This, as Geoffrey Colvin has pointed out, is a form of deep empathy. Because we humans are most moved by stories when we can evaluate the teller's trustworthiness, stories told authentically create a strong and enduring connection. In this way, stories connect us and engender trust.[21]

When trust is high, we are best situated for action toward the future, and this, too, is where the power of story is immense. As literary critic Martin Puchner has written, stories "change the way we see the world, and also the way we act upon it."[22] Framed this way, stories can go beyond clarifying and connecting to compel us toward life-giving futures. These stories that compel us forward provide the action that is key to the movement from traditionalism to traditioned innovation.

Stephen Denning, a lawyer who spent most of his career at the World Bank, which he helped refashion and reorient through the power of story, has coined a particular story genre he calls "springboarding." A spring-board story is one that enables the audience to leap in understanding so that it can grasp how an organization, community, or complex system might change or grow toward the future. In short, it compels action on the part of the hearers.

In this respect, a springboard story is less about transferring information than about catalyzing understanding. While elements of Denning's springboarding descriptions border on being too confiningly technique-y, the genre itself is extremely valuable, encouraging storytellers and hearers to visualize from a story in one context what is involved in transformation in an analogous one. It's like telling Simon Kapwepwe's story of a Land Rover hurtling through a glass storefront to inspire for Julia Chickamonenga an imagination for a strong-women's all-nude welcoming chorus.

According to Denning, stories that effectively springboard action in institutional contexts often need only enough texture or detail to show how the basic message might apply to the hearer's own particular context. Springboard stories epitomize or embody the change idea, almost like a premonition of what the future will be like. Typically, this involves a "happy," or better yet a hopeful, ending—one that springs the listener out of the negative, questioning, or skeptical frames of mind that our bewilderments can foster.[23]

To state that differently, a springboard story invites listeners out of the mindset that says "we can't because," and invites them into a reframing of "we can if." This mindset, write Adam Morgan and Mark Barden in their wonderfully handy little book, *A Beautiful Constraint*, is a vital dimension of building generatively toward the future. Because we all encounter constraints—be they bewilderments over the storms and fog on these wilder seas or the limits imposed by our predecessors or institutional contexts—the way we frame our constraints is important.

As Morgan and Barden observe, today's approaches are in effect yesterday's approaches, based on what was appropriate then, not necessarily now. Our orientations toward the future typically comprise bundles of beliefs, assumptions, and behaviors whose natures and rationales go unquestioned. As Dickens stated, "Men's courses will foreshadow certain ends, to which, if preserved in, they must lead." In other words, today's successes and failures blind us to new possibilities for tomorrow. And the only way out of this path-dependence is by reframing our present realities with "propelling questions" that hold together bold ambition and a realistic understanding of present constraints.[24]

Enter the *can-if*.

Scrooge might say "I can't change, because:

- my habits are too ingrained,

- the business must remain profitable, or

- the people already despise me too much."

Zambians might say, "We can't become independent, because:

- the Crown is too strong,

- we've learned helplessness under colonial rule, or

- colonization is all around us."

A form of compelling storytelling will reframe those constraints, catalyzing understanding and springboarding toward the future with *can-if*. "I can change if I honor Christmas in my heart and live in the Past, the Present, and the Future," Scrooge might say. Or "We can find independence if we outfox the colonizers and demonstrate the absurdity of their ways," the Zambians might say.

A compelling story punctuated by a *can-if* is full of immense potential, a key form of traditioning that, in allowing us to link stories of the past to stories of the future, facilitates the move from tradition to traditioned innovation. It keeps the conversation about *how* something could be possible, rather than *whether* it would be possible. It keeps hope and inquisitiveness alive at the same time. It forces everyone involved in the conversation to take responsibility for discovering answers, rather than identifying barriers, because no one asking *can-if* can note obstacles without looking for solutions in the same sentence.

Perhaps most important, it helps us understand ourselves as people who look for solutions, rather than as people preoccupied with problems and obstacles. As Morgan and Barden note, this "requires vision from a leader to cut through to the key challenges, and the understanding that [any] process is unlikely to stop at a single first can-if, but instead become a sequence in which one solution leads to another challenge, which, in turn, needs a solution, and so on."[25]

So if the sage advice is indeed *to be a Scrooge*, and if traditioning invites us into stories extending backward and forward that *clarify, connect*, and *compel* us, then what's left might be the hardest part. If a spirit of humility guides us back to the traditions, and if a posture and practice of gratitude invite a "faithful reception," then it's discernment, peppered with wisdom bent on action, that sits at the heart of the propelling, *can-if* orientation that turns tradition into a richer practice of traditioned innovation for the future.

What do we carry forward, and how and why and when and where do we carry it as we step toward the hopeful directions we've imagined? Just as Julia Chickamonenga captured the essence of Simon Kapwepwe's protest, so too might we try to discern and gather up the wisdom of the past for the sake of the future.

Poet and essayist Mary Oliver recalls that she once attended a lecture about the Whitney family, with particular focus on Gertrude Vanderbilt Whitney, whose status in two of America's wealthiest and most prominent families gave rise to a particularly charmed life—one she felt compelled to use for considerable good. The lecture was given by Mrs. Whitney's granddaughter, who used a phrase that struck Oliver as particularly fine, prompting Oliver to "[slip] the phrase from the air and put it into my own pocket!" The phrase was "inherited responsibility," interpreted in the family as a sense of calling to use their received wealth for the larger purposes of an enduring public good. It's a phrase that nods to Heclo's "faithful reception," but, significantly, it marks a shift from Heclo's passive to something more active.

As Oliver describes it, inherited responsibility "is precisely how I feel, who have inherited not measurable wealth but, as we all do who care for it, that immeasurable fund of thoughts and ideas, from writers and thinkers long gone into the ground."

"So here I am," Oliver says. She continues:

> walking on down the sandy path, with my wild body, with the inherited devotions of curiosity and respect. . . . Yes, it is a din of voices that I hear, and they do not all say the same thing. But the fit of thoughtfulness unites them. . . . Forebears, models, spirits whose influence and teachings I am now inseparable from, and forever grateful for. I go nowhere, I arrive nowhere, without them. With them I live my life, with them I enter the event, I mold the meditation, I keep if I can some essence of the hour, even as it slips away. . . . They were dreamers, and imaginers, and declarers; they lived looking and looking and looking, seeing the apparent and beyond the apparent, wondering, allowing for uncertainty, also grace, easygoing here, ferociously unmovable there; they were thoughtful.[26]

There is always a danger that efforts toward traditioning might lead to traditionalism, a stance that is not particularly useful for navigating the future. There surely are ways of unearthing and retelling the traditions that can deepen ideologies or permanently relegate forgotten elements to the junkyard. There are ways that present a utopian past; they pretend to be movements forward but are really just attempts to move backward. There are ways that can lead to exclusion or fail to account for the injustices that have brought us to the present, just as there are ways that can bring about a sense that the present was inevitable or foreordained. As well, we can unearth and retell the traditions in ways that substantiate what Gardner called "the straitjacket of unwritten rules that hems the individual in."[27]

When these warning signs present themselves, our engagement with tradition is probably not traditioning, but rather a lurch toward traditionalism.

Faithful traditioning is an ongoing journey of learning from, inquiring about, engaging with, and appreciating those who have gone before us, as well as the convictions, the practices, the institutions, that bear us into the future. That journey also involves discerning how to cast off all those convictions, practices, and institutions that were sinful and broken or have just outlived their usefulness.

Inherited responsibility looks inevitably toward the past, present, and future all at once, dynamically. Drawn by the future through our capacity for imagining, we also rely on the past to envision the future and to illumine the present. Traditioning forces us to assess what we've been doing, to question what we've been learning, and perpetually to contemplate who we've been becoming. Then it points all those questions, in one swift movement, to the present and the future, inviting us to consider all three tenses at once, to be a Scrooge who declares, "I will live in the Past, the Present, and the Future. The Spirits of all Three shall strive within me."

Chapter 6
Collaborating

In our efforts to build a new earth,
We have allowed our vision
Of the new Heaven to dim.

—*Sir Francis Drake*

Fortunately, we are not alone as we seek to cultivate an imagination sufficient to navigate wilder seas. If it were up to each of us alone, we would feel overwhelmed by the sheer weightiness of wisdom from the past, possibilities for and anxieties about the future, and the complexities of the present. As we suggested in the last two chapters, though, we can draw on friendships, institutions, networks, and collaboration to nurture a dynamic imagination and commitment to innovation that is deeply rooted in traditions.

To help foster imagination for our own lives as well as for the communities and institutions that enable us to flourish, we develop intrinsic relationships with others. We do that through holy friendships and unlikely ones, through vibrant institutions and the cultivation of new ones, through dense networks and weak ties, and through entrepreneurial collaboration as well as cross-sector learning. As we cultivate intrinsic relationships, we depend on and cultivate afresh important virtues such as trust, generativity, and wisdom.

147

All of these relationships and virtues require us to abandon an individualism that is false even though it is seductive. We tell ourselves that it is all about the individual, and that I can make of myself whatever I want without any need for anyone else, a narrative we perpetuate through our fascination with people we perceive, wrongly, to be successful lone geniuses—Steve Jobs, Bill Gates, Mark Zuckerberg, and the like. Though this picture continues to seduce people into a false imagination, we are living with the wreckage of "lost connections."[1] Social media, for example, shows mostly curated lives—the wins, successes, and images that portray our best selves. When we can't live up to what we perceive in others, we try to cope with the wreckage of lost connections through various forms of addiction, but that only numbs our psyche, creates false narratives about our past and future as well as present, or intensifies our brokenness.

A better picture of our humanity is provided by Augustine at the beginning of his *Confessions*: "Our hearts are restless until they rest in thee, O God." We are created for relationship with God, with one another, and with the whole creation. When we foster intrinsic connections and relationships, we discover the underlying contexts that make flourishing possible. This is as true for institutions as it is for people, as we will show in this chapter.

We begin, however, with the significance of friendships.

Friendships are central to a flourishing, well-lived life. They are crucial to keeping us connected to God and to others, and to discovering who we are. Friends help us make sense of our past, orient us toward a bright future, and discern what we ought to do in the present.

Friendship is a central means for describing the moral life in authors such as Aristotle, Augustine, and Thomas Aquinas in the West; it is also embedded in Central African images, such as *Ubuntu,* and Native American practices of developing strong connections to the land and the broader created world.

It is only in western modernity that we have managed to trivialize the significance of friendship in favor of individualistic decision-making and a preoccupation with the "self." In so doing, we have intensified problems of loneliness, anxiety, depression, and isolation that are now becoming epidemics in the United States. Johann Hari's book *Lost Connections* documents the challenges we face in the Anglo-American world with what he describes as our lost connections to such things as meaningful values, meaningful work, meaningful relationships, the natural world, and any sense of hope for the future. We struggle to navigate the future, much less to practice traditioned innovation, when we find ourselves isolated and missing connections.

This is as true for leaders of large institutions as it is for Sergio and other Homeboys and Homegirls working alongside Father G. Connections are as important for busy professionals as for the attachments that infants and toddlers need at Talitha Koum. Our communities flourish when we discover a roving listener like De'Amon at Broadway UMC, or when we are encouraged to work in teams at Matryoshka Haus. We get into trouble when we are isolated from others; we discover new life when we befriend—and are befriended by—others.

Here we highlight two types of friendships for cultivating imagination and discovering a flourishing life: holy and unlikely. They are both important and often overlap, and yet they are also significantly different kinds of relationships.

Holy friendships are intimate, enduring, and formative. They bear similarities to what Aristotle calls "character friendships," in that they require time to develop and sustain. They depend on levels of reciprocity that focus our attention. We can only sustain authentic holy friendships with a limited number of people because of the timefulness and depth of the relationships. We need to know one another well enough that we can see and say and hear things together that others can't. The intimacy of holy friendships carries risks; when distorted or not enriched by unlikely friendships and other networks and relationships, they can become problematic by being exclusive or elitist. But we can't flourish without them.

Holy friends do three important things: they help us dream dreams we otherwise wouldn't have dreamed, they help us affirm gifts we otherwise would be afraid to claim, and they challenge the sins we have come to love. They orient us toward the future in life-giving ways, helping us understand ourselves more clearly and faithfully. They inspire us, affirm us, and challenge us.

When Greg was asked to serve again as dean of Duke Divinity School in July 2018, it upended what he thought he was going to be doing for the next several years. Initially he wasn't sure it was the right thing to do or what he really wanted to do. He also wasn't sure he could trust his own feelings or thoughts about the matter. He sought guidance from holy friends who offered wisdom and clarity for his discernment from diverse perspectives.

One in particular, a business leader with experience in the academy, helped Greg dream how serving as dean again could enable him to address many of the bewilderments our world is facing. He helped Greg dream in different ways about continuities between what he had been doing in Armenia and in other roles with the platform that being dean of Duke Divinity School would provide. He said, don't just be the dean "of" Duke or a dean "at" Duke; be sure you also focus externally on being a dean "from" Duke. New horizons were set.

Another friend helped Greg see how his gifts align well with helping existing institutions imagine new possibilities. She observed how Greg could help talented people utilize their gifts to form new relationships and teams that offer exciting possibilities for their own vocations within and through those institutions. She noted that, while Greg was hesitant to move back into the stresses of a "line authority" role, it was a significant calling to lead an institution—especially one focused on forming and equipping people to lead Christian institutions—and that Greg had gifts better utilized in such a calling than in other things he "wanted" to do.

A third friend echoed some of the dreams and the affirmations, yet also challenged Greg about some of his sins. This friend noted that it would be a bad thing for Greg to do if he returned to a workaholic 24/7 routine; she insisted that he maintain healthy habits of eating and exercising and resting. She also observed that it would be important to focus on the possibilities for what Duke could become, and not get bogged down in the challenges and feelings of responsibility that could often lead Greg to discouragement. She noted that Greg would need to surround himself with some "unlikely" friends and team members who could help share the burdens, imagine the future, and create a multiplier impact.

These friends offered overlapping insights and wisdom, and it became apparent that Greg should accept the invitation to serve again. Yet he also knew, and continues to realize, that these weren't simply one-time pieces of advice. He continues to need to be reminded of the dreams, the affirmations, and the challenges. Holy friends offer these perspectives on an ongoing basis to and for each other; they often take on pivotal significance at prismatic decision points.

Indeed, if institutional leaders in both formal and informal roles are to practice traditioned innovation well, they need ongoing relationships with holy friends. One of the dangers of professional leadership, especially formal institutional leadership, is how isolating it can become. Leaders get caught up in the daily demands of decision-making, and they often are faced with knowledge of personnel matters, difficult challenges, and the sheer relentless demands of the job—including e-mail and other accelerated expectations of a technological era—so that they forget to attend to important relationships such as friendships.

Holy friends typically need to be at arm's length from our day-to-day responsibilities. They need to know enough about our daily life and demands that they have a window into what is really going on; but it is problematic if they are in a reporting relationship or otherwise too involved in the outcomes of decisions.

Often holy friendships arise out of connections made through church and other faith-based relationships that cut across sectors. One day Greg was introduced to a business leader in Texas. The business leader said, "I feel like I already know you." Greg was puzzled. The business leader pulled out his phone, and turned to a note—he then read the definition of "holy friendships" that he had read in an article that Greg had written. It turns out that this man is a part of a small group of Christian leaders of different types of organizations who use Greg's understanding of holy friendships as the framework for their gatherings. They meet weekly to help one another dream, to affirm one another, and to challenge one another.

This businessman then observed to Greg that those relationships had changed his life, reoriented his leadership, and had helped save his marriage. It was deeply moving to hear about the importance of the friendships in this person's vocation and in his life. These friendships were helping him navigate the future personally and professionally, and he was a more hopeful and imaginative person and leader as a result.

Holy friendships often have transformational impact in people's lives. They often can inspire actions that have multiplier impact, even at a level of global significance. Tsietsi Mashinini was a Black South African who felt significant discouragement as a teenager in the early 1970s. But a group of holy friends in a Methodist church in Johannesburg encouraged him to dream dreams he otherwise wouldn't have dreamed, affirmed gifts he was afraid to claim, and challenged sins he had come to love. At least partly because of their friendship, Mashinini became a crucial leader in the Soweto Youth Uprising on June 16, 1976, that is now marked as South Africa's Independence Day holiday.[2]

Holy friendships are profoundly formative for our imagination, and they also provide important connections and intrinsic relationships. They are intimate, and so we can only sustain a handful of those relationships.

They need to be complemented by cultivating multiple "unlikely" friendships across diverse contexts of our lives. Sometimes our closest holy friends are people who started out as unlikely friends—whether through a congregational context or any number of other ways in which people discover deeper connections with one another. Sometimes treasured relationships transform identities and imaginations for the future in highly unlikely ways.

For example, C. P. Ellis, a white man and member of the Ku Klux Klan, and Ann Atwater, a Black woman and civil rights activist, developed a relationship in the 1960s that began as a conversation between enemies and slowly became a transformational friendship.[3] In a more contemporary context, Robert P. George and Cornel West are close friends whose relationship is as unlikely as it is transformational. They disagree about many things in life, and yet they have deep appreciation for each other and now model that relationship in talks across the country—especially on college campuses to show how conservatives and liberals, Anglo-Americans and African Americans, Catholics and Protestants, can learn to engage each other constructively and charitably.

In many cases, though, unlikely friendships are more diffuse. They also require intentionality, but of a different sort than holy friendships. Their sheer "unlikeliness" means that we wouldn't discover them in the ordinary patterns of our daily lives. We must find ways to seek them out and cultivate them across time. Why do they matter?

First, they help us uncover our own blind spots and biases. Listening to those who are very different from us—whether on the basis of culture, race, religion, socioeconomic status, life experience, gender, sexual orientation, profession, or political/ideological convictions—can help us see things in new ways. Careful listening does not necessarily mean we will come to an agreement, nor does it mean we endorse the other's perspective or they ours. But we are less likely to have huge blind spots if we have diverse relationships.

Second, unlikely friendships often illumine our imaginations and are generative of new insights. They expand what Scott Page calls our "cognitive repertoire."[4] Page focuses on unlikely friendships among people with different cognitive backgrounds and experiences. Engineers and artists think and see the world differently. Page shows through careful analysis that there is a "diversity bonus" when people develop relationships that expand their cognitive repertoires.

This is also true when people develop unlikely friendships across domains other than the cognitive. Cross-cultural relationships as well as friendships among people who have learned to see the world in quite disparate ways, for whatever reason, enable us to be more generative and to cultivate wisdom. These friendships require trust and, when nurtured well, encourage further trust.

This points to a third reason why unlikely friendships matter: they build bridges that foster communal flourishing. The most important bridge-building relationships we can cultivate are what Marc J. Dunkelman calls "middle ring relationships" in his book, *The Vanishing Neighbor*.[5] He describes these relationships as the heart of community in American life. Inner rings describe our most intimate relationships, with families and close friends; outer rings describe casual acquaintances.

Middle-ring relationships are with the people with whom a person is familiar but not particularly intimate. They are central to fostering a sense of vitality as well as nurturing those meaningful disagreements that shape a healthy body politic. Typically, this middle ring comprises no more than 150 people because of the limits of our brains.

Dunkelman suggests that middle-ring relationships, which are so formative, are also those under the greatest threat. Our inner-ring relationships still exist, though they would be more formative and life-giving if they were cultivated more as "holy friendships." Our outer-ring relationships are enhanced by technology and can cultivate valuable loose ties.

Middle-ring relationships require intentionality that we have underplayed, and both personally and culturally we are suffering from their impoverishment. Unlikely friendships are a way to cultivate those middle-ring relationships and to nurture a healthier civic community.

Congregations, colleges, and other institutions ought to encourage unlikely friendships among their core constituencies. This is more than just checking a "diversity" box; it is rather nurturing gifts that diminish blind spots, enhance generativity, and enable us to tackle wicked problems with greater creativity and wisdom.

Friendships, both holy and unlikely, are crucial to creating and sustaining connections with God, with one another, and with the whole Creation. They also foster community and cultivate the kind of imagination we need to practice traditioned innovation. And while friendships are necessary and valuable, they are also not sufficient. We also need strong institutions to foster the kinds of collaboration that enable us to flourish as particular people and for broader cultures.

Modern Americans too often celebrate community without attending to the critically important roles that vibrant institutions play in nurturing friendships and enabling a community's practices to flourish. We take vibrant institutions for granted, forgetting they are crucial for creating spaces that shape and pattern human life and address fundamental human needs and yearnings.

Because we have ignored the crucial difference that vibrant institutions make in our lives and in the ecology of our wider social existence, we have allowed once-vibrant institutions to become lifeless bureaucracies. We have watched once-glorious spaces and organizations deteriorate and become shells of the vitality they once represented. When institutions deteriorate into bureaucracies, we discover that virtues become vices, hope becomes corroded by cynicism, and relationships fracture and diminish.

By contrast, vibrant spaces like churches, colleges, and libraries continually make room for wisdom to be nurtured over the course of time. They are part of our "social infrastructure" that is necessary if "social capital" is to be developed and sustained.[6] Social infrastructure includes those spaces that enable people to come together, develop relationships, engage disagreements about important matters, and nurture a commitment to goods held in common across disagreements and differences. Social infrastructure includes crucial institutions such as libraries, churches, child care centers, bookstores, and other "third spaces."

Eric Klinenberg notes the centrality of social infrastructure for the quality of our life together: "When social infrastructure is robust, it fosters contact, mutual support, and collaboration among friends and neighbors; when degraded, it inhibits social activity, leaving families and individuals to fend for themselves."[7] Klinenberg also notes that religious congregations, in part by their sheer ubiquity, offer an incredible context that could nurture social infrastructure and go a long way toward repairing our fraying social fabric.

We tend to underestimate how institutional spaces "speak" to people. Over the years, we have heard story after story about vocations discovered and renewed, relationships developed and reconciled, spiritual lives developed and deepened—all occasioned by particular institutional spaces, especially Christian ones.

But it is not only the space. It is also the way of life that those institutions nurture. At their best, institutions communicate and nurture vibrancy as bearers of tradition, laboratories for learning, and incubators of leadership. Institutions give form and structure to our convictions, enabling us to cultivate thriving communities to be signs, foretastes, and instruments of the reign of God. Seen in this light, our ability to nurture deep connections, to cultivate meaningful relationships, and to address challenging problems depends significantly on our ability not only to think about institutions but also to think appreciatively from within them—to cultivate the practice of thinking institutionally.

Why? Vibrant Christian institutions are bearers of tradition. These traditions are found in the architecture, in the rhythms of daily schedules, in the formal and informal norms of the people who work and pray there, in the ways positions are described, and in the ways decisions are made. This is most obvious in monastic communities that have lasted for decades and even centuries, but it is no less true of other institutions such as schools, congregations, L'Arche communities, hospitals, and hospices.

Vibrant institutions nurture traditioned innovation as a way of thinking and acting, and they make central the practice of ongoing learning. This includes honoring the gifts of our personal and collective pasts as well as repenting of sin, both personal and institutional. Traditioned innovation focuses on the future to which the Holy Spirit is calling us, reminding us that we need to be a learning organization if that future is to be faithful. Rather than pitting a romanticized community over against a sterile bureaucracy, or traditionalism over against newness, vibrant institutions are laboratories for learning traditioned innovation. Vibrant institutions create laboratories in which people unlearn brokenness and learn to be trusting, generative, and wise.

Vibrant institutions also serve as incubators of leadership. Their dynamic internal cultures attend to the diversity of people's gifts, nurturing people in their variety to develop the virtues, skills, and perspectives that make transformative leadership possible. Not all participants in an organization will have gifts for transformative leadership, but all participants play indispensable roles in the overall vibrancy of an institution's leadership. That is, incubating leadership makes each of the various parts of an organization stronger and makes the sum of those parts even greater. By contrast, bureaucracies, not to mention toxic organizations, can take even the best leadership capacities and turn them into mediocre mush or sinful sludge.

Vibrant institutions are not always born in vibrant times. For example, Valparaiso University was founded in 1859, on the cusp of America's Civil War; Duke Chapel emerged from the ground amid a national financial crisis in 1930. Such examples serve as a reminder that a crucial way of thinking institutionally is taking the risk to found new institutions that meet our deepest human needs—for worship, education, shelter, hunger, beauty, joy, and community.

We need to both renew our existing institutions to be more vibrant, and we also need to be cultivating new ones. We have too often, especially in recent years, become cynical about our dysfunctional institutions rather than rebuilding them or investing in new, creative institutions designed to address the challenges and wicked problems we currently face.

These institutions often start as experiments to meet pressing issues. City Seminary in New York was founded in order to reach immigrant populations that otherwise wouldn't have easy access to Christian education and pastoral formation. Saint Mellitus Seminary in London began as an experiment for new patterns of pastoral formation connected to parish life; it has proven so successful as a new institutional model that it has started other sites throughout England. The curricular innovations and the new patterns of learning have improved already the quality and quantity of people preparing for pastoral ministry.

Similarly, new institutions are emerging to work on important issues across sectors. These emerge both as nonprofits, for-profits, and organizations with hybrid business models. These include organizations to encourage entrepreneurs, such as Praxis (and Praxis Academy), as well as broader initiatives globally such as GAME (Global Alliance for Mass Entrepreneurship). New institutions are emerging across sectors to address major challenges locally, regionally, and globally.

We do not currently have the institutions we need to navigate the future well. We need to cultivate vibrant institutions that can foster trust, generativity, and wisdom; we also need to start new ones that draw creatively and innovatively on the best of our past. This is, as Yuval Levin and the venture capitalist Marc Andreesen have both suggested from very different perspectives, "a time to build."[8]

The kind of generativity we need is reflected in the familiar injunction to "plant trees under whose shade you will not sit." This kind of vision and long-term imagination has made our life today possible, born of immigrants in northern Indiana who founded Valparaiso in 1859 as well as committed philanthropists who made Duke Chapel possible in the early 1930s. It is the kind of imagination we need now across sectors and at the intersections of sectors as we create the new institutions that foster collaboration, connection, and embody traditioned innovation.

We need to be willing to create new institutions even in less than ideal circumstances—or especially in challenging circumstances. For it is when we recognize that institutions are crucial spaces for nurturing faithful and joy-filled living that we will take the risks of founding new institutions—and for caring for them in practices and commitments that enable their continual birth and rebirth over time.

Institutions are crucial to human life and flourishing. Yet they also exist in complex interrelationship with networks. And, in an increasingly fast-paced, technologically driven society, we also need to cultivate the importance of dense networks and loose ties in our collaborations.

Networks are crucial for nurturing conceptual breakthroughs, cultivating Christian imagination, and practicing traditioned innovation. The density of the networks matters in each case, especially given contemporary contexts and the challenges we face. These dense networks are complementary to, not a substitute for, vibrant institutions (and the need for new ones).

A variety of scholars have argued effectively that networks of people meeting regularly are crucial for intellectual breakthroughs, social change, and innovation. Randall Collins argues in *The Sociology of Philosophies* that small groups of people meeting for sustained periods of time have been the constant reality across cultures as well as across time. A similar argument is made by Steven Johnson in *Where Good Ideas Come From*, and more recently by Niall Ferguson in *The Square and the Tower*.

James Davison Hunter makes the basic point succinctly in *To Change the World*: "The key actor in history is not individual genius but rather the network and the new institutions that are created out of those networks. And the more 'dense' the network—that is, the more active and interactive the network—the more influential it could be. This is where the stuff of culture and cultural change is produced."[9] Hunter's point is important, and needs to be modified and enhanced.

The modification: The relationships among networks, institutions, and leaders are more of a "both/and" rather than an "either/or": while one could argue that the Clapham Circle was an exceptional, dense network that eventually brought the end of slavery in early nineteenth-century Britain, it also depended on the leadership of William Wilberforce. Conversely, while Thurgood Marshall gets enormous and justified credit for the arguments in *Brown v. Board of Education* that outlawed segregation in US public schools in 1954, it was the dense network cultivated by Howard University Law School in the 1930s that shaped Marshall's leadership.

The enhancement: the actors are not only networks and new institutions that are created out of those networks (as well as individuals); they are also those institutions that make the networks possible. Howard University Law School was a keystone institution in the 1930s whose leader, Dean Charles Houston, cultivated new networks that became the key actors in enabling Thurgood Marshall to emerge as a transformational leader.[10] To be sure, Howard was itself transformed by those interrelations; yet its identity prior to those networks was crucial to enabling the interrelations to emerge.

Dean Houston quickly discerned what was at stake: if African Americans wanted to achieve equal rights under the law, African American lawyers needed to be superbly prepared and ready to effect cultural change beyond winning cases. He began a multipronged strategy to ensure effective formation of African American lawyers. He pruned the Howard Law faculty, focused on full-time students, shut down the night school, invited the best legal minds as guest lecturers, and created the expectation that faculty and students would have bold ambitions and rigorous standards. Biographer Rawn James Jr. sums up Houston's leadership: "He enacted sweeping reforms that transformed Howard Law School from what the city's wealthiest black residents called 'a dummy's retreat' into an institution whose uncompromising rigor and singularity of purpose drew comparisons to the military academy at West Point."[11]

Houston knew that, like West Point, Howard Law had the lives of human beings at stake. And he recognized that, like West Point, Howard Law was doing far more than simply providing education for a particular profession: it was building a cadre of leaders for a vision of a transformed society, leaders who also were trained in skills to transform that vision into effective and strategic practice.

How did Houston do it? He worked closely with the NAACP on real cases, in some instances taking the lead in a case himself. He developed strong connections with lawyers and other African American leaders up and down the East Coast, cultivating a network of relationships and practices that built remarkable capabilities in Howard Law students as well as other leaders in the broader community.

In the early 1930s, Howard Law School became the keystone of a broad ecosystem of people and organizations working to effect change. Richard Kluger describes the impact in *Simple Justice: The History of* Brown v. Board of Education *and Black America's Struggle for Equality*: "Howard Law School became a living laboratory where civil-rights law was invented by teamwork. There were probably never more than fifty or sixty students enrolled at any one time, and that was all right with Houston, who was not after numbers but intensive training of young minds that shared his dream. They all worked on real briefs for real cases and accompanied Houston and other faculty members to court to learn procedure and tactics."[12]

Thurgood Marshall was Houston's prize student. He was an apprentice to Houston, and even more important, he was the beneficiary of an opportunity to engage in action-oriented learning as a part of the broader ecosystem. Marshall developed significant capacities while at Howard, and then he remained in close touch with the school and with Houston after he graduated. Through the ecosystem fostered by Howard Law School, Marshall developed the mindset, skills, and character that he would continue to nurture over the rest of his life.

Marshall was a student at Howard Law for a mere three years; Houston was there as dean for only six. But the ecosystem that was created during that time became an incubator for dramatic changes in American culture. Kluger's summary judgment of Houston's leadership at Howard Law School is instructive: "In the six years he stayed, he both built a creditable law school and injected enormous momentum into a social movement that has not yet ended."[13]

Houston knew how to draw on the traditions of Howard University even as he incubated innovative approaches. He combined a demanding rigor with the skills of a diplomat, masterfully attending to both the local context and the possibilities of wider and more transformational impact.

Too often, we underplay the keystone significance of institutions such as Howard Law—institutions that see themselves as organisms in an ecosystem, incubators of relationships (both personal and organizational), and practices that effect significant culture change.[14]

Part of Houston's genius was discovering that his leadership at Howard Law was more akin to being a gifted gardener than to being a technician or a politician. He aimed for cultural change, and preparing lawyers and winning cases were components of that broader vision. Houston and Marshall accomplished some change in the short term, during the 1930s. But their greatest impact, and the most significant change to the culture, came more than two decades later, and beyond.

Institutions matter more than we suspect for long-term cultural change, especially when they are blessed with a clear sense of mission, visionary leadership, and a commitment to cultivating intrinsic relationships and practices as a part of a wider ecosystem. That ecosystem flourishes when vibrant institutions foster networks within and across their organizations for the sake of deeper and richer patterns of flourishing.

Niall Ferguson argues that the tensions between networks and institutions are as old as humanity itself. There are complex interrelations among them in diverse contexts, cultures, and times. Technological advances across the centuries have also shifted which one tends to have the upper hand, at least in transitional periods. For example, in our current time advances in digital technologies have created a greater emphasis on networks.

Even so, it is a mistake to assume some sort of irreversible, anti-institutional transition toward networks as a replacement for institutions. Rather, networks and institutions will both continue to exist and develop in complicated interrelations, and we need to be intentional and creative in identifying the most life-giving possibilities for navigating these complexities. We need now to cultivate dense networks of people with deep and enduring relationships meeting across time in order to describe well the emerging issues and possibilities for networks and institutions—and the reinvigoration of institutions as those durable forms of our common life.

Dense networks are crucial to cultivating Christian imagination. Dense networks also thrive with multiple forms of diversity, especially through unlikely friendships. Such diversity and unlikely friendships are essential for the formation of a faithful, truthful, and effective imagination.

In addition, there is a distinctively Christian perspective and argument, namely that our convictions about God entail that we believe a Christian imagination is focused on what Kavin Rowe has called "the story of everything."[15] There is no domain of knowledge, no mode of inquiry, that is outside the scope of our interest.[16]

In our contemporary context's explosion of knowledge, information, and expertise, no person can exhibit the breadth and depth of imagination that many of our premodern forebears embodied. Even so, we need a more expansive vision of the scope of the imagination Christians are called to develop, and this means engaging wider arrays of disciplines and modes of inquiry, even—perhaps especially—those not explicitly identified as Christian. Dense networks of such people and institutions are crucial to fostering imagination.

This is particularly true in our contemporary world, and it is a central reason why dense networks are essential to practicing traditioned innovation. Nurturing dense networks of people who embody multiple forms of diversity is crucial given the wicked problems we face amid the turbulence and bewilderments of our time. There are multiple causes of that turbulence and those bewilderments, as we describe in chapter 3: They include technological advances (e.g., AI and machine learning), fractured social and political relations, institutional decay, and educational patterns that encourage hyper-specialization rather than dense networks across sectors. The global pandemic of 2020 only intensifies this turbulence.

Dense networks operating in collaboration with vibrant institutions are necessary to address our turbulence and bewilderment. In some cases these dense networks involve reinvigorating ecosystems of institutional and personal relationships that have existed for years. Those ecosystems may involve cross-disciplinary collaboration that marked many colleges and universities at their best. The "college" system in British universities has fostered cross-disciplinary inquiry, though increasing disciplinary power has often loosened those contexts.

The ecosystems also may stretch across generations and geographies in patterns that foster intrinsic relationships. These may include denominational ecosystems of camps, congregations, youth groups, colleges, and seminaries that exist, for example, in the Christian Reformed Church or in particular regions of larger denominations such as The United Methodist Church. They may also include those dense networks cultivated by African American communities, such as the Lott Carey Global Christian Missional Community. Lott Carey has fostered cross-cultural relationships and networks that enable people to understand and appreciate different challenges and opportunities that others face.

Within broader business contexts, these dense networks include supply chains as well as new patterns of collaboration within and across geographical regions. The importance of dense networks includes seeking out innovative initiatives for large organizations such as PwC to move beyond its traditional roles in order to facilitate new collaboration and convene key actors across sectors. PwC already embodies dense networks, yet traditioned innovation encourages the cultivation of new dense networks to address new challenges and to provide fresh angles on old ones.

The density of the network matters significantly. Periodic gatherings and conferences lack sufficient frequency and depth to cultivate the shifts in mindsets, habits, and skills we really need. Cultivating networks that are primarily transactional will not be sufficient either. Given the pace of change, the demands and expectations of institutions and roles, and the pressures of hyper-specialization (learned and lived typically across many years of education and practice), periodic gatherings are unlikely to achieve breakthroughs, cultivate imagination, or help us practice traditioned innovation.

What criteria are necessary for a dense network? They include the following:

- multiple forms of diversity;

- cross-sector engagement;

- frequent interactions to promote new mindsets, habits, and skills;

- opportunities to develop unlikely friendships that support new imagination;

- conceptual articulation and storytelling to connect traditioning and innovation; and

- attentiveness to conditions and practices that foster (Christian) imagination.

To be sure, technology and other forces are changing the patterns by which networks can be cultivated, sustained, and deepened. We need to be as attentive to creative possibilities for the future as we are to the long-standing relationships that have brought us to this point.

There is an opportunity to cultivate dense networks that bring together "unlikely institutions" in a manner similar to the role that unlikely friendships might play. For example, Duke Divinity School and Duke's Pratt School of Engineering are collaborating in developing initiatives in new ways. New dense networks might be developed for leadership development among people who are working on similar issues but are used to operating in very different sectors. Or, more globally, there is an urgent need to bring together wealthy people and organizations to find innovative ways to address major global challenges that are unlikely to be addressed by single organizations or governments.

Yet, as important as dense networks are, we also need to be cultivating what have come to be known as "weak ties." The original insight of the "strength of weak ties" came four decades ago in a paper by Stanford sociologist Mark Granovetter. The heart of his argument is that while strong relationships are crucial to building in-group coherence among networks, there is a strength in "weak ties" among people who know how to connect with people across networks. These connectors are crucial to continuing to diversify relationships and to continue to enhance Page's "diversity bonus."

Weak ties are crucial to cultivating "bridging capital" as a complement to "bonding capital." Bonding capital occurs in and through dense networks; bridging capital emerges across networks. Those who have significant weak ties are able to foster new patterns of collaboration. Those new patterns might eventually become dense networks in other contexts. The key is to recognize the power of both dense networks and weak ties, bonding as well as bridging capital.

Being intentional about the strength of weak ties introduces fresh perspectives into processes of traditioning and innovating. For example, Christians engaging contemporary Jewish scholars' interpretations of the New Testament have shed fresh light on interpretations of both Jesus and Paul that have dramatically affected how we understand the biblical story.[17] Similarly, Olin College of Engineering's appointment of a practicing artist to its faculty introduced new perspectives as well as networks in the ways engineers are formed and learn to see their vocation and the broader world.

The strength of weak ties also points to the diverse nodes that exist in broad and dynamic networks. People who relate across different networks and can bridge across sectors play a crucial role both in uncovering new patterns from the past and in cultivating new innovation in the future. These significant patterns of learning promote rich collaboration.

This learning is both entrepreneurial and cross-sector. It is rooted in what Carol Dweck calls a "growth mindset" (as opposed to a "fixed mindset") that is always looking for new connections across fields as well as ways of connecting past, future, and present together.[18]

Contrary to popular imagination, entrepreneurship is a team effort. It depends on people learning together from a variety of perspectives, and an entrepreneurial mindset is deeply connected to a range of disciplines, experiences, perspectives, and learning. In a world marked by problems that are truly wicked, we need patterns of learning that foster broad knowledge as well as expertise. An entrepreneurial mindset nurtures generativity both in one's own cognitive repertoire and in the cultivation of relationships and modes of learning.

David Epstein illumines the importance of thinking broadly and cultivating an entrepreneurial mindset in his book, *Range*: "The challenge we all face is how to maintain the benefits of breadth, diverse experience, interdisciplinary thinking, and delayed concentration in a world that increasingly incentivizes, even demands, hyperspecialization." As he notes later, "a rapidly changing, wicked world demands conceptual reasoning skills that can connect new ideas and work across contexts." It requires an ability to "roam freely, listen carefully, and consume omnivorously."[19]

Navigating the future amid the turbulence and bewilderments of the contemporary world involves a commitment to both collaboration and the importance of an entrepreneurial mindset. What are the key characteristics of such a mindset?

One set of characteristics of an entrepreneurial mindset are virtues that need to be cultivated. Key is a sense of curiosity and generativity. It is the ability to observe, to look for new ways of seeing, to imagine new possibilities. A commitment to curiosity and generativity begins by asking how things come to be and how they might be made better. Such creativity is fostered by creating new associations, across time (bringing the past and the future into creative construction), across sectors (bringing diverse disciplines and contexts into adjacencies), or across cultures (bringing disparate ideas, assumptions, and patterns into generative conversation).

An entrepreneurial mindset also depends on and cultivates a commitment to wisdom. There are endless associations that can be pursued, but only some of them are worthwhile. Developing an ability to identify what is worth pursuing and what analogies are most fruitful is a virtue that can be cultivated.

We often identify a willingness to fail as an important ingredient in an entrepreneurial mindset, and there is truth in that. But there is no virtue in failing per se. The virtue is found in learning from failure, and learning in ways that make problematic forms of failure less and less likely. Such learning depends on and cultivates wisdom.

Because entrepreneurship depends on teamwork and relationships across time, sectors, and cultures, trust is also a crucial virtue for an entrepreneurial mindset. Trust does not require agreement, as a certain sort of contrarian questioning is important to discovering breakthroughs. But it does require an interpretive charitableness and an ability to recognize that others are a crucial part of a team's ability to work together. Cultures that encourage skepticism are fruitful; ones that breed distrust undermine collaboration and creativity.

A second set of characteristics are activities and skills that an entrepreneurial mindset cultivates. Foremost among these are the following, gleaned from multiple insights and lists:[20]

- willingness to get off "home court" to learn from others,

- nurturing a high tolerance for ambiguity,

- focus on making connections and creating value,

- thinking in (eco)systemic patterns,

- listening and observing to expand imagination, and

- ability to cross borders across multiple domains.

These are all activities and skills that can be nurtured, yet they require intentionality if they are to become part of our daily lives. Unfortunately, many of our educational practices, in both formal institutions and informal patterns, actually work against cultivating such activities and skills. So nurturing an entrepreneurial mindset will often require countercultural practices and intentionality in order to foster new default patterns.

This also suggests the importance of institutions that provide contexts to encourage entrepreneurial mindsets. Gary Pisano highlights the complexities of what it takes to foster a DNA of sustained innovation in specific organizations and in institutions more generally. He notes it requires an innovation strategy, an innovation system, and an innovation culture. Here we highlight his emphasis on an innovation culture because it is so crucial to nurturing an entrepreneurial mindset (we return to his other themes later).

Pisano notes that there are conventional descriptions of activities that are important to innovation: tolerance for failure, willingness to experiment, psychological safety, collaboration, and flat organizations. But he rightly emphasizes that they are necessary but not sufficient. He emphasizes the paradoxes that are necessary for an institutional culture to cultivate innovation and entrepreneurial mindsets that are productive and effective:

- Tolerance for Failure but No Tolerance for Incompetence

- Willingness to Experiment but Highly Disciplined

- Psychologically Safe but Brutally Candid

- Collaborative but Individually Accountable

- Flat but with Strong leadership.[21]

The paradoxes of innovative cultures show that nurturing and sustaining an entrepreneurial mindset require leaders who practice traditioned innovation and have a capacity for opposable thinking and living.[22]

How do we cultivate the kinds of collaboration that foster entrepreneurial mindsets in and through innovative organizational cultures? We need to promote the kind of curiosity and generativity that is rooted in cross-sector learning. Such learning is found at the intersections. It is nurtured when we ask questions about the conditions for flourishing—as people, as communities, as ecosystems. It requires a deep study of the natural world, as we are learning from the study of ecology and new approaches, such as biomimicry.[23] It involves engagement with the past and our traditions, including paying attention to particular "geographies," such as ancient Greece, the medieval Song Dynasty in China, Renaissance Florence, or contemporary Silicon Valley, where cultures sparked creative innovation because of the intersections of specific relationships and learning.[24] It also involves engaging in contemporary experiments in specific locales and regions, such as what James and Deborah Fallows did in diverse towns and cities across the United States. Their experiments are strong examples of what it means to work across sectors and foster thriving communities.[25]

Sometimes that cross-sector learning involves new experiments and education in unfamiliar terrain. The Reverend Mark Elsdon was struggling to discern how best to offer a hope-filled future at the Presbyterian campus ministry at the University of Wisconsin. The campus ministry is set in a central part of the campus, a strategic location for both ministry and real estate. He was looking for a creative way to use the land and buildings of the campus ministry. He began conversations with the synod about utilizing the synod's assets to get the capital needed for a major initiative around on-campus housing next to the campus ministry.

Along the way, Rev. Elsdon discerned that getting an MBA would help him understand the issues he was wrestling with in broader and deeper ways. He developed new partnerships and networks, and this cross-sector learning also enabled him to become more persuasive in his conversations with funders and in his negotiations with the state government around policy issues. As a result of these initiatives, the ministry has grown, has become more stable, is reaching more people, and is also able to focus on caring for those with mental health issues in better and deeper ways.

Elsdon developed a breakthrough, transformational idea through cross-sector learning, both informal and through a degree program. More generally, Steven Johnson shows how such cross-sector learning recurrently generates good ideas that are often transformational. In the terms we have been developing, breakthroughs depend on conversations among holy friends and unlikely friends; relationships embedded in practices within institutions and cultivated in new ones; opportunities discovered in dense networks and among weak ties; insights that emerge through an entrepreneurial mindset and cross-sector learning.

Johnson observes: "When one looks at innovation in nature and in culture, environments that build walls around good ideas tend to be less innovative in the long run than more open-ended environments. Good ideas may not want to be free, but they do want to connect, fuse, recombine. They want to reinvent themselves by crossing conceptual borders. They want to complete each other as much as they want to compete."[26]

We can best navigate the future, including the turbulence and be-wilderments we experience, when we collaborate through traditioned in-novation. It involves a variety of paradoxes and holding together commit-ments, practices, and relationships that others often put into opposition. No ship captain sails alone through a storm or fog. She needs a crew with diverse skills and ideas, along with the gathered wisdom of previous voy-agers who have already mapped a way.

Through collaboration, we can cultivate multiplier effects, embodying the intersections of friendships, institutions, networks, and entrepreneur-ial leadership that enable us to navigate the future faithfully and effec-tively. Given the uncertainties, ambiguities, and bewilderments we face, doing so will also require that we cultivate both an improvisational spirit and the institutions that can sustain that spirit through turbulent times.

Chapter 7
Improvising and Sustaining

Push into the future
In strength, courage, hope, and love.

—*Sir Francis Drake*

Do schools kill creativity? Does vulnerability foster human connection or trustworthy leadership? What do introverts uniquely bring to the world? Why is it wise to "start with why"? How does "power posing" inspire confidence?

These appear to be completely unrelated questions that, fitted together, might form an interesting riddle. However, it is likely that you could find people on the street who know how these questions are related. Perhaps you've already figured it out. If not, here's a hint: these questions have been asked by Sir Ken Robinson, Brené Brown, Susan Cain, Simon Sinek, and Amy Cuddy, respectively. Still not sure? Try this: the answers to these questions have all famously been deemed "ideas worth spreading." That's right. They're from TED talks—five of the most famous TED talks, each with millions of views and a kind of currency and traction that might never have been possible except for the improvisational ability of TED.

In their book, *New Power: How Power Works in Our Hyperconnected World—and How to Make It Work for You*, Jeremy Heimans and Henry Timms tell a fascinating history of TED's evolution. Having begun in 1984 as a regular gathering in Long Beach, California, where attendees

173

could pay a premium price to hear new ideas about technology, entertainment, and design (hence the name "TED"), TED hit its stride around 1990, when it annualized the assembly. Parts of what we recognize today as the TED ethos were in place back then: the organization was always scanning for new trends and always looking to be at the vanguard of how the world might be made better through the power of ideas. The difference—and this is a key one—was that TED operated solely on a model of exclusivity. The "ideas worth spreading" we know about today were limited by the filter of who could afford the trek to Long Beach, had the connections to get in the door, had the cachet to be part of what TED itself framed as a kind of secret society—"a growing and influential audience," as they described it, "from many different disciplines . . . united by their curiosity and open-mindedness—and also by their shared discovery of an exciting secret."[1] The program lineup was curated by a small team who kept a tight rein on which ideas about technology, entertainment, and design were worthy of the TED stage.

As with many things, the tech revolution of the early 2000s nearly upended TED, forcing what Heimans and Timms call the original "closed-shop elitist model" into a bit of an existential crisis that was tinged with irony: should TED embrace the business model the collaborative, democratized, interconnected world often imagined by TED speakers, or maintain the cool exclusivity and profitability of the status quo? The ubiquity of the internet and the rise of social media presented a significant decision point—and an invitation to improvise, which TED did.

What's interesting is that when TED opted to move in new directions, it didn't abandon the essence of what had made it effective; it still wanted to maintain its air of elitism and spread only the ideas it thought were worth spreading. So, it didn't fling off the doors Facebook-style, allowing anyone with a keyboard and a video camera unfettered access to its platform. Instead, quite adeptly and improvisationally, it created a paradox, doubling down on its core conference model, which became more inaccessible than ever (now in Vancouver, people pay as much as

$25,000 for one of the twelve hundred seats at the flagship event), while also establishing its brand and its "products" as among the most popular, shared, and open-sourced in the world—all free to anyone across the globe, so long as they have access to the internet.

It did this because British entrepreneur Chris Anderson practiced traditioned innovation when he assumed leadership in the early 2000s. He went out of his way to respect the unique culture of TED, promising to keep intact the vibe so beloved by veteran TEDsters. Yet, as he listened to talks from the TED stage that described how significantly the world was changing, he knew that TED must change, too. In effect, he said: "Yes, the world is different. And we will adjust and be different, too—so long as we remain true to ourselves."

Rather than meddling with the core model, he made adjustments by shifting other things, like the business model (nonprofit instead of for-profit) and by looking outward, building new communities around the conference. Heimans and Timms note, "If [Anderson] succeeded, each would create value in its own right; each would feed value back to the core."[2] Succeed he did.

The decision to post TED talks—the organization's sole intellectual asset—online and for free risked undermining the business model of ticket sales. But what happened was the opposite: the first talks went up online in June 2006, and by September they had racked up more than a million views. Today that number is in the billions, and all the increased awareness of the TED brand has drastically reshaped the market—decidedly in TED's advantage—for TED events all over the country. Corporate sponsors line up to have their brands associated with TED, and people pay big money for the chance to attend TED gatherings. And far more important, ideas worth spreading have spread the world over. More of us know that it matters to start with "why." We're aware of the power of vulnerability in leadership. We've rethought the place of creativity in education and started to listen better to the introverts among us. Perhaps we've even "power posed" to tap into a strength and confidence that got us successfully through a big meeting.

For that we have TED to thank. TED's ability to improvise—not to abandon who it was or to just make stuff up, but instead to honor its past and say "yes, and" to new opportunities—has truly made a difference in the world. TED is a vibrant institution, able to sustain and scale its work and to inspire improvement and flourishing, for people, organizations, and societies around the world.

Throughout the book thus far, we have argued that traditioned innovation is a mindset that best equips us for navigating the wilder seas of a turbulent future. Traditioned innovation requires us to orient toward our most important purposes—the promotion of flourishing, the highest forms of excellence for the people, institutions, and communities that surround us. Traditioned innovation likewise summons us to understand and account for the world's inevitable complexities and our frequent bewilderments amid the storms and fogs of these wilder seas. It requires, thereby, our very best efforts toward imagining, traditioning, and collaborating, so that we might navigate in ways that achieve transcendent, ultimate purposes.

In this concluding chapter, we explore two equally important dimensions—the work of *improvising*, as TED did, when conditions change and opportunities arise, as well as the work of *sustaining* our innovative, improvisational work. In navigational terms, improvising and sustaining are like adapting to the seas as they change and tending to our vessels so they stay afloat and on course as we progress toward our destination. Our argument, in short, is that we need to cultivate vibrant institutions that are equipped and continually renewed for the work that awaits them as the future unfolds.

❖ ❖ ❖ ❖ ❖ ❖

It's there, on the latter point, that we want to begin. To think effectively about navigating the future requires us to give serious consideration to *how* the future unfolds—if, indeed, we want to arrive at that future destination that has inspired us on this journey in the first place. In chapter 4, as we explored the indispensable art of imagining, we examined research on imaginative prospection by Peter Railton in which he argued that imagining involves both envisioning the landscape lying ahead of us and mapping the array of possible pathways that will enable us to pass through that landscape. Recall Railton's story about the hungry primitive man in winter, whose imagination helped him consider fish as a food source and then fashion the tools to catch the fish below the ice. Railton's technical summary of such a process was that "intelligent action over time involves not only taking choices in light of a causal model of possibilities, but *creating* possibilities— 'working backwards' from distant goals to the proximate actions that are preconditions for them, and 'working forward' by conceiving and acting upon ideas and ideals that will sustain new ways of acting in the future."[3]

While chapter 4 focused on the imagining part—the "working backwards from distant goals" that occurs mostly in our minds—this chapter focuses on the "working forward," the art of acting on ideas and ideals and sustaining that action toward the futures we imagine as they unfold. As we think about that action, about how we practice traditioned innovation by improvising and sustaining vibrant institutions into the future, it's important to take stock of how we conceive of the future and our role in navigating through its inevitable turbulence. This prompts us to ask a series of questions:"?

- How do our language and mental images invite us to think about how the future unfolds?

- When we look toward the future, what do our language and its associated images ask us to see?

- What do our language and images prevent us from seeing or cause us to distort?

- What do they enable us to see that we otherwise might not?

- And perhaps most important, as we attempt to deploy our imaginations toward the actual work of human flourishing
  How might we form images that will best equip us for the right kind of "forward movement"?

In short, we need to consider our metaphors.

As Alan Jacobs has argued—though he is certainly not the first to do so—we ought to work hard to understand the weight of the terms and images we deploy, as well as how we use them to direct our attention. Literary critic Kenneth Burke has suggested that we tend not to even notice the ways language influences reality or causes us to perceive it, something that is important because metaphorical expressions in our language can actually structure how we understand our lives.[4]

Take our everyday language about time, as just one example identified by George Lakoff and Mark Johnson in their book, *Metaphors We Live By*, which has proved seminal in our understanding of the profound impact of metaphorical language. In English, usually without even realizing it, we talk about time in economic or monetary terms:

- How do you *spend* your time?

- I've *invested* a lot of time in this project.

- *Budget* your time wisely.

- Stop *wasting* my time.

- That's hardly *worth* my time.

- He's living on *borrowed* time.

- Use your time *profitably*.

- This product is guaranteed to *save* you time.

178

Consider this for a moment: time is not something we can actually *save* or *borrow*. It is not a monetary asset of any sort really, yet we use or hear those phrases every day, and they significantly affect the way we understand and live our lives. We even go to great lengths in accounting to monetize time.

There are others like this that go unnoticed: argument as war (she attacked his argument; but he shot down her arguments quickly), happiness as up and sadness as down, or love as something we fall into.[5]

This language can have profound effects, particularly when we passively comply with our metaphorical language and constructs and fail to examine what they do to us. The militarized metaphors of argument are a good example. According to Jacobs, we lose something of our humanity by the very act of dehumanizing the person on the other side of the argument, and people cease to be people because they are, to us, merely representatives of the position we want to *demolish* or *wipe out* or *shoot down*.[6]

So what does this have to do with improvising and sustaining vibrant institutions as we navigate the future? Our metaphors, especially when they pass below our notice, start to collect and form what Mary Midgley has called "imaginative patterns, networks of powerful symbols that suggest particular ways of interpreting the world."[7] Others have called these patterns and networks "mental models," a technical term that refers to our "psychological representations of real, hypothetical, or imaginary situations," to borrow a proper definition advanced by Princeton's Mental Models and Reasoning Lab. Put differently, these are the small-scale models of reality that our minds construct, which we then use to anticipate events, to reason, to explain things, or even to motivate our actions. Take the adage that when we walk around with only a hammer, everything looks like a nail. Our mental models of reality have real-world, practical, everyday consequences.[8]

In this way, our mental models shape the meaning we give to the world and, in turn, the ways we approach our "working forward" toward the future. Often, our mental models are hereditary, in the sense that they're passed down from the people who came before us. You and I didn't invent time-as-money, for example, even though that concept influences how we conceive of time.

One set of metaphors or mental models that has proven to have far-reaching effect, and which we'd like to suggest dispensing with, is the prevalent imagery of machines as a guiding metaphor for human endeavors. We too frequently use mechanistic images to describe complex entities, such as societies and institutions. This is something we have inherited from French Enlightenment thought, which suggested that these complex human interactions were things to be built, taken apart, and reengineered—things that comply, in other words, with the predictable laws of physics.

Traces of this mental model still reside with us today, often problematically, when we talk about top-down, bottom-up, centralized, or decentralized organizations or societies. We even use this construct to talk about ourselves—our bodies as machines, for example, which scientists increasingly resist as we discover the dynamism and interdependence of body systems.[9] As Midgley has observed, we even extend machine metaphors to talk about our inner lives, seeing ourselves "as pieces of a clockwork: items of a kind that we ourselves could make, or might decide to remake if it suits us better."[10] Think about it: How often have you used a phrase such as "I know what makes him tick"?

In her book about the relationship between parents and children, developmental psychologist Alison Gopnik has noted how problematic it is to think mechanistically about the role of a parent. And we would like to suggest that this applies to any role in which a person leads others. Carpentry, Gopnik notes, provides the metaphors we often use to think about how to mold and construct the people under our care and prepare them for the future. Of course, when you're a carpenter, you devote some attention to the kind of material you're working with, and that material may well influence what you try to build. But, by and large, your job as a carpenter is to shape that material into a final product that will fit the scheme you already had in mind when you began the project. Typically, you do your work in a shop that is spared from the elements. And the way you assess the job you've done is to look at the final product. *Is the door true? Is the chair steady? Do the cabinets close correctly?* To a carpenter, precision and control are highly prized, while messiness and variability are unacceptable. *Measure twice, cut once.*

It's easy to see why this mechanistic model for parents or leaders is problematic. We've probably all known people who were each pushed by their parents to select an esteemed career during childhood, found and entered a top college to prepare for that career, and arrived in adulthood deeply unhappy, having never considered individual gifts, passions, dreams, or alternatives. This is because people aren't like wood and metal, and the conditions of their development are never as predictable or controllable as the carpenter's shop. We can't just sketch what we want, measure carefully, and expect to end up with the right final product simply because we followed the blueprints.[11]

Hopefully, the implications of Gopnik's insight are clear: as we lead and work with human beings, it matters what kinds of images and mental models we use to understand our movement toward the future. It would be difficult to overstate the importance of how our mental models inform our understanding of how we pursue human flourishing in our lives, work, and institutions. Mental models inform not just how we envision the landscape that is ahead of us—which, unlike a chair or a cabinet, can never accurately be described until we see it—but also the ways we understand and pursue the pathways through that landscape. Our mental models form how we "work forward" toward human flourishing.

In human endeavors, mechanistic thinking simply won't do. That's because the pursuit of flourishing is not just a matter of setting the right goal and making the right measurements. The world is too messy, the seas too wild and turbulent for such a model.

Quite simply, we can't engineer or construct the future, try though we might.

So, with that in mind, we want to stand on the shoulders of people like Midgley and Gopnik and the philosophers of the English (rather than the French) Enlightenment, who argued the irrationality of considering human nature, human development, and human affairs of all sorts in mechanistic terms. In this way, our mental models for thinking about the work of human flourishing should always be *dynamic*, involving some things under our influence and many things outside our control. That's the way the world works, after all.

So what might that look like? One subset of dynamic mental models is organic in nature. Gopnik, for example, sees working in a garden as an effective model for thinking about the role of a parent—and we think that can extend to the realm of institutional leadership. When we work in a garden, we create what Gopnik calls "a protected and nurturing space for plants to flourish." Gardening takes labor, a lot of exhausted digging, and sometimes a little wallowing in manure. And as any gardener knows, our plans are always foiled—we're never able to predict drought or unseasonable heat, a late freeze or incessant rain. Aphids swarm, snails snack, and spider mites spin webs on our precious leaves and flowers. The seeds we thought would flower pink occasionally come up orange, and the ivy sometimes forgets it's supposed to climb.

And yet, as Gopnik observes, the compensation is that our greatest horticultural triumphs and joys also come when the garden escapes our control, when the weedy white Queen Anne's lace unexpectedly shows up to border something colorful, when the grapevine that was supposed to stay hitched to the arbor takes a mind of its own and runs riot through the trees. In fact, she says, there's a deeper sense in which such accidents are a hallmark of good gardening, and our ability to improvise and adapt speaks volumes about our horticultural prowess. Take a meadow or a cottage garden: the glory of a meadow is its messiness, the fact that different grasses and flowers will flourish or perish as circumstances change, and there's no guarantee that any individual plant will turn out exactly as we'd hoped. Still, the overall product is splendid—perhaps precisely for that reason.

The good gardener works to create fertile soil that can sustain a whole ecosystem of different plants with different strengths and varying beauty. And never can we *make* things grow just as we want them to—at least not if we want them to sustain health and beauty over time. Unlike the carpenter of a good chair, a good gardener is always changing as she adapts to the circumstances of the seasons, the unpredictable weather, or even parasites. And in the end, that kind of "varied, flexible, complex, dynamic system" will prove robust, adaptable, and beautiful.[12]

In this sense, we might reformulate the image that Levin and Andreessen propose that it is "time to build."[13] Perhaps we might better say it is time to cultivate ecosystems of institutions and tend to their interrelations.[14]

Throughout this book, we've relied heavily on a different sort of dynamic model, nautical and navigational rather than organic. Something similar holds true with this metaphor, given the ways we can influence, but never fully control, the dynamics at play in nautical navigation on wilder seas. Thinking about navigating under these circumstances, particularly in the ways described by Sir Francis Drake, enables us to think about:

- *purpose*: Why are we on this sea, and how might we orient our institutional vessels toward our destination (flourishing)?

- *bewilderment*: What are the forces beyond our control—the storms and the fogs of a world in flux—that will influence our navigation on these wilder seas?

- *imagining*: Where are we going, what might it look like, and how might we discover the best ways to get there?

- *traditioning*: How might we draw from wisdom, experience, and knowledge to inform our navigation, studying the maps and the accounts of others who have gone before us and using all we have learned from our own formation and experience?

- *collaborating*: How might working with others better equip us to fulfill our purpose and navigate toward the destination, when surely we can't effectively do it alone?

183

It's easy to understand why dynamic mental models of leadership prove much more useful and instructive than mechanistic ones in these complex times. Given the world's complexity and unpredictability, and given the ways the universal laws and predictive models of a laboratory, factory, or workshop aren't likely to account for these factors, we'd do well to envision more dimensions of our lives, institutions, relationships, and societies through models that account for dynamic complexities. The work of leadership for human flourishing is dynamic work, always requiring us to adapt.

We discussed in chapter 3 that the wisdom of traditioned innovation can be found in its ability to avoid the pathologies of traditionalism and the follies of futurism. As we find ourselves here and now on these wilder seas, and as we seek to fulfill our deep longing for the flourishing that is our destination, escaping back to the shore is not a valid option. It simply won't do to long for the past, to be swept up in nostalgia or unexamined habits, or to exercise our obstinance and demand that the ways of the past are sufficient for the future.

Likewise, we can't assume that innovation techniques will save us, or that the future can be made to fit our blueprints and plans. We wouldn't expect a boat captain to reach a destination just by being inventive or disruptive or innovative. Those things might help, sure, but we'd like to trust that she's drawing from the maps and the stories of prior passages as she prepares for wilder seas. We'd also like to think that her formation and provision would prepare her for the sort of artistry and creativity and fortitude that will be required for the always-new voyage of the here and now.

One thing we ought to note before proceeding any further is that our nautical metaphor also has limitations. The problem with human affairs and the "destination" of human flourishing is that we never actually "arrive," as we expect a sailing ship to do. Human flourishing is not a place where we can dock the boat, disembark, and call the journey a success. And yet, while this suggests a limitation to our metaphor, we make the case that this is precisely its strength. The reason is that the pursuit of a destination we'll never attain once and for all should point us back, perpetually, to the place where we started: the "why." The elusive quality of our destination forces us into deeper why questions: Why is human flourishing worth our pursuit? Why do we go to all this effort to understand and account for the storms and fogs and various bewilderments? Why bother imagining? Why tradition? Why collaborate?

And so, here we find ourselves, out on these seas, tending these institutions, and navigating toward a destination we must continually remember is worthy of our pursuit.

As we head now down the back stretch of this book, we want not only to think about how we think about the future, as important as that is. We also want to discuss the importance of improvising and sustaining vibrant institutions that are up to the task of navigating these wilder seas, that will help us keep on striving. That requires us to ask: How might we adapt and improvise? And how might we attend to our institutional vessels in ways that sustain our navigation?

The place to start is improvisation, an art that we can best understand by turning to its most accomplished practitioners: jazz and comedy performers.[15]

As Miles Davis huddles close to his performing partner, a bass player, jazz colors begin to mix. The fuchsia of Davis's trumpet slides in front of his partner's electric-green leopard-print bass. The bass player's canary-yellow shirt blends with Davis's green robe, which is speckled itself with canary-yellow polka dots and a pattern of cerise flowers that match the bass player's head wrap. Bright, bold colors vie for visual supremacy but manage to blend, mimicking, to a degree, the music. You can almost *hear* in the visual—intersecting lines of trumpet, bass, piano, and drums, each pointing to, and responding to, bright traces of the other. It's almost too fitting, too fabricated, as if these performers were posing for a picture on the cover of some book or article called *Seeing Jazz: Sound in Color*.

If the color scheme lends this moment a sense of fitting fabrication, the performers' bodies seem to do just the opposite. They reveal the authenticity and some of the spontaneity of the moment. The bass player furrows his brow, deep in concentration, while a hint of a smile sneaks from behind Davis's trumpet: muted bliss. Both musicians' eyes focus deeply on some unseen space between us and their instruments, as though the air is filled with visual magic, something a little unexpected and deeply right. Davis and his partner are here and now, caught up in a moment that transcends them both but requires them both. They give themselves away with full attention, but in doing so have very clearly received something back: a truer, freer version of the musical selves they gave away when the performance began. This moment wasn't an accident, but neither was it fully expected—at least not exactly like *this*. And yet, unmistakably, something important is occurring that is far better than any plans they might have conjured if they'd viewed jazz performance as a recital or the rote execution of something scripted and planned. But jazz, we know, is not *that*.

This sublime moment is captured in a photo that sits atop a 2013 cnn.com article about the surprising similarities between the minds and habits of the best jazz musicians and organizational leaders. Its author, management professor Frank J. Barrett, offers readers a condensed version of his instructive book, *Yes to the Mess: Surprising Leadership Lessons from Jazz Improvisation*, in which he contends that many of us might benefit from a "jazz mindset" in organizational contexts—balancing freedom and constraints, learning by doing, and performing and experimenting simultaneously, to name a few of the applicable jazz customs. By making these practices part of their lives, Barrett argues, leaders can invent novel responses and take the kinds of calculated risks that help them unleash new potential and navigate quickly evolving contexts. We concur.[16]

Barrett does many things right, in the article and in the book, with his descriptions of jazz and with the connections he draws between jazz and organizational leadership. Yet a curious exchange in the "comments" section of his CNN piece highlights the importance of how musicians think about improvisation.

The quibble is over Barrett's very first suggestion, which, indeed, ought to strike as odd anyone who has ever closely observed jazz musicians or played jazz themselves. "Master the art of unlearning," Barrett urges, since, in his view, jazz musicians "guard against the seductive power of routines and habits." Connecting this to leadership, Barrett suggests the countless ways institutions can become "locked in a dominant design," where people "find themselves trapped in roles," resulting in ruts, where "dynamism is lost." To be sure, most of us have seen this kind of pattern take root in institutions. Routines and habits *can* lock and trap and make us unhealthfully path dependent. But Barrett seems to miss something in the very essence of jazz that the best jazz improvisers know well—specifically that routines are often the source of good jazz, the place where musicians develop skills that liberate them to improvise well.

Maintaining habitual routines helps jazz musicians develop skills, while also immersing themselves in the language and learned vocabulary of jazz. That is, the freest playing—the most improvisational—only comes after a long apprenticeship in learning to "speak jazz." The most accomplished and skilled jazz musicians are quick to tell you that their best improvisations are built on material they have already mastered through habit and routine.

To understand this is to realize that, instead of rejecting habits and routines, Miles Davis immersed himself in the traditions of jazz, drilling its scales, learning its language, and apprenticing himself to its experts. He innovated *through* and *with* jazz tradition. He was able to improvise something new because he had internalized the old.

This surely translates in ways that Barrett missed with his rejection of routine. Without the fluency gained through habit, attempts at improvisation descend into chaos. The problem isn't habit or routine, in other words; it's failing to utilize what those habits and shared grammars can produce. Only when we steep ourselves in these things can the right kinds of surprising new improvisations emerge.

Imagine, for example, a junior high band teacher handing each student a different instrument on the first day of class and instructing them to begin a creative jazz number. Musicians in this kind of situation, such as they are, don't improvise; they guess and make things up. Even if they know how to sight-read or play a scale, they don't play together or build off one another, because they're too busy trying to figure out what's going on with their own instruments. This kind of cacophony couldn't be more different from what Miles Davis and his bassist offer. Davis and his bassist didn't know exactly what might come next—but we can rest assured it wasn't the hellish dissonance of a middle school band debut.

That's because improvisation—and this is a key insight for any would-be improvisers—is not the same thing as making stuff up. Improvisation isn't an art for novices. It's not even about "being original, clever, witty, or spontaneous," to quote Sam Wells.[17] And most certainly, improvisation isn't about "master[ing] the art of unlearning." It's actually quite the opposite.

Improvisation, instead, is a learned and practiced art that requires immersion in tradition and a continual anchoring back to it. As Wells offers, "It's about being so soaked in a tradition that you learn to take the right things for granted. People who train in improvisation train in a tradition. They learn to trust one another and to say [or do or play] the obvious thing."[18]

In this way, improvisation is also the primary mode by which traditioned innovation occurs—the "acting out," or the "working forward," so to speak, of traditioned innovation. All of the traditioning and forming that occurs backstage—the mindsets developed, the stories internalized, the character traits cultivated, the maps learned and memorized, the skills acquired through habit—all of these come together to enable leaders to improvise freely and innovatively in performance. Gaining skills through habitual repetition enables performative freedom, a key dimension of improvisation, even as more is needed for true improvisation to occur.

In fact, it's almost certain that one must inhabit and understand a coherent tradition that gives their art—music or leadership or something else entirely—a larger framework of reference. Imagine if Miles Davis and his band practiced the ten thousand hours minimally required for peak skill, an insight discovered by psychologist Anders Ericsson and popularized by Malcolm Gladwell, but did so only in isolation. Each would have an individual routine—go to the practice room, warm up the instrument, run through some scales, work on various pieces of repertoire, experiment with them in various ways, keep the fruitful experiments and discard the failures, polish the pieces, prepare for performance. Even after ten thousand hours of individual practice, however, they would find meshing difficult. Their artistry would likely be intensely personal and expressive but would lack any "togetherness." That's because, when skilled performers collaborate—something we all aspire toward in our institutional contexts—they need the glue that tradition provides.[19]

Tradition gives them language and grammar, a "learned vocabulary." In the case of jazz, that learned vocabulary and shared tradition come from listening to the tradition and rehearsing it together. When skilled jazz performers come together to improvise, they can only do so because they speak a similar language, fluent in shorthand concepts like "block chords," "cross-rhythms," and "side-slipping." They share a tonal vocabulary, so everyone understands when someone wants to modulate up or down. Or when one member of the group solos, others might recognize a particular "lick" that prompts them to latch on and follow the song in a new direction. This isn't to say that every jazz musician shares in some single tradition that has a clearly definable language. It is true, however, that there are jazz traditions that enable diverse people to share enough of a language to make improvisation possible, even people who hardly know one another.

189

Tradition also gives improvisers shared reflexes and impulses, which become habitually ingrained in a community of performance. This is especially true among improv comedy performers, such as Stephen Colbert—a truly astonishing improviser—who has described at length a basic reflex he learned during his training at Second City in Chicago. In short, that reflex was to "say 'yes' as often as you can," and allow the acceptance and openness that "yes" provides to avail the group to something masterful and expectedly unexpected.

Colbert recalls that when he started at Second City, there was only one rule: the "yes-and." Through the "yes-and," improvers build a world worth inhabiting. They accept what the other improvisor initiates and add to it. If your partner says you are a doctor, then you are a doctor. You might then respond by saying, "We're doctors and we're jumping from an airplane." As Colbert observes, "You have to keep your eyes open when you do this. You have to be aware of what the other performer is offering you, so that you can agree and add to it." And once you've done that, once you and your partner build the trust to accept and "yes-and" one another, you can improvise a whole scene, with neither person in full control. It becomes, in Colbert's words, a process of "mutual discovery," in which the scene is often as much a surprise to the actor as it is to the audience.[20]

Indeed, anyone familiar with *The Colbert Report* (or, more recently, *The Late Show with Stephen Colbert*) has witnessed, Colbert's relentless "yes-anding," especially in the interview portion of the show. While much of the show's early material was planned and scripted, the final interview portion inevitably took off in unexpected directions. In this highly improvisational arena, Colbert displayed his seasoned reflexes; he almost *always* "yes-anded," and the success or failure of these interviews usually depended on Colbert's guest "yes-anding" back. The episodes that really *went somewhere* were the ones that grew out of a mutual commitment to "yes-anding" and surprised everyone involved. It shouldn't be a surprise, then, that many of the funniest interviews come from fellow actors and comedians, some of whom were schooled at Second City.

Colbert—an adept philosopher, we should note—actually connects the practice of "yes-anding" to the cultivation of wisdom, something he expounded upon in a graduation speech at Knox College. "Now will saying 'yes' get you in trouble at times?" he asked. "Will saying 'yes' lead you to doing some foolish things? Yes it will. But don't be afraid to be a fool." People who avoid foolishness are usually just cynics, and in Colbert's view, cynicism "masquerades as wisdom, but it is the farthest thing from it." The reason is because cynics refuse to learn; they simply choose to stay blind, choosing to reject opportunities out of fear. "Cynics always say no," according to Colbert. But "saying 'yes' is how things grow. Saying 'yes' leads to knowledge."[21]

Beyond Colbert, well-schooled "yes-anders" from Second City include Steve Carell, Tina Fey, Amy Poehler, Mike Myers, Chris Farley, the Belushi brothers, Bill Murray, and Dan Aykroyd. Their habit of "saying yes" has led to some of the most innovative forms of comedy: the office-place mockumentary genre exemplified by Carell in *The Office* and Poehler in *Parks and Recreation*, for example, which were known to improvise their way to multiple Emmys. The habitual reflex of accepting, of saying yes, is how growth happens and new possibilities are created. That's what happened when the folks at TED said "yes, and" to the dawn of the internet age.

The alternative to accepting with a yes is something often referred to as "blocking," which essentially is saying no. An improv actor might, for example, point two fingers at someone and yell, "Bang!" That friend could *accept* the offer in any number of ways—diving out of the way, clutching the wound, or turning into Superman, bouncing the bullet off his chest—and where the scene goes from there is an endless expanse of possibility. Or, just as easily, he could *block* the offer, stifling possibility. Blocking rejects the offer by discontinuing the premise of the other's offer (that he has shot a gun). He might block by responding with "That's not a real gun!" or "No, no, no, you don't have a gun. I do!" and pointing his own fingers back. He might even commit the cardinal sin of improvisa-tion: running away.

That is, he might reject the dawn of the internet age while working at TED, doubling down on conferences without adapting and sharing. He might lead a university and think that higher education will endure with-out "yes-anding," neglecting to see its opportunities in an era that invites us to rethink knowledge and information and the pursuit of wisdom. He might view his leadership of a health system through a lens of decreasing profit margins, running away from an invitation by patients concerned with holistic care rather than maximal efficiency.

There may be times when blocking is necessary—in theater, in jazz, in leadership, in life—but invariably, whenever a blocking move is made, improvisation comes to a screeching halt. If that's our choice, we must be clear about the consequences.

Sam Wells suggests, like Colbert, that we should always put the bur-den on blocking—that in life, as in improv theater, we should assume that the right answer is probably not no. In a compelling thought experi-ment, Wells wonders on behalf of Christians: what if we never blocked? If blocking generally assumes a context of violence, or at very least a stance that is "subtly aggressive and undermines the space of the other," in which the attainment of one person's good requires the denial of another's, then perhaps we ought to avoid it at nearly any cost.[22]

After all, a blocking stance assumes shortsightedly and wrongly that we live in an environment only of scarce resources, as if a finite amount of "the good" exists, and each person must struggle to gain his or her zero-sum share. *If you do something I don't like, I must block you*, this stance instinctively assumes. This is often, Wells suggests, a function of trying to control or even manipulate the future, to assume that we alone are respon-sible for making the story "come out right." It assumes we are carpenters or engineers, not gardeners. Surely this is not right.[23]

And although we might assume that accepting or blocking constitute the two primary choices in improvisation, there are actually more choices, as Wells sees it. In fact, an imaginative ability to transcend yes or no when we encounter what comes to us from beyond our control can actually lead to the most transformative action. Looking beyond the binary of accepting or blocking, Wells proposes a positive entailment: *What if we accepted all offers and looked for ways to transcend and reshape the bad ones?* He calls this a posture of "overaccepting," which requires some explanation.

Accepting usually assumes a context of trust. It assumes that we live in an environment of abundant resources, where the resources that truly matter are inexhaustible (recall Matryoshka Haus's imaginative decision to consider resources as entailing far more than money), and where individuals don't seek *their own share* but instead seek *to share*. Actors on an improv stage tend to assume these things, and they are able to accept because they, and their partners, won't seek to control or manipulate the future. Everyone on stage, it can be trusted, is open to unexpected surprises.

That is well and good when the context is one of trust, like the improv stage, and where actions and intentions can be assumed benevolent or, at worst, neutral. Yet we live in a world where that isn't often the case, where not all offers are good, and saying yes to certain offers ranges from naivety to foolishness to outright cooperation with evil. Accepting all offers in life might seem dubious, naive, and imprudent, and we must consider how to both avoid blocking and maintain integrity.

A natural and understandable impulse is simply to block "bad" offers when we can't assume trust or when we know the offer to be malicious. When that happens, we tend to believe that a terse no is the only appropriate response, something that is especially true in "call-out cultures," where too often the only appropriate response to wrong or injustice is a public shaming of its perpetrators. But as Wells notes, every no comes with costs: shrinking the imagination, relinquishing the capacity to interpret the world in a charitable light, or, perhaps most important, shutting down avenues toward redemption and flourishing.

In these situations, simple acceptance is problematic, but so is blocking. So, as Wells suggests, problems offer the improviser possibilities for development and exploration; one simply has to learn to see problems as opportunities. The effort, then, ought to transcend the binary either/or of yes or no, accepting or blocking. We ought to try, instead, to overaccept.

"Transcend" is a key word here because that's not the same thing—let us be clear—as simple acceptance or even compromise. The right improvisational response in difficult situations isn't usually to find some common ground *between* accepting and blocking. Instead, we improvise most fruitfully, according to Wells, when we think *beyond* both accepting and blocking and voyage into the arena of overaccepting. Overaccepting is an attempt to fit the smaller story that has come our way—which often we didn't invite or go looking for—into a "larger story" we find ourselves part of. When presented with problematic offers, that means looking for ways to help guide those offers toward redemptive purposes—toward flourishing.[24]

> Overaccepting is accepting in the light of a larger story. The fear about accepting is that one will be determined by the gift and thus lose one's integrity and identity. The fear about blocking is that one will seal oneself off from the world and thus lose one's relevance and humanity. Overaccepting is an active way of receiving that enables one to retain both identity and relevance. It is a way of accepting without losing the initiative. This often involves a change of status.[25]

Wells illustrates this with a compelling story about a concert pianist who was set to begin a performance, when suddenly a scream rose from the audience. It was a child, who bolted from the seat beside his parents and took off running around the auditorium. The concert pianist stepped away from the piano in order to compose herself and maintain focus, when the child ran up the steps and onto the stage, sat himself down on the bench, and began to hammer away at keys on the piano. As the hushed audience began to gasp in horror and embarrassment (*someone block this child!*), the pianist walked quietly toward the child and stood behind him as he hammered the keys. The pianist leaned over him and, without disturbing the child, placed right and left hands outside his two small hands on the keyboard. The pianist then began to play in response to the child's notes, weaving his discordant sounds into an improvised melody. And suddenly, a moment of horror became a moment of beauty.

To have run backstage would have been to commit the cardinal sin of the improviser. To have thrown the child out would have been to block shortsightedly. To have let him bang away at the keyboard would have been simple acceptance of something not really worth accepting. But to enter his action, and to weave a beautiful melody around him, was to receive the child as a gift, to see his behavior as an opportunity—to overaccept his action, in other words, into a larger story that could be redeemed for something better and transcendent. It's easy to imagine everyone in the audience going home touched that night, with a story to share that was even more beautiful than the scheduled Beethoven concerto.[26]

This, precisely, is the kind of reflex and action we ought to embody as we seek to lead and improvise new ways forward on the wilder seas of our turbulent times. We shouldn't settle for the tribalism, mistrust, and conflict that have seized our public life (the child's play, if you will), but neither should we reflexively block those things or run backstage. We shouldn't assume that all technological advancement will yield human advancement, even as we shouldn't reject it out of hand as a threat to human flourishing. There are many things that complicate our perilous journey on these wilder seas. If we view them correctly, we will see them as opportunities.

The stage improvisors of jazz and comedy can teach us this: our traditions have prepared us, anchored us, guided us, formed us, and inspired us. We owe them a great deal, and we can continue to rely on how they've prepared us. Yet our moment is new. The tradition hasn't seen it exactly like this before. The story is unfolding in a dynamic environment, and our "work forward" is full of opportunity to improvise new life.

Their greatest lesson might be the knowledge that nearly anything that comes our way can be answered, "yes, and . . ."[27]

❖ ❖ ❖ ❖ ❖ ❖

Sustaining this way of being—to cultivate cultures and systems and habits of improvisation and innovation that permeate and animate a vibrant institution or a society across time—is another challenge. That's where we now want to turn our attention, to the ways we design and sustain our institutions so they endure as vibrant and improvisational vessels capable of navigating these wilder seas.

Sustainability has become a buzzword, a concept we throw around with ease. The reality, of course, is that sustainability—best defined for our purposes as a way of operating that meets the needs of the present without compromising the ability of those who follow us to operate in a way that meets their needs—is extremely difficult in practice. As we've mentioned from the beginning of this book, faddish innovation techniques often sprout up. They can start to function a bit like a diet of 5-Hour Energy shots: great as a spark, but terrible as a means of sustenance.

So how might our leadership and our institutions maintain vibrancy and sustain a habit of traditioned innovation? How might we ensure that innovation is not a 5-Hour Energy shot and improvisation is not just a beautiful moment in a concert hall, but both are ways of being that allow us to "work forward" sustainably into the future?

Gary Pisano has spent considerable energy unraveling the paradox that innovation spurs growth in institutions, growth leads to scale, and scale, in turn, can make innovation more difficult. Studying some of the world's most well-established and endowed organizations, many of which desperately want to spur and sustain innovation, Pisano has found that most efforts are fruitless. Established organizations, after all, are often marked by hours of meetings, labyrinths of policies and procedures, and byzantine organizational matrices for decision-making. Because of these challenges, it's actually the case that some of the most underappreciated creativity occurs when people in existing institutions learn how to navigate their inherited structures and arrange those structures for the work of ongoing innovation. Start-up entrepreneurship is like building a new house from the ground up, he suggests (not easy, but people willingly do it all the time) while designing and maintaining existing organizations for the work of innovation is like renovating a home while living in it (much more difficult)! That is why we must think well about how to maintain institutions that can sustain innovation.

As Pisano argues, "innovation initiatives" are destined to fail because a sustainably innovative way of being requires a long-time horizon and profound cultural changes—a nutrient-rich diet rather than a shot of 5-Hour Energy. It's also true that innovation within existing organizations comes with inherent trade-offs: How do we effectively invest in existing capabilities versus new ones? And the real issue, more than the scale or size of an organization, is its complexity. Friction impedes mobility in organizations as in physics, and complex organizations have many moving parts that need synchronizing if they are to sustain the vibrancy of innovation. The more moving parts, the more likely the friction.

The good news, Pisano reports, is that organizational ecosystems can be altered by our actions. If we so choose, and if we properly commit to it, even the most complex institutions can sustain innovation—and can thus maintain the vibrancy that will propel it toward its ultimate destination on these wilder seas. How?

Pisano's research suggests three things, and we add an essential fourth. First, Pisano says, an institution must systematically create an innovation strategy. Second, it must design an innovation system, creating structures and governance that align the strategy with the organization's capabilities. Third, it should build an innovation culture. And finally, the piece we'd add is that the organization must practice self-renewal that is continually traditioning and improvising to draw new sources of life. Each of these merits unpacking.[28]

A strategy, Pisano notes, is nothing more than "a commitment to a set of coherent, mutually reinforcing policies or behaviors aimed at achieving a specific goal."[29] An innovation strategy specifies how an organization intends to use innovation to create and capture value. It's what an organization can use to clarify its priorities when many different opportunities or paths forward exist.

A good strategy, in Pisano's estimation, serves two purposes. First, it helps clarify the tradeoffs an organization is willing to make between what he calls the "short-term exploitation" of existing resources versus the "long-term exploration" of new opportunities. Second, a good strategy helps align diverse parts of an organization around common priorities, making even large organizations less complex for innovation. Without an explicit innovation strategy, written and articulated for the organization at large, no one knows what kinds of innovation, or innovation toward what ends, are actually important to an organization—or sometimes, whether innovation is even important at all. An effective innovation strategy can be used to focus the organization's resources and energy on building the right set of capabilities.[30]

Strategy is useless, of course, without the second important part of sustaining innovation: the systems and structures needed to implement srategy. Pisano calls this the "innovation system," a benign term that seems intended to obscure the fact that this is about matters of organizational governance and the exercise of power.

Power is a scary word these days, but it needn't be, not when it is held in proper perspective. As John W. Gardner has written, power shouldn't be confused with status or prestige or dictatorial designs. It's simply the capacity to ensure the outcomes one wishes and to prevent the ones one does not wish. It's a key dimension of effective leadership. "Many good people," Gardner writes of power, "persuade themselves they want nothing to do with it. The ethical and spiritual apprehensions are understandable. But one cannot abjure power."[31] Without power—in an institution, in a society, in anything really—nothing happens. So the key, as Gordon T. Smith points out, is that effective institutions have intentional and transparent structures for the exercise of power. Power is simply leverage, the capacity of people to do what they are called to do, individually and collectively.

Power is what marshals our intellectual, moral, and material resources to a common end. Taken that way, it doesn't sound so bad.[32]

Power is tricky, though, as Gardner points out. As political philosophers have noted throughout history, perhaps none as articulately as the great statesman James Madison, power must always be regulated, lest we find ourselves always on a quest to gain more for ourselves and leave less for our neighbors. Power, in this respect, must be accompanied by discipline, virtue, accountability, and transparency—and perhaps, as Madison would have it, a few checks and balances. As Smith notes, simultaneously leveraging and moderating power is the key to the effectiveness of any institution. Accountability and transparency, for example, are not the same thing as disempowerment; they're simply part of the calculus of the proper stewardship of power.

Power needs to be considered and understood in institutional contexts because effective innovation strategies require practices for knowing what needs to be done, who needs to do it, and what mechanisms are most appropriate for doing it. Leaders up and down and across the organization need to make and implement good decisions if the organization is to promote, as we've suggested, the sort of flourishing toward which the organization and its constituents are called. Proper governance, oversight, and administration of the organization—boring as those might sound to the imaginers and innovators—prove essential so that the "main things" can be cultivated and take root.[33]

So what has this to do with sustained innovation and institutional vibrancy? As Pisano notes, an organization's capacity for innovation stems to a significant degree from its systems and structures. To sustain innovation, an organization needs a coherent set of interdependent processes and structures that dictates how it searches for and finds new problems and solutions, how it synthesizes ideas into value propositions, and how it selects the projects or initiatives to prioritize. Sustained innovation requires tight alignment between the innovation strategies and the organization's capabilities.[34]

Unfortunately, there are no universal "best practices" for how to achieve this, because all practices, in all contexts, present trade-offs. Creating sustainable systems and organizational capabilities for innovation is more like bespoke tailoring than buying off the rack, notes Pisano. The leadership challenge is thus to design the particular systems and power structures that will work for an individual organization and a particularized innovation strategy.

In other words, we can't tell you exactly how to do that in your institutions. It requires an attuned political sensitivity and an understanding of the delicate ways power ought to be stewarded, exercised, leveraged, and checked. In just about any case, advises Pisano, innovation systems and power structures should do three things: they should *search* for novel and valuable problems and solutions, they should *synthesize* diverse streams of ideas into coherence (combining ideas in new ways), and they should discern how to *select* among multiple opportunities for innovation.[35]

In this respect, sustainably innovative and vibrant institutions not only get things done, they get the *right* things done. They build structures, habits, and practices designed to access knowledge, wisdom, insight, and imagination. They create open lines of conversation throughout the organization that allow ideas to circulate. They acknowledge that ideas, creativity, and insight don't always follow the lines of the organizational chart or the maze of the decision-making bureaucracy and that sometimes communication across the institution leads to a fruitful cross-pollination of ideas. And, just as important, they acknowledge that not all the answers are internal. Learning and collaborating outside the institution, even outside the industry or sector, are vital.[36]

And so, building the right systems and structures for innovation is essential. But it's not the only thing, since innovation is a deeply human activity shaped by more than power and structure and strategy. It's also shaped by culture, the third of Pisano's essential elements.

Culture, to borrow from social psychologist Geert Hofstede's concise definition, is simply the "collective programming of the mind which distinguishes members of one group or category of people from another."[37] To quote Helen Spencer-Oatey, it's "a fuzzy set of basic assumptions and values, orientations to life, beliefs, policies, procedures and behavioural conventions that are shared by a group of people, and that influence (but do not determine) each member's behaviour."[38] Culture shapes how people think, behave, and feel, and thus profoundly shapes how innovation happens and how institutions maintain vibrancy. But because culture is "fuzzy" and diffuse, it can be extremely difficult to change, especially in large, complex, or aged organizations. The important reality, however, is that strategies and systems mean little without a culture that supports them.[39]

All institutions have cultures, and all teams within institutions do too. The key is to develop a culture that helps support the things we want to achieve, a culture that is conducive to the work of vibrancy, flourishing, and innovation. As Gordon Smith describes it, it's the culture that provides our institutions and communities with social energy, and the goal is a culture that fosters and animates our capacity to fulfill our mission and purpose.[40]

Healthy institutional cultures are generative; they are places where the character of the people permeates the feel of the place, where people are willing to plant trees under whose shade they might not sit. We've argued throughout this book for the importance of certain character traits and virtues—love, hope, curiosity, humility, gratitude, discernment, trust, generativity, wisdom—and implicit in this argument has been a belief that these traits not only help us practice traditioned innovation, they also indelibly shape the tone and feel of the spaces we inhabit. As David Brooks argues, character formation is not an individual task or something that is achieved on a person-by-person basis, the product of sitting in a room thinking about the difference between right and wrong. Instead, it occurs when we "build a thick jungle of loving attachments," when we commit ourselves to others and to causes that transcend ourselves. We have opportunities in the institutions we inhabit to cultivate what Brooks calls "moral ecologies," places where certain values are prioritized, certain ways of being are expected, certain expectations subtly guide everything from how we dress and talk to what we admire and disdain, or even how we define our ultimate purposes.[41]

If we want to cultivate vibrant institutions that are up to the challenges of these wilder seas, we need to ask ourselves key questions: Are our institutions truly places where we value kindness and gratitude? Are they places where we prize boundless curiosity and humor? Is our culture, our moral ecology, marked by mutuality, respect, and grace when our failures are born of earnestness or experimentation? Do we value hard work, even as we value people as *whole* people, beyond their utility and productivity? Do we exercise all that is in our power to minimize fear and celebrate courage? Are we focused on nurturing practical wisdom in all we are and do? Is ours a place with a "Three Musketeers" ethos, where we are truly one for all and all for one?

It's not just that these things make for better institutions or more enjoyable workplaces. That's true, and certainly worth a lot. But it's also the case that institutional culture is an indispensable dimension of how innovation happens. When asked what's more important, shaping the culture or the formal systems of an organization, Pisano says unequivocally that "the answer is both: systems and culture are inextricably linked. Each reinforces the other."[42] And as Peter Drucker famously noted, culture eats strategy for breakfast. Certainly, that "fuzzy" thing called culture merits our time and attention if we are to sustain innovation.

Even so, a fourth thing—beyond the innovation strategy, the innovation systems and power structures, and the innovation culture of Pisano's matrix—is vital to sustaining innovation. That is a continual self-renewal, an ongoing and dynamic habit of traditioning and improvising and traditioning and improvising again.

As John Gardner suggests, even the strongest institutions that hold themselves to the highest of standards are inevitably prone to the complacency that foreshadows decline. "I once believed," Gardner writes, that it might be possible to design an ever-renewing organization, one that would never run down, never lose its vitality. It would provide for dissent, it would institutionalize the devil's advocate, it would provide the seedbeds for new ideas and new solutions. It would never cease learning and developing.

But it was not to be:

After many years, I concluded that human beings are much too firmly wedded to the status quo to let anyone get away with such a scheme. They will discount the devil's advocate. They will work the blandishments of comradeship on the dissenter. They will root out the seedbeds.[43]

Gloomy, right? Our institutions, like our bodies and minds, are prone, at some point, to deterioration. As Gardner points out, many people want to assume that the factors that produce deterioration within institutions can be wished out of existence or held at bay by wealth, power, status, or rules—the things that, paradoxically, grant the security that often leads to deterioration. These are also many of the things, we should point out, that lead increasing numbers of people, young and old, to be suspicious of institutions.

What, then, should we do, if this is our fate? How might we infuse renewal into the lives of our institutions so that innovation and vibrancy can be sustained against our bent toward deterioration?

There are practical things, some of which bleed into our previous discussions of strategy, systems, and culture, but which also merit exploration on their own.

First, we must unleash human potential within our institutions. That sounds simple, but it's not. "Nothing is more vital to the renewal of an organization," Gardner writes, "than the system by which able people are nurtured and moved into positions where they can make their greatest contribution."[44] This means creating what Robert Kegan and Lisa Laskow Lahey call "everyone cultures" and "deliberately developmental organizations," places where both the institution and the people who inhabit it see themselves as "resources to support each other's flourishing." These are places like Next Jump, a tech company that sums up its belief system with an equation:

Better Me + Better You = Better Us

This equation, which risks bordering on trite, is actually full of profound truth: *Better Me* signals the importance of an appetite for constant improvement. *Better You* is about the meaning people derive from their work through helping others, inside and outside the company. And *Better Us* is the payoff for the company, the community, and ultimately the world; it's the outcome toward which everyone in the company can aspire; it's the flourishing toward which all of us strive.[45]

As simple as this sounds, it's rare. Gardner notes: "Given the importance of [this dynamic], one might expect organizations to provide special rewards for those executives who are 'people developers,' but it rarely happens." Instead, we usually reward our leaders for production or charisma or confidence, for balancing the budget or satisfying the shareholders.[46]

So if unleashing human capability in our institutions is order number one, then an important way we can do that is, number two, to reassign people or let them vary their duties. This is radically practical and fundamentally impactful. We've seen this in organizations like Decurion, which we described in chapter 1, as it allowed Cristina to rotate jobs from day to day in the ArcLight theater, all as preparation for her goal to be a Hollywood set designer, the aspiration at the end of her "line of sight." Younger people, in particular, benefit from this kind of practice, as new tasks can pose new challenges that help hone skills, broaden experience, and develop the underappreciated value of becoming a generalist. This, in fact, not only keeps institutions in a mode of renewal; it also helps them adapt and improvise more capably. As David Epstein has discovered, in most fields—especially those that are complex and unpredictable—generalists, not specialists, are the ones who are primed to excel. They're more creative, more agile, and able to make connections their more specialized peers often don't see.[47]

We saw this play out when we visited Fisher Middle School in Greenville, South Carolina, where faculty not only work together in surprising ways, they also extend themselves into new areas of instruction. They're content experts, sure, but as Essie Taylor, an eighth-grade (formerly sixth-grade) social studies teacher pointed out to us, the school's project-based learning approach keeps the learning fresh for faculty and students alike, while also extending everyone's range and ability to make connections. That happens because teachers train differently from the start, with a STEAM approach and a view of the whole system. "It's totally different from other schools and other training," she noted, and that makes all the difference. She then adds, "Being here, I enjoy my work much more [than work in previous schools]. We work together, doing something different here that is focused on students' thriving."[48]

This approach, letting people vary outside their "lane," is not without its risks, though: it might just cause the organization to rethink itself, to slip from the bondage of the status quo and embrace "what might be," since people (especially younger people) who are given license to roam often don't lack ideas. Varied experiences, it seems, have a way of generating them. And this kind of "risk" is exactly the point: renewal and vibrancy are hard to avoid when we allow new people to breathe new life into new corners of our institutions.[49]

Number three is closely related: to create institutions marked by self-renewal, it is beneficial to develop what our friend Tiziana Dearing calls "open circles," the capacity to welcome new stakeholders into our work and to allow existing stakeholders to evolve into different or multiple roles over time. This is like the collaborations we discussed in the last chapter, only here we want to note that these collaborations are an important source for renewal and vibrancy. Gardner was apt to suggest we might open the doors and windows so that outsiders might relieve us of our propensity for insularity. That is because even the best of us—*especially* the best of us—succumb at times to groupthink: a strong conviction in a group that "we're right," that our shared rationalizations support our convictions, and that any threats to our convictions ought to be systematically rejected.

We succumb to this when we conform, censor doubters, close the ranks, and belittle outsiders, critics, and competitors. Famous cases abound, especially in political administrations, where groupthink leads to war—American ventures into Vietnam or Iraq spring to mind. When this happens in our own institutions, we stagnate at best, hasten catastrophe at worst. And the answer, to fend off this risk and avail ourselves of the renewal required of sustained innovation, is to practice open circles both within and beyond our own institutions.[50]

Finally, and perhaps most important, a source of renewal that can sustain a vibrant institution is the ongoing and dynamic interaction between traditioning and innovating. We have discussed both of these themes at length, and we'd like to underscore that this ongoing interaction is the key, not only to sustaining a vibrant institution but also to navigating the wilder seas of the future.

Gardner argues that organizations and societies that stagnate do so because people have lost sight of their goals, becoming preoccupied with the procedures and routines of the present. We've all seen it, the path-dependent people and organizations that do things as they've always done them because that's the only thing they know to do. These are the people and institutions that nudge us to lose faith in institutions themselves, to devolve into assumptions that we'd best go it alone since institutions can't evolve or can't be trusted. People who carry these assumptions about stagnant, languishing, and stiffly bureaucratic institutions often aren't wrong. But the answer isn't rejection; it's renewal. It's "yes, and" steeped in the tradition.

Traditioning is a gift. It's an invitation to rediscover and revive those animating goals and purposes that prompted people before us to plant the trees under whose shade we now get to sit. It's an opportunity to recapture the life-giving hope of the people who planted and tended the institutions we inhabit today. It's a chance to bottle the energy that allowed our organizations to exist and endure and to channel that energy into new possibilities for a life-giving future. It's a summons to explore the best of our traditions and to discover there what Marjorie Thompson has called "a feast for hungry hearts." "Indeed," she notes, "I might caution against gluttony!"[51]

As we capture the vibrancy that traditioning can transmit, we have no choice but to say: "Where next?" "What now?" "Yes, and." To become an improviser, in this respect, is to be, as Sam Wells put it, "like a man walking backwards." That's because "the only given in this life" is what we see behind us as we march toward the future, the traditions of which we are a part that have equipped us for what is ahead; that which has borne us to the present so we might enjoy a radical openness to the changes that will carry us forward toward future flourishing.[52]

To sustain innovation, then, requires us to develop the right strategies, systems, and cultures that foster it within our institutions. But it is also to go continually back to the well, to practice a kind of renewal that captures the benevolent impulses that brought our institutions into being, sustained them through the years, and equipped them for the work that we now, in this moment, have the privilege to lead and to do.

These are wild seas indeed. The world is changing, because that's what the world has always done. And yet, for many of us, there's a sense that the future isn't what it used to be, that where we're headed is toward seas even wilder than the ones we know now. Often, we start to believe that we are destined to sink. So let us then be reminded of the words of the psalmist, who said that "We will not fear, though the earth should change, though the mountains shake in the heart of the sea; though its waters roar and foam, though the mountains tremble with its tumult" (Ps 46:2-3, NRSV).

At the same time, let us not also assume that we are merely here to be passengers on this sea, here to endure until our time is up. We have a purpose, a telos, a destination, a "why" whereby we are called to promote the flourishing of one another, to help one another begin to taste the life that really is life. As we set out on a course toward that destination, we are sure to become bewildered on these wilder seas by the storms and the fog and the elements beyond our control. When this happens, we have gifts, blessings on which we can rely to help us navigate the future: well-endowed imaginations marked by hope, curiosity, and humility; rich traditions that we can mine with gratitude and discernment; and one another—an ability to work together through holy and unlikely friendships, dense networks and loose ties, and entrepreneurial collaborations. In all this, the invitation is to improvise new life, to discover new ways in which the past might inform our capacity to create a better future.

Indeed, let it be so.

Notes

Traditioned Innovation: An Introduction

[1] Julian Barnes, *Nothing to be Frightened Of* (New York: Knopf, 2008), 3.

[2] See William Butler Yeats, *The Second Coming*.

[3] See C. Kavin Rowe, *Christianity's Surprise* (Nashville: Abingdon Press, 2020).

[4] For a significant diagnosis of our attitude toward institutions, with a profound call for the need to reinvigorate institutions, see Yuval Levin, *A Time to Build* (New York: Basic Books, 2020). This important analysis was published just as we were completing this book.

[5] David Epstein, *Range: Why Generalists Triumph in a Specialized World* (New York: Riverhead Books, 2019), 49.

[6] Note, for example, the epigraph to *Beloved*, which is a citation from the book of Romans that includes an internal citation to the Old Testament book of Hosea. It is a complex narrative, and yet one that abides in hope.

[7] See Charles Taylor, *A Secular Age* (Cambridge, MA: Harvard University Press, 2007), 539ff.

[8] See Jeremy Begbie, *Resounding Truth* (Grand Rapids: Baker, 2007).

[9] Vaclav Havel, "The Need for Transcendence in the Postmodern World," delivered in Independence Hall, Philadelphia, PA, July 4, 1994. Accessed online at http://www.worldtrans.org/whole/havelspeech.html.

[10] Michael Ignatieff, *The Ordinary Virtues* (Cambridge: Harvard University Press, 2017), 25.

[11] Ignatieff, *The Ordinary Virtues*, 203.

[12] Ignatieff, *The Ordinary Virtues*, 219.

[13] See praxislabs.com for this quotation and further description of the organization's use of this term.

[14] Cormode, forthcoming. The quotation is taken from a prepublication version of the typescript.

Chapter 1
Navigating

[1] Sergio's story appears in Gregory Boyle, *Barking to the Choir: The Power of Radical Kinship* (New York: Simon & Schuster, 2017), 52–54.

[2] Cristina's story is told in Robert Kegan and Lisa Laskow Lahey, *An Everyone Culture* (Boston: Harvard Business Review Press, 2016), 144–45. Information about Decurion, including what is written here, can be found throughout the book. This quote from Bryan Ungard is on p. 102.

[3] For a rich discussion of this congregation, on which we draw, see Michael Mather, *Having Nothing, Possessing Everything* (Grand Rapids: Eerdmans, 2018). We also have benefited from ongoing conversations with Mike and De'Amon over several years.

[4] See Lex Rieffel, "Institutions Are under Existential Threat, Globally," June 28, 2018, https://www.brookings.edu/blog/up-front/2018/06/28/global-institutions-are-under-existential-threat/.

[5] See Christian Miller, *The Character Gap: How Good Are We?* (New York: Oxford University Press, 2018), 36–47.

[6] Wisława Szymborska, *The three oddest words*, trans. S. Baranczak and C. Cavanagh, NobelPrize.org, accessed September 8, 2020, https://www.nobelprize.org/prizes/literature/1996/szymborska/25558-poetry-1996-7/.

Chapter 2
Purpose

[1] William Damon, *The Path to Purpose* (New York: Free Press, 2008), 31–32.

[2] Paul Froese, *On Purpose* (New York: Oxford University Press, 2016), 21.

[3] Damon, *The Path to Purpose*, 31–33.

[4] See David Brooks, "Anthony Kennedy and the Privatization of Meaning," *The New York Times*, June 28, 2018.

[5] Tip of the cap to Simon Sinek, whose TED talk and subsequent book, *Start with Why*, has given currency to this phrase.

[6] Dan Heath, "Writing a Mission Statement That Doesn't Suck," https://www.youtube.com/watch?v=LJhG3HZ7b4o.

[7] Although this is a widely cited case, we borrowed the idea from Simon Sinek, *Start With Why* (New York: Portfolio/Penguin, 2009), 50.

[8] See Jim Collins and Jerry I. Porras, "Building Your Company's Vision," *Harvard Business Review*, September–October 1996, https://hbr.org/1996/09/building-your-companys-vision?referral=03758&cm_vc=rr_item_page.top_right.

[9] Graham Kenny, "Your Company's Purpose Is Not Its Vision, Mission, or Values," *Harvard Business Review*, September 3, 2014, https://hbr.org/2014/09/your-companys-purpose-is-not-its-vision-mission-or-values.

[10] These statements might not reflect current company vision statements because of how quickly companies tend to change them. That, in part, helps prove our point: organizations need something larger to anchor to.

[11] John P. Kotter, *Leading Change* (Boston: Harvard Business School Press, 1996), 68–69.

[12] See A. G. Lafley and Roger L. Martin, *Playing to Win* (Boston: Harvard Business Review Press, 2013).

[13] Richard Gunderman, *We Make a Life by What We Give* (Bloomington: Indiana University Press, 2008), 160.

[14] See L. Gregory Jones, "Overcome Mission Drift by Practicing Traditioned Innovation, Faith and Leadership," November 17, 2015, https://www.faithandleadership.com/l-gregory-jones-overcome-mission-drift-practicing-traditioned-innovation.

[15] Pope Benedict XVI, *Deus Caritas Est*, available in *Giving Well, Doing Good*, ed. Amy A. Kass (Bloomington: Indiana University Press, 2008), 63.

[16] Marguerite Barankitse, "Love made me an inventor," *Faith & Leadership*, December 16, 2013, https://faithandleadership.com/marguerite-maggy-barankitse-love-made-me-inventor.

[17] All quotations in this section are from an interview with Susan Cowley, conducted by Andrew P. Hogue and Sarah J. Fala on January 18, 2018.

[18] Kelle's story appears in Shelly Conlon, "Leading the Way: University High Senior Poised to be the First from Talitha Koum Program to Graduate," *Waco Tribune-Herald*, May 20, 2018, https://wacotrib.com/news/education/university-high-senior-poised-to-be-first-from-talitha-koum-program-to-graduate/article_6a7a9f3f-3439-5d57-a9b2-d9c283b25387.html.

[19] See Dave Packard, "1960—Packard Speeches, Box 2, Folder 39—General Speeches, Supervisory Development Program, HP, Palo Alto," March 8, 1960, https://historycenter.agilent.com/packard-speeches/ps1960. See also Bruce Jones, "The Difference between Purpose and Mission," *Harvard Business Review*, February 2, 2016, https://hbr.org/sponsored/2016/02/the-difference-between-purpose-and-mission.

[20] Gunderman, *We Make a Life by What We Give*, 32.

21 See Adam Grant, *Give and Take* (New York: Penguin, 2013), 4–15, 157–158.

22 Damon, *The Path to Purpose*, 40. None of these points should be surprising to Christians, yet our own imagination has too often been stunted by distortions and contractions in our own beliefs and practices.

23 Damon, *The Path to Purpose*, 44.

24 Shakespeare, William, *Romeo and Juliet*, 2.2.133-35.

25 See Christian Smith and Hilary Davidson, *The Paradox of Generosity* (New York: Oxford University Press, 2016).

26 See Miller, *The Character Gap*, 37.

27 Grant, *Give and Take*, 15.

28 Gunderman, *We Make a Life by What We Give*, 33.

Chapter 3
Bewilderment

1 Charles P. Pierce, "The Head vs. The Heart: There Are Plenty of Reasons for the Thinking Fan to Disown College Football, and Yet, Every Fall . . ." *Sports Illustrated*, September 10, 2018, 38.

2 See the analysis and provocative title of Blair H. Sheppard et al., *Ten Years to Midnight* (Oakland: Berrett-Koehler, 2020).

3 Gregory Boyle, *Tattoos on the Heart* (New York: Free Press, 2010), 2.

4 See Blair H. Sheppard et al., "Adapting to a New World," *Strategy and Business*, May 13, 2020, https://www.strategy-business.com/article/Adapting-to-a-new-world?gko=5b5d.

5 Quoted in Thomas L. Friedman, *Thank You for Being Late* (New York: Farrar, Straus and Giroux, 2016), 187.

6 See Friedman, *Thank You For Being Late*.

[7] See "The Creed of Speed," *The Economist*, December 5, 2015.

[8] Geoff Colvin, *Humans Are Underrated* (New York: Portfolio/Penguin, 2015), 3.

[9] See Galina Zapyanova and Anders Christiansen, "Hope, Trust Deficits May Help Fuel Populism," April 7, 2017, https://news.gallup.com/poll/207674/hope-trust-deficits-may-help-fuel-populism.aspx.

[10] Pew Research Center, "Little Change in Overall Public Views of the Impact of Nation's Institutions," July 10, 2017, http://www.people-press.org/2017/07/10/sharp-partisan-divisions-in-views-of-national-institutions/1_2-13/.

[11] See Zapyanova and Christiansen, "Hope, Trust Deficits May Help Fuel Populism."

[12] Joseph L. Badaracco, *The Good Struggle* (Boston: Harvard Business Review Press, 2013), 2–3.

[13] Duke Corporate Education, "Leading in Context," 2013 CEO Study.

[14] Friedman, *Thank You For Being Late*, 198.

[15] Avivah Gottlieb Zornberg, *Bewilderments* (New York: Schocken, 2015).

[16] John W. Gardner, *Self-Renewal* (New York: W. W. Norton, 1964), 9–10.

[17] Jaroslav Pelikan, *The Vindication of Tradition* (New Haven: Yale University Press, 1984), 65.

[18] Neel Burton, "The Meaning of Nostalgia: The Psychology and Philosophy of Nostalgia," *Psychology Today*, November 27, 2014, https://www.psychologytoday.com/blog/hide-and-seek/201411/the-meaning-nostalgia.

[19] F. Scott Fitzgerald, *The Great Gatsby* (New York: Scribner, 2004), 180.

[20] Charles Duhigg, *The Power of Habit* (New York: Random House, 2012), 12–19.

[21] See Tom Kelley and David Kelley, *Creative Confidence* (New York: Crown Business, 2013).

[22] Carol S. Dweck, *Mindset* (New York: Ballantine Books, 2007).

[23] See Kelley and Kelley, *Creative Confidence*, 49.

[24] Erik Brynjolfsson and Andrew McAfee, *The Second Machine Age* (New York: W. W. Norton, 2014), 106.

[25] Pelikan, *The Vindication of Tradition*, 6.

[26] Gardner, *Self-Renewal*, 3.

[27] Gardner, *Self-Renewal*, 6.

[28] See Richard A. Swenson, *Margin* (Colorado Springs: NavPress, 2004).

[29] These quotations from Ignatius of Loyola and about the Jesuit order are available from https://www.jesuits.org/about-us/ignatius-of-loyola/.

[30] Boyle, *Barking to the Choir*, 3.

[31] Portions of Homeboy's history are told in Boyle, *Tattoos on the Heart*, 1–8. Additionally, some of these stories come from an interview Greg conducted with Father G in 2016.

[32] Pelikan, *The Vindication of Tradition*, 81–82.

[33] Steven Johnson, *Where Good Ideas Come From* (New York: Riverhead Books, 2010), 31.

Chapter 4
Imagining

[1] See Martin Seligman, preface to *Homo Prospectus*, by Martin E. P. Seligman, Peter Railton, Roy F. Baumeister, and Chandra Sripada (New

York: Oxford University Press, 2016), xi. See also R. F. Baumeister, K. D. Vohs, and G. Oettingen, "Pragmatic Prospection: How and Why People Think about the Future," *Review of General Psychology,* vol. 20, no. 1 (2016): 3.

[2] Martin Seligman, *The Hope Circuit* (New York: PublicAffairs, 2018), 349. See also Steven Johnson, *Farsighted* (New York: Riverhead Books, 2018), 80.

[3] Liz Essley Whyte, "Giving It All," *Philanthropy Magazine* (Spring 2014), https://www.philanthropyroundtable.org/philanthropy-magazine /article/spring-2014-giving-it-all.

[4] See Alan Barnhart, "God Owns Our Business," *Generous Giving,* accessed September 16, 2020, https://generousgiving.org/media/videos /alan-barnhart-god-owns-our-business.

[5] Barnhart, "God Owns Our Business."

[6] Christian Smith and Hilary Davidson, *The Paradox of Generosity* (New York: Oxford University Press, 2014), 1.

[7] Barnhart, "God Owns Our Business."

[8] Whyte, "Giving It All."

[9] Barnhart, "About," accessed September 16, 2020, https://www.barn hartcrane.com/about/.

[10] See Seligman et al., *Homo Prospectus.*

[11] See Peter Railton, introduction to *Homo Prospectus,* 6. See also Martin E. P. Seligman and John Tierney, "We Aren't Built to Live in the Moment," *New York Times,* May 19, 2017.

[12] Seligman, *The Hope Circuit,* 350–51.

[13] See Railton, introduction to *Homo Prospectus,* 22. See also Peter Railton, "That Obscure Object: Desire," *Proceedings and Addresses of the American Philosophical Association* 86 (2012): 22–46.

[14] Railton, introduction to *Homo Prospectus,* 22.

[15] Agustin Fuentes, *The Creative Spark* (New York: Dutton, 2017), 1.

[16] Stephen T. Asma, *The Evolution of Imagination* (Chicago: University of Chicago Press, 2017), 2.

[17] Fuentes, *The Creative Spark*, 1–2.

[18] Asma, *The Evolution of Imagination*, 39–41. See also Jeff Dyer, Hal Gregersen, and Clayton M. Christensen, *The Innovator's DNA: Mastering the Five Skills of Disruptive Innovators* (Boston: Harvard Business Review Press, 2011), 55.

[19] See Asma, *The Evolution of Imagination*, 39–41; Fuentes, *The Creative Spark*, 2, 8.

[20] See Railton, introduction to *Homo Prospectus*, 21–22. Although the important parts of Railton's "fisherman" story remain intact, we have modified the story slightly (and added a little texture) in order to serve our purpose, which is subtly different from his. That is, Railton tells the story in order to demonstrate the link between prospection and motivation, which he merely hints is useful for human innovation. We are most interested in how prospection leads to innovation, so we have slightly modified the details in order to emphasize this point.

[21] Baumeister et al., "Pragmatic Prospection," 3.

[22] Asma, *The Evolution of Imagination*, 231.

[23] See *Matryoshka Haus* (Matryoshka Haus, 2017), 13–15.

[24] See Mark Sampson, "Stumbling Towards an Alternative Imagination," *The Thread*, https://thethread.ptsem.edu/leadership/alternative-imagination.

[25] Sampson, "Stumbling Towards an Alternative Imagination."

[26] Sampson, "Stumbling Towards an Alternative Imagination."

[27] *Matryoshka Haus*, 13–15.

[28] *Matryoshka Haus*, 13–15.

[29] David Brooks, *The Social Animal* (New York: Random House, 2012), 247–48.

[30] Michel Foucault, quoted in Mario Livio, *Why?* (New York: Simon & Schuster, 2017), 9.

[31] See Isaiah Berlin, *The Hedgehog and the Fox*, 2nd ed. (Princeton: Princeton University Press, 2013). Thanks to David Brooks for prompting us to consider this essay, which he discusses in *The Social Animal*, 249–50.

[32] See Livio, *Why?* 3–5, 14.

[33] Johnson, *Where Good Ideas Come From*, 75–83.

[34] Dyer, Gregersen, and Christensen, *The Innovator's DNA*, 56–57.

[35] Johnson, *Where Good Ideas Come From*, 75–83.

[36] Johnson, *Where Good Ideas Come From*, 75–83.

[37] Johnson, *Where Good Ideas Come From*, 75–83.

[38] Barnhart, "God Owns Our Business."

[39] Johnson, *Where Good Ideas Come From*, 75–83.

[40] Steven Johnson has noted in an interview that he can only keep hunches alive if he writes everything down and revisits the half-baked hunches over time. He has kept a single document, full of hunches, where he has jotted down nearly every hunch over the last ten years. Whether it's a book idea, or an idea for a start-up, or a magazine article idea, or whatever, he just writes it down. At present, the document runs ninety thousand words, longer than any of his nine books, though he is quick to acknowledge that "half of [the ideas] make no sense. Half of them are dumb ideas. Maybe a quarter of them are promising. Then a quarter of them have actually borne fruit and turned into big ideas in my little world." He tries to go back and read the document every six months or so, and what happens is that an idea that didn't make much sense when he wrote it in 2009—because he didn't understand something about the world, or technology hadn't evolved to a certain place at that time— suddenly starts to make sense and become full of potential a decade later.

Or it connects to some other hunch he had in 2013, another unrelated one in 2015, and then in a strand of hunches begins to emerge into a really good idea. See "Why Slow Hunches Can Beat Fast Ideas," interview with Steven Johnson, American Express OPEN Forum, https://heleo .com/conversation-slow-hunches-can-beat-fast-ideas/15059/.

[41] See Edmund Burke, *Reflections on the Revolution in France* (New York: Penguin, 1986).

[42] Daniel Kahneman, *Thinking, Fast and Slow* (New York: Farrar, Strauss and Giroux, 2011), 254.

[43] Simone Weil, *First and Last Notebooks* (Eugene, OR: Wipf & Stock, 2015), 111.

[44] David Brooks, "The Big Test," *The New York Times*, February 23, 2009.

[45] He expanded this idea in David Brooks, *The Social Animal*, 245.

[46] Kahneman, *Thinking, Fast and Slow*, 262.

[47] Kahneman, *Thinking, Fast and Slow*, 262.

[48] See Daniel Kahneman, "Why We Contradict Ourselves and Confound Each Other," *On Being with Krista Tippett*, October 5, 2017, https://onbeing.org/programs/daniel-kahneman-why-we-contradict-our selves-and-confound-each-other-jan2019/#transcript.

[49] See Jean Bethke Elshtain, *Who Are We?* (Grand Rapids: Eerdmans, 2000), 63. See also Brooks, *The Social Animal*, 46.

[50] Nathan Hill, *The Nix* (New York: Knopf, 2016), Part Nine, Chapter 34, Kindle edition.

[51] See Horst W. J. Rittel and M. M. Webber, "Dilemmas in General Theory of Planning," *Policy Sciences* 4 (1973): 155–69.

[52] Alan Watkins and Ken Wilber, *Wicked and Wise* (Romsey, Hampshire, UK: Urbane, 2015), xiii.

[53] See Kahneman, *Thinking, Fast and Slow*, 264–65.

[54] See Brooks, *The Social Animal*, 246–47.

[55] Wendell Berry, quoted in Kathryn Shattuck, "Out on the Prairie, Moon, Music, and Lectures, Too," *New York Times*, October 2, 2012, https://www.nytimes.com/2012/10/03/us/prairie-festival-draws-crowds -to-land-institute-in-kansas.html.

[56] See, for example, Martin Seligman, *Learned Optimism* (New York: Vintage, 2006), 111–15.

[57] Michael Lamb, "Aquinas and the Virtues of Hope: Theological and Democratic," *Journal of Religious Ethics* 44 (May 19, 2016): 2:303. Also see Michael Lamb, "Between Presumption and Despair: Augustine's Hope for the Commonwealth," *American Political Science Review* 112 (November 2018): 4:1036–49.

[58] Quoted in Lamb, "Between Presumption and Despair," 1036.

[59] Shane J. Lopez, *Making Hope Happen* (New York: Atria, 2013). This story is also adapted in Shane J. Lopez, "Making Hope Happen," *The Huffington Post*, May 5, 2013, https://www.huffingtonpost.com/shane-j -lopez-phd/making-hope-happen_b_2812859.html.

[60] Our information on 3M comes from two main sources: the vast trove of information on the company's website, as well as Jonah Lehrer, *Imagine* (New York: Houghton Mifflin Harcourt, 2012), 25–30. All items quoted here are from Lehrer's book. One additional note: Lehrer's book was pulled from shelves over a plagiarism controversy in which it was revealed that Lehrer fabricated certain quotes in the book. Those charges focused on sections of the book that do not include this one.

[61] See James Clear, *Atomic Habits* (New York: Avery, 2018).

Chapter 5
Traditioning

[1] Orlando O. Espín, *Idol and Grace* (Maryknoll, NY: Orbis, 2014), 9.

[2] Railton, "Introduction," *Homo Prospectus*, 15.

[3] Seligman and Tierney, "We Aren't Built to Live in the Moment."

[4] Walter Brueggemann, *An Introduction to the Old Testament* (Louisville: Westminster John Knox, 2003), 8.

[5] See Charles Dickens, *A Christmas Carol and Other Christmas Writings* (New York: Penguin Classics, 2003). Portions of this retelling are borrowed from Richard Gunderman, *We Come to Life with Those We Serve* (Bloomington: Indiana University Press, 2017), 84–96.

[6] Railton, introduction to *Homo Prospectus*, 15.

[7] See Charles Taylor, *Modern Social Imaginaries* (Durham, NC: Duke University Press, 2003).

[8] Alexis de Tocqueville, *Democracy in America*, ed. and trans. Harvey C. Mansfield and Delba Winthrop (Chicago: University of Chicago Press, 2000), 489–92.

[9] See Hugh Heclo, *On Thinking Institutionally* (New York: Oxford University Press, 2008), especially chapter 4.

[10] See Miller, *The Character Gap*, 200–201.

[11] See James Davison Hunter, *To Change the World* (New York: Oxford University Press, 2010), 76–78.

[12] See Gordon T. Smith, *Institutional Intelligence* (Downers Grove, IL: InterVarsity Press, 2017), 3–5.

[13] Levin, *A Time to Build*, 19.

[14] Jane Addams, *Democracy and Social Ethics* (New York: Macmillan, 1907), 273.

[15] See Vern Huffman, "Stories from the Cha Cha Cha," in *The Impossible Will Take a Little While*, ed. Paul Rogat Loeb (New York: Basic Books, 2004), 161–62. See also John E. Jessum, *An Encyclopedia of Conflict and Conflict Resolution, 1945—1996* (Westport, CT: Greenwood, 1998), 375.

[16] See Alasdair MacIntyre, *After Virtue* (Notre Dame, IN: University of Notre Dame Press, 1981). See also Gary Riebe-Estrella, "Tradition as

Conversation," in *Futuring Our Past*, ed. Orlando O. Espín and Gary Macy (Maryknoll, NY: Orbis, 2006), 141–56.

[17] For a provocative narrative about Jewish traditioning and arguments related to the founding of Israel, see Chaim Potok, *The Chosen* (New York: Simon & Schuster, 1967).

[18] Elshtain, *Who Are We?* 5.

[19] Gardner, *Self-Renewal*, xii.

[20] Wiley Cash, "Owning the Past," *Salt Magazine*, February 28, 2018, http://www.saltmagazinenc.com/owning-the-past/.

[21] See Geoffrey Colvin, *Humans Are Underrated* (New York: Portfolio/ Penguin, 2015), 146–52.

[22] Martin Puchner, *The Written World* (New York: Random House, 2017), 4.

[23] See Stephen Denning, *The Springboard* (Boston: Butterworth Heinemann, 2001), 197–98.

[24] Adam Morgan and Mark Barden, *A Beautiful Constraint* (Hoboken: John Wiley & Sons, 2015), 38.

[25] Morgan and Barden, *A Beautiful Constraint*, 80–81.

[26] Mary Oliver, *Upstream* (New York: Penguin, 2016), 56–58.

[27] Gardner, *Self-Renewal*, 45.

Chapter 6
Collaborating

[1] Johann Hari, *Lost Connections* (New York: Bloomsbury, 2018).

[2] See L. Gregory Jones, *Christian Social Innovation* (Nashville: Abingdon, 2016), chapter 3, for more details on Mashinini's story in relation to the theme of holy friendship.

[3] See Osha Gray Davidson, *The Best of Enemies* (New York: Scribner, 1996), for the full story of Ellis's and Atwater's relationship.

[4] Scott E. Page, *The Diversity Bonus* (Princeton: Princeton University Press, 2017), 11.

[5] Marc J. Dunkelman, *The Vanishing Neighbor* (New York: W. W. Norton and Co., 2014).

[6] See Eric Klinenberg, *Palaces for the People* (New York: Crown, 2018), for an excellent discussion of the significance of social infrastructure for enabling social capital.

[7] Klinenberg, *Palaces for the People*, 5.

[8] Levin, *A Time to Build*; see Marc Andreessen, "It's Time to Build," April 18, 2020, https://a16z.com/2020/04/18/its-time-to-build/. Andreessen wrote his piece in the wake of the global pandemic of 2020.

[9] James Davison Hunter, *To Change the World* (New York: Oxford University Press, 2010), 38.

[10] This example is described a bit more fully in L. Gregory Jones, "Why Institutions Matter for Culture Change," *Faith and Leadership*, October 18, 2016, https://faithandleadership.com/l-gregory-jones-why -institutions-matter-culture-change.

[11] Rawn James Jr., *Root and Branch* (New York: Bloomsbury, 2010), 21.

[12] Richard Kluger, *Simple Justice* (New York: Random House, 1975), 128.

[13] Kluger, *Simple Justice*, 125.

[14] See L. Gregory Jones, "Metaphors Matter," *Faith and Leadership*, May 31, 2016, https://faithandleadership.com/l-gregory-jones-met aphors-matter.

[15] See C. Kavin Rowe's forthcoming book, *Christianity's Surprise* (Nashville: Abingdon, 2020), especially chapter 2.

[16] Sam Wells illumines the significance of this kind of Christian imagination in his book *Improvisation* (Grand Rapids: Brazos, 2004).

[17] For one influential example, see Daniel Boyarin, *A Radical Jew: Paul and the Politics of Identity* (Berkeley: University of California Press, 1994).

[18] Carol S. Dweck, *Mindset*.

[19] David Epstein, *Range* (New York: Riverhead Books, 2019), 13, 53, 228.

[20] For examples of diverse lists that nonetheless point to similar activities and skills, see David Epstein, *Range*; Abbie Griffin et al., *Serial Innovators* (Palo Alto, CA: Stanford University Press, 2012); Clayton M. Christensen et al., *The Innovator's DNA* (Boston: Harvard Business Review Press, 2011); Gary Pisano, *Creative Construction* (New York: Public Affairs, 2019).

[21] Pisano, *Creative Construction*, 182–95.

[22] The image of "opposable" thinking and living is taken from Roger L. Martin. See, for example, the book he cowrote with Jennifer Riel, *Creating Great Choices* (Boston: Harvard Business Review Press, 2017).

[23] See Donyelle Meadows, *Thinking in Systems* (White River Junction, VT: Chelsea Green, 2008); Janine Benyus, *Biomimicry* (New York: Harper, 1997); Robin Wall Kimmerer, *Braiding Sweetgrass* (Minneapolis: Milkweed, 2015).

[24] See Eric Weiner, *The Geography of Genius* (New York: Simon & Schuster, 2016) for a fascinating journalistic account of several of these cultures and what can be learned from them.

[25] James Fallows and Deborah Fallows, *Our Towns* (New York: Pantheon, 2018).

[26] Steven Johnson, *Where Good Ideas Come From*, 22.

Chapter 7
Improvising and Sustaining

[1] Jeremy Heimans and Henry Timms, *New Power* (New York: Doubleday, 2018), 204.

2 Heimans and Timms, *New Power*, 205.

3 See Railton, "Introduction," *Homo Prospectus*, 21–22.

4 Alan Jacobs, *How to Think* (New York: Currency, 2017), 91.

5 George Lakoff and Mark Johnson, *Metaphors We Live By* (Chicago: University of Chicago Press, 2003).

6 Jacobs, *How to Think*, 98.

7 Mary Midgley, *Myths We Live By* (London: Routledge, 2004), 1. Thanks to Jacobs for pointing us to Midgley.

8 Shane Parrish, "Farnam Street: Mental Models," uploaded August 4, 2016, https://vimeo.com/177585900.

9 See Randolph Nesse, "The Body Is Not a Machine," February 4, 2016, https://evmed.asu.edu/blog/body-not-machine.

10 Midgley, *Myths We Live By*, 1.

11 See Alison Gopnik, *The Gardener and the Carpenter* (New York: Farrar, Straus and Giroux, 2016), 18–19.

12 Gopnik, *The Gardener and the Carpenter*, 18–19.

13 See Yuval Levin, *A Time to Build* (New York: Basic Books, 2020); Marc Andreessen, "It's time to build," April 18, 2020, https://a16z.com/2020/04/18/its-time-to-build/.

14 Interestingly, General Stanley McChrystal proposes the image of a gardener for leadership in the military. See *Team of Teams* (New York: Portfolio/Penguin, 2015).

15 In what follows we are indebted to Nathan J. Jones, who helped us understand intricacies of both musical and theatrical improvisation—and who helped us write this section.

16 Frank J. Barrett, "What the Best Jazz Musicians and Business Brains Have in Common," March 5, 2013, http://www.cnn.com/2013/02/21/opinion/route-to-top-jazz-business-success.

[17] See Samuel Wells, "Improvising Leadership," *Faith and Leadership*, March 26, 2012, https://www.faithandleadership.com/multimedia/samuel-wells-improvising-leadership.

[18] Wells, "Improvising Leadership."

[19] See Anders Ericsson and Robert Pool, *Peak* (Boston: Houghton Mifflin Harcourt, 2016). David Epstein points to limitations of the ten-thousand-hour rule in *Range*.

[20] "Stephen Colbert Commencement Address," Knox College, June 3, 2006, http://departments.knox.edu/newsarchive/news_events/2006/x12547.html.

[21] "Stephen Colbert Commencement Address."

[22] Wells, *Improvisation*, 108, 128.

[23] Wells, *Improvisation*, 109.

[24] Wells, "Improvising Leadership."

[25] Wells, *Improvisation*, 131.

[26] Wells, *Improvisation*, 131–32.

[27] Wells also illumines in his book how Jesus practices overaccepting throughout his ministry. Further, Jesus's resurrection is a paradigmatic example of God overaccepting our attempts at blocking. Christians living as Easter people is a part of what makes Christian witness recurringly "surprising" to a world used to patterns of blocking.

[28] See Gary P. Pisano, *Creative Construction* (New York: PublicAffairs, 2019), 1–15.

[29] See Gary P. Pisano, "You Need an Innovation Strategy," *Harvard Business Review*, June 2015, https://hbr.org/2015/06/you-need-an-innovation-strategy.

[30] Pisano, *Creative Construction*, 19–26.

[31] John W. Gardner, "Leadership and Power," *Leadership Papers* (Washington, DC: Independent Sector, 1986), 3.

[32] Smith, *Institutional Intelligence*, 53–57. See also Andy Crouch, *Playing God* (Westmont, IL: InterVarsity, 2013), for insightful discussion of a Christian approach to power.

[33] Smith, *Institutional Intelligence*, 53–54.

[34] Pisano, *Creative Construction*, 27, 109.

[35] Pisano, *Creative Construction*, 109–110.

[36] Some of these ideas draw on the insights of Gordon Smith. See *Institutional Intelligence*, 75–83.

[37] Geert Hofstede, "The Business of International Business Is Culture," *International Business Review* 3 (March 1994): 1–14.

[38] Helen Spencer-Oatey, "What Is Culture?" *GlobalPAD Core Concepts* (2012): 3.

[39] See Pisano, *Creative Construction*, 179.

[40] Smith, *Institutional Intelligence*, 109.

[41] Brooks, *The Second Mountain*, xix–xx, 4.

[42] Pisano, *Creative Construction*, 216.

[43] John W. Gardner, "Renewing: The Leader's Creative Task," *Leadership Papers*, no. 10 (Washington, DC: Independent Sector, 1988), 13.

[44] Gardner, "Renewing: The Leader's Creative Task," 8.

[45] Kegan and Lahey, *An Everyone Culture*, 2, 20-21.

[46] Gardner, "Renewal: The Leader's Creative Task," 8.

[47] See Epstein, *Range*.

[48] Essie Taylor, Interview with authors, December 6, 2018.

⁴⁹ See Kegan and Lahey, *An Everyone Culture*, 26–41; Gardner, "Renewal: The Leader's Creative Task," 10.

⁵⁰ See Tiziana C. Dearing, "Managing for Return on Social Innovation (ROSI): Pillars for Sustainable Social Impact," in *Managing for Social Impact*, ed. Mary J. Cronin and Tiziana C. Dearing (Springer International, 2017), 6.

⁵¹ Marjorie Thompson, *Soul Feast* (Louisville: Westminster John Knox, 1995), 13.

⁵² Wells, *Improvisation*, 148.

Printed in the USA
CPSIA information can be obtained
at www.ICGtesting.com
LVHW030054090524
779737LV00006B/453